W9-AUD-826

DATE DUE

Demco, Inc. 38-293

US FOREIGN POLICY AND THE PERSIAN GULF

US Foreign Policy and Conflict
in the Islamic World

Series Editors:
Tom Lansford
The University of Southern Mississippi-Gulf Coast, USA
Jack Kalpakian
Al-Akhawayn University, Morocco

The proliferation of an anti-US ideology among radicalized Islamic groups has emerged as one of the most significant security concerns for the United States and contemporary global relations in the wake of the end of the Cold War. The terrorist attacks of September 11, 2001 demonstrated the danger posed by Islamic extremists to US domestic and foreign interests. Through a wealth of case studies this new series examines the role that US foreign policy has played in exacerbating or ameliorating hostilities among and within Muslim nations as a means of exploring the rise in tension between some Islamic groups and the West. The series provides an interdisciplinary framework of analysis which, transcending traditional, narrow modes of inquiry, permits a comprehensive examination of US foreign policy in the context of the Islamic world.

Other titles in the series

A Bitter Harvest
US Foreign Policy and Afghanistan
Tom Lansford
ISBN 0 7546 3615 1

US-Indonesian Hegemonic Bargaining
Strength of Weakness
Timo Kivimäki
ISBN 0 7546 3686 0

Crossing the Rubicon
Ronald Reagan and US Policy in the Middle East
Nicholas Laham
ISBN 0 7546 3961 4

Strategic Preemption
US Foreign Policy and the Second Iraq War
Robert J. Pauly, Jr. and Tom Lansford
ISBN 0 7546 4357 3 (Pbk)
ISBN 0 7546 3975 4 (Hbk)

US Foreign Policy and the Persian Gulf

Safeguarding American Interests through Selective Multilateralism

ROBERT J. PAULY, JR

Norwich University and Midlands Technical College, USA

ASHGATE

DS
326
P38
2005

c, 1

57010216   1-7-09

© Robert J. Pauly, Jr 2005

All rights reserved. No part of this publication may be reproduced, stored in a retrieval system or transmitted in any form or by any means, electronic, mechanical, photocopying, recording or otherwise without the prior permission of the publisher.

Robert J. Pauly, Jr has asserted his right under the Copyright, Designs and Patents Act, 1988, to be identified as the author of this work.

Published by
Ashgate Publishing Limited
Gower House
Croft Road
Aldershot
Hants GU11 3HR
England

Ashgate Publishing Company
Suite 420
101 Cherry Street
Burlington, VT 05401-4405
USA

Ashgate website: http://www.ashgate.com

British Library Cataloguing in Publication Data
Pauly, Robert J., 1967-
    US foreign policy and the Persian Gulf : safeguarding
    American interests through selective multilateralism. - (US
    foreign policy and conflict in the Islamic world)
    1.War on Terrorism, 2001- 2.Intervention (International
    law) 3.United States - Foreign relations - Persian Gulf
    Region 4.Persian Gulf Region - Foreign relations - United
    States 5. United States - Foreign relations - 1989-
    6.Persian Gulf Region - Foreign relations 7.United States -
    Foreign relations - Iraq 8.Iraq - Foreign relations -
    United States 9.Iraq - History - 1988-
    I.Title
    327.7'3053

Library of Congress Cataloging-in-Publication Data
Pauly, Robert J., 1967-
    US foreign policy and the Persian Gulf : safeguarding American interests through
selective multilateralism / by Robert J. Pauly, Jr.
        p. cm. -- (US foreign policy and conflict in the Islamic world series)
    Includes bibliographical references and index.
    ISBN 0-7546-3533-3
    1. Persian Gulf Region--Foreign relations--United States. 2. United States--Foreign
relations--Persian Gulf Region. 3. United States--Foreign relations--1989- 4. International
cooperation. 5. International relations. I. Title: US foreign policy and the Persian Gulf.
II. Title. III. Series.

    DS326.P38 2004
    327.73053'09'049--dc22   2004025168

ISBN 0 7546 3533 3

Printed and bound in Great Britain by MPG Books Ltd, Bodmin, Cornwall

Contents

Acknowledgments

This book would not have been possible without the assistance and support of a wide range of colleagues, family members and friends. In particular, I would like to express my gratitude to the following individuals for their roles in helping me to bring the project to fruition: my editor, Kirstin Howgate, for her encouragement and support throughout the editorial process; Halima Fradley and Emily Poulton for their assistance during the editorial review and marketing processes; Sarah Horsley for her diligent copyediting of the manuscript; Tom Lansford and Jack Kalpakian for the opportunity to participate in the *US Foreign Policy and Conflict in the Islamic World* book series; my Norwich University Master of Diplomacy students for their informed opinions on the Second Iraq War and its aftermath; Steve Wills for his friendship; the late Doyle Smith for his friendship and dedication to the University of Virginia men's lacrosse program; the staffs at the Flying Saucer, Kelly's Deli and Pub, and Willy's Oyster Bar and Grill in Columbia for their kindness and hospitality in providing a few welcome breaks from the research and writing processes; and to Peggy, Bob, Mark, Chris, Sami, John and Missy Pauly for their perpetual love and support in all of my personal and professional endeavors.

For my grandparents

Chapter 1

Introduction

US Foreign Policy and the Persian Gulf: Breaking with the Past

In June 2004, President George W. Bush used his commencement address to the graduating class of the US Air Force Academy to articulate a long-term strategy designed to reduce the threats posed to American interests by transnational terrorist organizations and their sponsors. In that speech, which was delivered approximately three months prior to the third anniversary of Al Qaeda's attacks on the World Trade Center in New York and the Pentagon on the outskirts of Washington, D.C., on 11 September 2001, Bush made three fundamental points. First, the US-led pursuit of the democratization of the Greater Middle East is—and will remain—central to the effective prosecution of the war against terrorism. Second, the conduct of nation-building operations in Iraq since the liquidation of former President Saddam Hussein's regime in April 2003 represents the first step in the wider economic and political transformation of the broader Arab and Islamic worlds. Third, the maintenance of a sustained American commitment to the above objectives is indispensable to providing for the security of the United States at home and safeguarding its interests abroad.[1]

Most significantly, in linking the democratization of Iraq—and, eventually, the Greater Middle East as well—to the war on terror, Bush stressed that "[f]ighting terror is not just a matter of killing or capturing terrorists. To stop the flow of recruits into terrorist movements, young people in the region must see a real and hopeful alternative— a society that rewards their talent and turns their energies to a constructive purpose." Consequently, he continued, the "vision of freedom has great advantages. Terrorists incite young men and women to strap bombs on their bodies and dedicate their deaths to the deaths of others. Free societies inspire young men and women to work, and achieve, and dedicate their lives to the life of their country. And in the long run, I have great faith that the appeal of freedom and life is stronger than the lure of hatred and death."[2]

In casting Saddam's removal from power through the conduct of Operation Iraqi Freedom in March and April 2003 and ongoing efforts to develop representative political and free market economic institutions in the new Iraq as key parts of the war on terrorism, Bush drew parallels to past American conflicts with opponents of freedom across the globe. In particular, he emphasized that "it resembles the great clashes of the last century—between those who put their trust in tyrants and those who put their trust in liberty. Our goal, the goal of this generation is the same: we will secure our nation and defend the peace through the forward march of freedom."[3] Furthermore, he noted that the extension of the pursuit of freedom beyond Iraq represents an innovative new approach toward the region, one that reverses

Washington's long-time support for authoritarian leaders in the Arab world. In conclusion, he explained that

> [For] decades, free nations tolerated oppression in the Middle East for the sake of stability. In practice, this approach brought little stability, and much oppression. So I have changed this policy. In the short term, we will work with every government in the Middle East dedicated to destroying the terrorist networks. In the longer term, we will expect a higher standard of reform and democracy from our friends in the region. Democracy and reform will make those nations stronger and more stable, and make the world more secure by undermining terrorism as its source. Democratic institutions in the Middle East will not grow overnight; in America, they grew over generations. Yet the nations of the Middle East will find, as we have found, the only path to true progress is the path of freedom and justice and democracy.[4]

Bush's remarks at the Air Force Academy reiterated a theme upon which the president and his advisors consistently placed an emphasis during the diplomatic prologue to, and prosecution of, the Second Iraq War, and the subsequent implementation of US-led nation-building operations in Iraq: the long-term pursuit of economic and political reform processes across the Greater Middle East.[5] In an address at the American Enterprise Institute just under a month prior to the launch of Operation Iraqi Freedom, for example, Bush stressed that

> The nation of Iraq—with its proud heritage, abundant resources, and skilled and educated people—is fully capable of moving toward democracy and living in freedom. The world has a clear interest in the spread of democratic values, because stable and free nations do not breed the ideologies of murder. They encourage the peaceful pursuit of a better life. And there are hopeful signs of a desire for freedom in the Middle East. Arab intellectuals have called on Arab governments to address the "freedom gap" so their peoples can fully share in the progress of our times. Leaders in the region speak of a new Arab charter that champions internal reform, greater [political] participation, economic openness, and free trade. And from Morocco to Bahrain and beyond, nations are taking genuine steps toward [political] reform. A new regime in Iraq [will] serve as a dramatic and inspiring example of freedom for other nations in the region.[6]

Notwithstanding the extent to which the Bush administration's objectives are realistic—a question open to debate and unlikely to be answered convincingly for years, if not decades, to come—its approach to the Persian Gulf is indeed a revolutionary one. It was developed in large part as a result of the events of 9/11, which prompted the administration to develop a preemptive National Security Strategy designed to eliminate future threats to US interests posed by terrorist organizations and their state sponsors (most notably Al Qaeda and Iraq) before such dangers become imminent and thus unavoidable.

Ultimately, that strategy breaks with past US policymaking in the Persian Gulf, an undertaking that itself dates to the 1830s.[7] A brief review of American engagement in the Gulf is all that is required to demonstrate that point. That review is broken down temporally in three contexts—the pre-Cold War, Cold War and post-Cold War eras, each of which is touched on below.

Pre-Cold War Years

Prior to the outbreak of the Cold War, US interests in the Persian Gulf were primarily, albeit not exclusively, economic in orientation. Initially, American engagement in the region was limited to the cultivation of a new market for US goods. The development and deepening of commercial relationships with actors such as the Persian Empire and Oman coincided with the progression of the American Industrial Revolution over the latter half of the twentieth century. Linkages between private interests in the United States and the states of the Gulf (most notably Saudi Arabia) grew stronger with the discovery and exploitation of petroleum deposits across the region during World War I and the interwar years.[8]

Increasing American reliance on the Persian Gulf for oil, in turn, led to a growing impetus for the expression of US diplomatic influence therein. Ultimately, the diminution of the British presence in the Middle East as the United Kingdom focused on domestic rather than colonial interests in the aftermath of World War left Washington to play the West's lead role in the Gulf—politically and, if necessary, militarily. As historian Michael Palmer asserts:

> Americans naively expected to supplant the British commercially without having to accept old-world-style political or military responsibilities. ... The evolution of American involvement in the Gulf paralleled the British pattern—a long period of solely commercial, followed by the more rapid development of strategic and geoeconomic interests. By the 1940s, Americans had replaced the British as the most important economic power in the Persian Gulf. Unfortunately, though not surprisingly, with that newfound commercial dominance came considerable diplomatic and military involvement.[9]

Cold War Years

During the Cold War, the "diplomatic and military involvement" to which Palmer refers was conditioned primarily by US efforts to minimize, if not eliminate, Soviet involvement in the region. However, the ethnic, political and religious complexity of the Middle East also demanded the pragmatic cultivation of often-transitory collaboration with given states at a particular historical juncture.

The nature of the relationships between Washington and Iran on one hand, and Iraq on the other, is a case in point. The United States maintained a close relationship with Iran until the government of Shah Reza Pahlavi was overthrown by supporters of fundamentalist Islamic cleric Ayatollah Ruhollah Khomeini in 1979. In the 1980s, by contrast, the United States backed Saddam's regime in its war against Iran. It supplied the Iraqis with armaments—as did the rival Soviets—and failed to discourage Baghdad's development, and use, of chemical weapons of mass destruction (WMD). Above all, those policies enhanced Iraq's capacity to threaten regional stability, which it did, to

Washington's detriment, during the 1990s and 2000s. As historian Charles Tripp notes,

> By the mid-1980s, not only had Iraq re-established full diplomatic relations with the United States, but it was also benefiting from the material support of a range of Western states, most notably the United States itself, France and Great Britain. Some of this assistance came in the form of financial credits, some in consumer goods and some in military supplies directly useful to Iraq's war effort. Iraq found itself in the happy position of being courted by both superpowers and their allies, successfully enlisting its support for their war effort in the waters of the Gulf and on the land front.[10]

Post-Cold War Years

More than any state in the Persian Gulf, Iraq has been central to American policymaking in the region throughout the post-Cold War era to date. The defining event in the Gulf during President George H.W. Bush's tenure in the White House, for instance, was the American-led prosecution of Operation Desert Storm, which unfolded between January and February 1991 on the heels of the conclusion of the Cold War via the collapse of Communist regimes across Central and Eastern Europe in 1989-90 and the reunification of Germany in October 1990.[11] Bush responded to the act of provocation that triggered the conflict—Iraq's invasion of Kuwait in August 1990—with a mixture of prudence and resolve.

From the outset, he was determined not to allow Saddam's aggression to stand. However, Bush also recognized the need to avoid unilateral American action in a region generally averse to Western culture and influence. In order to achieve that end, he set about the construction of a broad coalition of Western, Asian and Middle Eastern states that would act only under the auspices of the United Nations (UN) and thus mitigate, if not avoid completely, the perception that the United States was acting solely in its own interest. Capitalizing on the personal and professional relationships Bush and Cabinet members such as Secretary of State James Baker, Secretary of Defense Richard Cheney and National Security Advisor Brent Scowcroft had cultivated with world leaders in the past, the administration mobilized international support against Iraq more rapidly than would likely have been the case had a set of individuals lacking their collective experience been in office at the time.

Throughout the 1990-91 Persian Gulf crisis, the administration focused on the use of personal diplomacy—whether over the telephone or through frequent airplane shuttles from Washington to European and Middle Eastern state capitals—in order to maintain cohesion within the coalition by ensuring that each of its members' needs were met sufficiently. Baker's September 1990 trip to procure financial contributions from coalition partners both to offset the costs of the military buildup and offer aid to states making significant sacrifices to enforce the economic sanctions against Iraq, and his subsequent mission to mobilize support for the passage of a UN use-of-force resolution, were two notable examples. These consultations were effective primarily because they demonstrated Bush's personal commitment to the coalition and the objectives that entity sought to achieve.

Put simply, the administration skillfully cobbled together a coalition based on a confluence of the myriad interests listed above. However, Bush recognized that the coalition would remain united only so long as its members deemed its existence beneficial. As a result, he set limited objectives, all of which were codified explicitly in UN resolutions. Bush understood that once the coalition had achieved its principal goal—the expulsion of Iraqi forces from Kuwait—that entity would lose its principal source of legitimacy. Thus, he did not press for a removal of Saddam from power through a sustained military offensive in Iraq itself. The administration managed the crisis masterfully given the circumstances; Bush and his advisors also displayed the requisite geopolitical prudence to retire the coalition before it collapsed under its own weight. However, Bush's decision not to seek Saddam's removal from power also left nearly intact a source of long-term instability in the Gulf, one with which his successor, President William J. Clinton, would have to contend.

Over the course of Clinton's two terms in office, his administration sought to limit Saddam's potential to develop nuclear, chemical and biological WMD and, perhaps, eventually transfer those munitions to terrorist organizations, by relying upon the UN to dispatch weapons inspectors to Iraq and oversee Baghdad's use of proceeds from the sale of its petroleum resources for humanitarian items such as food and medicine. It also employed limited military force against Iraq on several occasions from 1993-98, the most robust of which came in response to Saddam's expulsion of the weapons inspectors in December 1998. According to Kenneth Pollack, the point man on Iraq on National Security Advisor Samuel Berger's staff, "Bill Clinton was certainly not looking to make Iraq the centerpiece of his foreign policy. And when the President found himself in domestic political turmoil as a result of the Monica Lewinsky affair, avoiding foreign policy crises became an even greater priority."[12] Consequently, Clinton attempted to contain the threats posed by Iraq on the cheap in terms of economic and political capital, domestically as well as internationally. As journalists and public policy analysts Lawrence Kaplan and William Kristol assert, the "Clinton administration avoided confronting the moral and strategic challenge presented by Saddam, hoping instead that an increasingly weak policy of containment, punctuated by the occasional fusillade of cruise missiles, would suffice to keep Saddam in his box."[13]

Clinton's only substantial—and somewhat sustained—response to Saddam's consistent unwillingness to adhere to a series of UN resolutions to which he acceded at the conclusion of the Persian Gulf War (including, most notably, prohibitions against the development of nuclear, chemical and biological WMD and sponsorship of terrorist groups) was a brief flurry of cruise missile strikes in the context of Operation Desert Fox in December 1998.[14] Those strikes, which came after Saddam's expulsion of UN weapons inspectors the previous month, did not result in the inspectors' return. Instead, once completed, they left Saddam free to defy the United States without repercussions until the events of 9/11 contributed to the expression of a renewed American willingness to take bold action against Iraq.

President George W. Bush articulated that shift in tone, if not formal policy (as the Clinton administration had also repeatedly stressed verbally that it was committed to regime change in Iraq), through the promulgation of a broader approach to the issue of the state sponsorship of terrorism in his January 2002 State of the Union Address. In the wake of the liquidation of the Al Qaeda-sponsoring Taliban regime in Afghanistan through the successful completion of Operation Enduring Freedom the previous month, Bush used the address to impress upon those states with a history of support for terrorism that the United States would not tolerate such behavior. In particular, the president characterized three states (Iraq, Iran and North Korea) as members of "an axis of evil, arming to threaten the peace of the world." Furthermore, he referred explicitly to the threats posed by states determined to develop WMD and maintain relationships with terrorists, including, but not limited to, bin Laden and his global network, concluding that Iraq, Iran and North Korea "pose a grave and growing danger. They could provide these arms to terrorists, giving them the means to match their hatred. They could attack our allies or attempt to blackmail the United States. In any of these cases, the price of indifference would be catastrophic."[15] Essentially, that address provided the rhetorical foundation for the planning and prosecution of the Second Iraq War.

Statement of Research Questions

With the above observations providing a necessary contextual foundation, this book addresses the following research questions:

- First, what were the fundamental economic, military and political causes of the 1990-1991 Persian Gulf War? Were such causes primarily regional or global in character?
- Second, who were the principal actors—individual, national and international—in the contexts of the 1990-1991 and 2001-2003 Persian Gulf crises and conflicts? To what extent did each of these actors drive events in the Gulf from 1990-2004?
- Third, what roles did American leaders—and the policies they developed and implemented play—in both the 1990-1991 and 2001-2003 Persian Gulf crises and conflicts?
- Fourth, how effectively did the George H.W. Bush administration manage the 1991 Persian Gulf War and its aftermath?
- Fifth, how effectively did the Clinton administration define, articulate and pursue US interests in the Persian Gulf from 1993-2001? What were the short- and long-term costs and benefits of its diplomatic, economic and military policies toward the region?
- Sixth, how effectively did the George W. Bush administration define, articulate and pursue US interests in the Persian Gulf from 2001-2004? What were the short- and long-term costs and benefits of its diplomatic, economic and military policies toward the region?
- Seventh, what steps must American leaders take to safeguard US interests in the Persian Gulf in the future?

Statement of Theses

In addressing its research questions, the book will present the following theses:

- First, the George H.W. Bush administration's management of the 1990-1991 Persian Gulf crisis was both prudent and effective when assessed in the short term. However, while the administration did a laudable job constructing a broad-based coalition and using that entity to expel Iraqi forces from Kuwait and thus reduce Baghdad's capacity to threaten regional stability in the short term, its failure to eliminate Saddam's regime has proven shortsighted and extraordinarily costly over the long term.
- Second, the Clinton administration's reliance on the UN Security Council to enforce a series of resolutions proscribing Saddam's development of WMD programs and sponsorship of terrorist organizations, and its limited use of force in response to Iraq's repeated violations of those strictures, were relatively ineffective means to safeguard US interests in the Persian Gulf from 1993-2001.
- Third, the George W. Bush administration's use of a preemptive strategy to confront Iraq over its development of WMD and sponsorship of terrorist groups and forcibly remove Saddam from power was both necessary and effective given the fundamental shift in the nature of the threats posed to the security of Americans at home and abroad in the aftermath of Al Qaeda's attacks on the World Trade Center and the Pentagon on 11 September 2001.
- Fourth, ultimately, it is essential that US policymakers consider the liquidation of Saddam's regime and subsequent nation-building process in Iraq as useful first steps rather than endpoints in the democratization of the Persian Gulf and broader Greater Middle East over the long term. The pursuit of such a vision for change will ensure that history deems the Second Iraq War successful in both military and political terms.

Structure of the Book

The book addresses the research questions and theses through the presentation of five main chapters and a concluding chapter that examine the following issues:

- Chapter 2 summarizes the history of the Persian Gulf, placing an emphasis on US foreign and security policy toward that region during the nineteenth and twentieth centuries.
- Chapter 3 examines and evaluates the George H.W. Bush administration's policies toward the Persian Gulf from 1989-93, placing an emphasis on the planning and prosecution of the 1990-91 Persian Gulf War.
- Chapter 4 examines and evaluates the Clinton administration's policies toward the Persian Gulf from 1993-2001.

- Chapter 5 examines and evaluates the George W. Bush administration's policies toward the Persian Gulf from 2001-04, placing emphases on the planning and prosecution of the Second Iraq War in 2002-03 and the conduct of nation-building operations in Iraq in 2003-04.
- Chapter 6 recommends an interconnected diplomatic, economic and security policy framework for the pragmatic pursuit of American interests in the Persian Gulf in light of insights drawn from the strengths and weaknesses of the George W. Bush, Clinton and George H.W. Bush administrations' respective approaches to that region.
- Chapter 7 revisits the research questions and elaborates on the theses in light of the evidence presented in the five main chapters of the book.

A detailed breakdown of the manner in which each of those chapters is structured follows.

The United States and the Persian Gulf: A Historical Overview

This chapter presents a brief historical overview of US policy toward the Persian Gulf in order to orient readers. It does so in five sections. The first section builds a foundation for the subsequent sections by discussing the ethnic, political and religious diversity of the Gulf and the centrality of history in driving the behavior of states and individuals in the region. The second, third and fourth sections review US diplomatic, economic and security policies toward states within the Gulf in the pre-Cold War, Cold War and post-Cold War eras, respectively. The fifth section summarizes the commonalities and divergences in those policies.

George H.W. Bush Administration and the Persian Gulf, 1989-1993

This chapter examines the George H.W. Bush administration's policies toward the Persian Gulf in four sections. The first section discusses the challenges of US policymaking against the backdrop of the closing stage of the Cold War generally and in the Gulf specifically. The second section reviews the administration's definition of US interests in the region and subsequent development, articulation and implementation of policies therein, placing emphases on the diplomatic prologue to, and prosecution of, the 1991 Persian Gulf War. The third section examines the strengths and weaknesses of those policies. The fourth section assesses the relative costs and benefits of the resultant policy outcomes.

Clinton Administration and the Persian Gulf, 1993-2001

This chapter examines the Clinton administration's policies toward the Persian Gulf in four sections. The first section discusses the challenges of US policymaking in the post-Cold War era generally and in the Gulf specifically. The second section reviews the administration's definition of US interests in the region and subsequent development, articulation and implementation of policies therein. The third section examines the strengths and weaknesses of those policies. The fourth section assesses the relative costs and benefits of the resultant policy outcomes.

George W. Bush Administration and the Persian Gulf, 2001-2004

This chapter examines the George W. Bush administration's policies toward the Persian Gulf in four sections. The first section discusses the challenges of US policymaking given the changing perception of threats to US interests in the post-9/11 era. The second section reviews the administration's definition of US interests in the region and subsequent development, articulation and implementation of policies therein, placing emphases on the diplomatic prologue to, and prosecution of, Operation Iraqi Freedom, and the subsequent conduct of nation-building operations in Iraq. The third section examines the strengths and weaknesses of those policies. The fourth section assesses the relative costs and benefits of the resultant policy outcomes.

Policy Prescriptions for the Future

This chapter considers the future of US policymaking in the Persian Gulf in four sections. The first section presents a methodological discussion of the use of the relative strengths and weaknesses of the George H.W. Bush, Clinton and George W. Bush administrations' approaches to the Persian Gulf as a means to help develop a more effective framework for the pursuit of American interests therein over the balance of the 2000s and beyond. The second section assesses the current and probable forthcoming threats to American economic, political and security interests in the region. The third section proposes a pragmatic interest-based US policymaking strategy vis-à-vis the Gulf. The fourth section promulgates a series of short- and long-term policy prescriptions for the implementation of that strategy.

Conclusions

This concluding chapter presents four sets of related observations. The first section discusses the extent to which American policy toward the Persian Gulf will condition the evolution of the relationships between the United States and the states of the Greater Middle East over the long term. The second section offers a set of brief responses to the research questions in light of the evidence presented in the main chapters of the book. The third section evaluates the theses. The final section considers the significance of the book's findings as pertains to the broader relationship between the Islamic and Western worlds.

Notes

1. George W. Bush, "Remarks by the President at the United States Air Force Academy Graduation Ceremony," 2 June 2004, *White House Office of the Press Secretary*

(www.whitehouse.gov).

2. Ibid.
3. Ibid.
4. Ibid.
5. For an in-depth account of the diplomatic prologue to, and prosecution of, Operation Iraqi Freedom and the subsequent conduct of nation-building operations in Iraq, see Tom Lansford and Robert J. Pauly, Jr., *Strategic Preemption: US Foreign Policy and the Second Iraq War* (Aldershot, UK: Ashgate Publishing Limited, 2004).
6. George W. Bush, "Statement by the President Regarding the United Nations Security Council and Iraq," 6 February 2003, excerpted in *We Will Prevail: President George W. Bush on War, Terrorism and Freedom* (New York: Continuum, 2003), 226-27.
7. For an in-depth account of American engagement in the Persian Gulf during the nineteenth century, see Michael A Palmer, *Guardians of the Gulf: A History of America's Expanding Role in the Persian Gulf, 1893-1992* (New York: Macmillan, 1992), 1-19.
8. Ibid.
9. Ibid., 244.
10. Charles Tripp, *A History of Iraq* (Cambridge: Cambridge University Press, 2000), 240.
11. For an in-depth account of the 1990-1991 Persian Gulf Crisis and War, see Steve Yetiv, *Explaining Foreign Policy: U.S. Decision-making and the Persian Gulf War* (Baltimore: Johns Hopkins University Press, 2004).
12. Kenneth M. Pollack, *The Threatening Storm: The Case for Invading Iraq* (New York: Random House, 2002), 86-87.
13. Lawrence F. Kaplan and William Kristol, *The War Over Iraq: Saddam's Tyranny and America's Mission* (San Francisco: Encounter Books, 2003), 37.
14. Pollack, *Threatening Storm*, 87-94.
15. George W. Bush, "President's State of the Union Address," 29 January 2002, excerpted in *We Will Prevail*, 108.

Chapter 2

The United States and the Persian Gulf: A Historical Overview

Introduction

Similar to many regions of the developing world, the contemporary Persian Gulf—and, for that matter, the surrounding Greater Middle East—feature characteristics illustrative of both continuity and change. Above all, those characteristics reflect the geography and history of the Gulf and its periphery as well as the distinctive identities and interests of the peoples who have established, governed and inhabited the myriad empires and states therein over the centuries. Inevitably, the names of individual leaders and their supporters and adversaries have changed from era to era. By contrast, however, the region's ethnic, religious and political diversity has remained relatively constant. As Bernard Lewis, one of the most authoritative modern historians of the Middle East, notes,

> Unlike India, China, or Europe, the Middle East has no collective identity. The pattern from the earliest times to the present day, has been one of diversity—in religion, in language, in culture, and above all in self-perception. The general adoption at the present time, in countries east and west and north and south of the so-called Middle East, and even in the Middle East itself, of this meaningless, colorless, shapeless, and for most of the world, inaccurate term is the best indication of the lack of a perceived common identity, either at home or abroad.[1]

The diversity to which Lewis refers has mitigated the capacity of the states and peoples of the Persian Gulf and broader Arab and Islamic worlds to forge the common bonds and interests necessary to ensure enduring economic prosperity and political stability. In the process, it has also led to perpetual complications in the relationships between states situated in the Western and Islamic worlds generally, and American and European leaders and their counterparts in the Gulf and across the Greater Middle East in particular. Consequently, a brief examination of the fundamental factors at play in the evolution of the identities of the states and peoples of those regions will provide an instructive foundation for the introductory discussion of US policymaking therein that ensues. That examination touches on the issue areas of geography, ethnicity, religion and politics.

Geography

In general terms, the Persian Gulf is situated in the heart of the Greater Middle East.

While the names and rulers of the political entities bordering the Gulf have changed repeatedly over time, the territory of which the region is composed has remained relatively unchanged. Geographically, it ranges from the inhospitable deserts of Saudi Arabia and rocky coastline of Oman in the south to the birthplace of Mesopotamia between the Tigris and Euphrates Rivers surrounding modern Baghdad and the mountains of northeastern Iraq and northwestern Iran. While lacking substantial expanses of arable land, the region is blessed with vast petroleum reserves, a resource initially uncovered early in the twentieth century and one upon which the economies of nearly all of its states are based. Regrettably, that dependence on oil has contributed to a dearth of economic diversification with potentially crippling consequences once the reserves have been expended.

The waters of the Gulf itself meet the coastlines of eight states—Iran, Iraq and Saudi Arabia, as well as Bahrain, Kuwait, Oman, Qatar and the United Arab Emirates. Those states, in turn, either directly abut or are situated in the geographic vicinity of Egypt, Israel, the Gaza Strip and West Bank, Jordan, Lebanon, Syria, Turkey and Yemen, all of which have consistently had an impact on the region's economics, politics and security for at least the past half-century, and, in most cases, far longer. The roles of each of those political entities and at least some of their peripheral regional neighbors in Northern Africa and Central Asia are addressed to differing degrees in the balance of the book.

Ethnicity and Religion

Prior to discussing the issues of ethnicity and religion in the Persian Gulf, a primer on the formation of identity in the Greater Middle East is essential. Lewis offers precisely such a primer in his 1999 work, *The Multiple Identities of the Middle East.*[2] Specifically, he views the phenomenon of identity construction in a bifurcated manner. In historical terms, he emphasizes two relevant clusters of factors in the development of an individual's identity, which are associated with birth and allegiance to leadership, respectively. The first cluster includes blood, place and religious community. Those three elements are then subdivided, with blood determined by family, clan, tribe and ethnic nation, place by village, neighborhood, district, province and country, and religious community by a combination of local and immediate bonds. The second cluster features loyalty to a head of state, governor of a province, administrator of a district and headman of a village. According to Lewis, these related clusters have grown closer over time, in large part through the ongoing globalization process. As he explains, in "modern times, under the influence of the West, a new kind [of identity] is evolving between the two—the freely chosen cohesion and loyalty of voluntary associations, combining to form what is nowadays known as civil society."[3]

When defined broadly, as is the case here, the Persian Gulf houses individuals who possess a variety of ethnic and religious backgrounds. Its five most prevalent ethno-religious groups are Arabs, Iranians, Kurds and Turks—the vast majority of whom practice either Sunni or Shia Islam—and Jews with familial origins in such wide-ranging places as Europe, North Africa, Russia and the United States. Additional minority groups in the region include Assyrians, Coptic and Maronite Christians, as well as a variety of guest workers and other migrants from South and Central Asia.[4] Further subdivisions on the basis of clan, tribal and religious affiliation have contributed to a social picture that is relatively, if not fully, homogeneous in some states (the Arabs of Saudi Arabia and miniature neighbors such as Bahrain, Kuwait and Qatar, for example) and more heterogeneous in others (most notably the mixtures of Kurds and Arabs in Iran and Iraq).[5] As scholar Mordechai Nisan, who specializes in the study of the minorities of the Middle East, explains, the "image of a totally Arab Muslim Middle East reflects only a partial picture of reality. ... In the some twenty Arab-defined countries there are approximately 280 million people of whom, nonetheless, about forty million could be defined as either non-Arabs ethnically or nationally, or non-Muslims religiously."[6]

The case of Iraq is especially useful in illustrating the ethnic and religious differences evident across the region. Ethnically, the Iraqi population is divided primarily among Arabs (75-80 percent) and Kurds (15-20 percent) and a range of other groups, including Turkomen and Assyrians (five percent). With respect to religion, it is 97 percent Muslim (60-65 percent Shiite and 32-37 percent Sunni) and approximately three percent Christian.[7] Geographically, the Kurds reside in the north, along Iraq's borders with Turkey and Iran, while most Shiites and Sunnis live in the south and north-central sections of the former state, respectively. Historically, members of these groups have rarely mixed socially and continue to remain suspicious of one another.

Although the vast majority of Muslims in the Persian Gulf share a common belief in the five pillars of Islam,[8] Sunnis and Shias are divided over the basis for the practice of that faith. The former focus on the principles originally outlined by the prophet Muhammad in 610 AD and the latter on the line of succession for leadership of the community dating to Muhammad's death in 632.[9] Similarly, across the globe, adherents to the two principal strains of Islam interpret that faith's holy book (the Koran) in a variety of ways. In the Gulf in particular, Muslims are divided on the role of Islam in society and governance. Religion plays a predominant role in the political systems of some states and a less significant one in others. The Sunni and Shia interpretations are central to daily life in Saudi Arabia and Iran, respectively. Turkey, on the other hand, has a secular government. John Esposito, director of Georgetown University's Center for Christian-Muslim Understanding, for example, notes that Islam has "incorporated a variety of beliefs and activities that grew out of religious and historical experience and the needs of specific Muslim communities. ... The inherent unity of faith, implicit in statements like 'one God, one book, one [final] prophet,' should not deter one from appreciating the rich diversity that has characterized the religious (legal, theological and devotional) life of the Islamic community."[10]

Politics

The politics of the contemporary Persian Gulf reflect both the traditional pursuit of diplomatic, economic and security interests by the governments of the states therein and the impact of ethnicity and religion on those interests. Consider the 1991 Persian

Gulf War. The diplomatic prologue to, and subsequent prosecution of, that conflict demonstrated that most Muslim-majority states define their security primarily in traditional realist—as opposed to nascent civilizational—terms and act on that basis. Rather than side with Iraq against the American-led coalition in the Gulf War, a diverse array of Arab states including Egypt, Saudi Arabia and Syria aligned themselves with the West, assisting in the expulsion of Iraqi President Saddam Hussein's forces from Kuwait. Additionally, while Kuwait was the only Arab state to offer overt support for the George W. Bush administration's liquidation of Saddam's regime in April 2003, regional opposition was relatively muted, particularly at the inter-governmental level.

On the other hand, the economic, political and security challenges to the US-led conduct of nation-building operations in Iraq since the conclusion of the Second Iraq War continue to illustrate that ethnic and religious imperatives are all but certain to have a marked impact on intra- and inter-state relations in the Persian Gulf and broader Islamic world over both the short and long terms. With respect to the case of Iraq specifically, the legacy of Saddam's quarter-century in power has further complicated the contemporary relationships among that state's Sunnis, Shiites and Kurds. During that time, Saddam and his Sunni-dominated Baath Party systematically repressed and exterminated hundreds of thousands of Kurds, Shiites and other political opponents. Perhaps the most brutal period of repression came in the aftermath of the 1990-91 Persian Gulf War when Saddam's army crushed Kurdish and Shiite revolts that had been encouraged but not supported militarily by the George H.W. Bush administration. Since the end of Operation Iraqi Freedom in May 2003, for example, coalition forces have uncovered more than 300,000 bodies in mass graves across Iraq. That number is likely to increase substantially given that nearly one million Iraqis disappeared concurrent with Baathist repression of Saddam's opponents in the 1980s and 1990s.[11] As Sandy Hodgkinson, a US State Department expert who spent a year working on the issue of mass graves in Iraq, explains, "There will be graves people haven't seen or don't remember. It will be a long time before we determine how many sites there are and where they are."[12]

Once Saddam's regime had been eliminated, it was left to a US administered Coalition Provisional Authority (CPA) to establish the basis for an enduring representative democracy in Iraq. American diplomat L. Paul Bremer spent his year at the head of the CPA working on two major political projects. First, he orchestrated a process through which an initial Iraqi Governing Council (IGC) composed of members from each of Iraq's principal ethnic and religious groups (the Shiites, Sunnis and Kurds) drafted an interim constitution to serve as the foundation for long-term democratization. Second, he developed a plan for the progression from an interim Iraqi governing body in June 2003 to a transitional government by January 2005 to a permanent elected government by the end of December 2005.[13]

Conceived as an interim body with an indeterminate tenure, the IGC had two fundamental weaknesses, both of which reflected deeper challenges to the democratization process within Iraq. First, while broadly representative of Iraq's diverse ethnic and religious composition, the IGC lacked any leader capable of commanding widespread support among Shiites, Sunnis and Kurds. The one figure capable of generating such respect among majority Shiites, for instance, was (and remains) the Grand Ayatollah Ali Sistani. Yet, as is the case with most mainstream Shiite clerics, he prefers to focus on religion and play a more indirect role at the political level within Iraq. According to Reuel Marc Gerecht, a fellow at the American Enterprise Institute and expert on Shiism, "clerics like Sistani ... understand that clerics cannot become politicians without compromising their religious missions."[14] Second, the divergent interests of its members—and their respective constituencies—complicated the interim constitution drafting process. Initially opposed by the IGC's five Shiite members, the constitution was eventually approved via negotiated compromises to include a provision on minority rights for the Kurds, Sunnis and women, and another recognizing Islam as the central source of Iraqi law in March 2004. Its long-term viability, however, remains very much in question.[15]

The constitutional dilemma is one of the more problematic issues that John Negroponte, who Bush appointed as the first post-Saddam US Ambassador to Iraq, will have to help the Iraqis to address effectively.[16] Others include the aforementioned timetable for the progression from interim to transitional to permanent governance in Iraq between June 2003 and December 2005 and what role, if any, the UN will play in that process. An interim Iraqi government is scheduled to serve from 30 June 2004 through the establishment of a transitional National Assembly and executive and judicial councils by 31 January 2005. The executive will be composed of a three-member Presidency Council to include a prime minister responsible for the day-to-day management of governmental affairs. The Presidency Council will appoint both the prime minister and a nine-member Supreme Court.

The 275-member National Assembly will be responsible for drafting a permanent constitution, which must be approved in a national referendum no later than 15 October 2005. Assuming that deadline is met, elections for a permanent government will follow, with the members of that body scheduled to assume office by 31 December 2005 and manage the future of the new Iraq thereafter. Whether that timeline is followed to the letter remains open to question and will likely be a product of both the security environment in Iraq and economic progress—or lack thereof—in that context in 2005.[17] What is clear, however, is that the character of the political entity that emerges in Iraq and its maintenance over the long term will be conditioned primarily by the relationships among and decisions made by the Iraqis themselves. Those decisions, in turn, will help to determine whether democratic governance has a future at broader regional level.

Ultimately, these observations serve as a useful point of departure for a summary of the history of US policy toward the Persian Gulf. That synopsis, which is designed to serve as a general introduction to (and thus not a comprehensive examination of) the topic, is presented in four sections that unfold in the following manner:

- The first section opens with a summary of the history of the Gulf, then reviews American diplomatic, economic and military policies toward that region prior to the onset of the Cold War in the aftermath of World War II. The latter review places an emphasis on the opening half of the twentieth century, and the section closes with a synopsis of the short- and long-term consequences of US engagement with Gulf states during that period.

- The second section reviews American diplomatic, economic and military policies toward the Gulf during the Cold War. It concludes with a synopsis of the short- and long-term consequences of those policies.
- The third section reviews American diplomatic, economic and military policies toward the Gulf since the end of the Cold War. It concludes with a synopsis of the short- and long-term consequences of those policies. This section will be considerably shorter than the initial two sections given that Chapters 3, 4 and 5 all focus in great detail on the US role in the Gulf in the post-Cold War era.
- The final section assesses the most significant similarities and differences in US diplomatic, economic and security policies toward the Gulf over the course of American history.

US Foreign Policy and the Persian Gulf—Pre-Cold War Era

The history of the Persian Gulf dates to the emergence of the Mesopotamian Civilization in approximately 3000 BC as a result of the settlement of the fertile valley between, and adjacent to, the Tigris and Euphrates Rivers by an ancient people known as the Sumerians. The region in which the Sumerians settled—referred to by modern historians as the "Fertile Crescent"—is sandwiched between the Taurus and Zagros Mountains in the north and Arabian desert in the south, and bordered by the Gulf in the east and the Mediterranean Sea in the west. It includes parts of present-day Iraq, Kuwait, Turkey, Syria, Jordan, Israel and the Palestinian Authority-administered territories of the Gaza Strip and West Bank.

Mesopotamia progressed politically from the development of a series of autonomous city-states to the establishment of three successive empires, the second of which was headed by an astute Babylonian politician and warrior named Hammurabi. During his reign from 1792-1750 BC, Hammurabi established an "eye-for-an-eye" system of justice and achieved military success by dividing and then conquering his opponents.[18]

The Mesopotamian world's most enduring legacy was that it demonstrated the capacity of the Fertile Crescent to sustain a given human population over multiple centuries. Ultimately, the fragmentation and eventual disappearance of any semblance of a cohesive Mesopotamian empire by 539 BC was the first in a series of geopolitical transitions in the Persian Gulf and across the broader Middle East in the contexts of which internal and external actors grappled for control over those regions. As Nisan points out in describing the Greater Middle East,

> This strategically critical and historically significant region of humanity has been the home of many diverse peoples, some of whom should be considered indigenous inhabitants, others as foreign conquerors, still others as travelers across its formidable expanse that serves as an international crossroads. Empires have come and gone, and the remnants of

earlier epochs resonate in archaeological fossils and places of epic and mythological memory. The spiritual flights of mankind hover above and the military exploits of warriors are not forgotten. The past is never completely out of sight, and indeed the present may only be the most contemporary chapter of the past, which never dies.[19]

A chronological review of the transitions touched on above unfolds in the ensuing sub-sections, which focus on the pre-Islamic, Islamic and European colonial eras.

Pre-Islamic Era

Prior to the genesis of the Islamic faith in the seventh century AD in Arabia, a range of distinctive political actors battled for, and then exercised territorial control over, all or parts of the Persian Gulf and the surrounding regions. Those actors included three of the most historically significant empires of the Greater Middle East: the Persians, Macedonians and Romans. As Egyptian historian Zahi Hawass asserts, "[w]ith the arrival of the Persians on the world stage, a new era of empire began. The Near East became in many ways a single unit, to be passed around by a succession of local and foreign armies. The various native cultures preserved many of their distinctive traits, but they became mixed with foreign influences to form an intricate series of mosaics."[20]

One of the last Babylonian Kings to preside over territory in Mesopotamia was a man named Nebuchadnezzar. In 586 BC, Nebuchadnezzar razed the Hebrew capital of Jerusalem and sent the Jewish people into exile, an act that has since served as one of many historical sources of contemporary conflict between the Israelis and their Arab neighbors. Less than a century later, the Babylonians themselves were defeated by Cyrus the Mead, who went on to establish a Persian Empire that, at its height, had borders stretching from Central Asia to the periphery of the Greek world. Broadly similar to the Jews, the early Persians also practiced a monotheistic faith, one that focused on the prophet Zoroaster.[21]

The Persians, some of whose descendants now reside in Iran, proved unable to stop the expansion of the Macedonian Empire to the East under the leadership of one of the most effective military leaders in ancient history—Alexander the Great. Upon ascending to the throne as a result of the assassination of his father, Philip I, in 336 BC, Alexander set out to enlarge the empire. Over the ensuing 13 years, he extended Macedonian control from the Balkans in the west to what is now known as India in the east. He died at age 33 in 323 BC at a palace in the Fertile Crescent after a short illness and his empire subsequently fragmented into several smaller kingdoms, the most enduring of which was administered by the Ptolemaic dynasty of Egypt.[22]

Alexander exposed much of the Greater Middle East to the traditions of Greek Civilization, albeit for a relatively limited period of time. With the gradual decline in power of the Hellenistic kingdoms, a nascent empire emerged further to the West and eventually moved in to fill part of the regional power vacuum. Its capital was in Rome. While the Romans never controlled as much of the Persian Gulf itself as Alexander did, their impact on the region proved more enduring for one fundamental reason: the development of Christianity, one of the contemporary world's three most practiced monotheistic faiths (Islam and Judaism are the others). The Romans crucified Jesus Christ, the prophet of Christianity, in 30 AD, and initially persecuted the followers of that faith. Despite that persecution, Christianity continued to spread and was eventually adopted of the official religion of Rome and its territories by Emperor Theodosius in 378.[23]

By 395, the Roman Empire had split into Western and Eastern segments, the latter of which (branded by modern historians as Byzantium), established a capital in Constantinople and continued to exert Christian influence on the Persian Gulf and broader Middle East. The division of the empire, however, reduced its power markedly and left both its flanks open to challenges from rival peoples and religions.[24] Neither of the two claimants to power in the east—the Byzantines or Persian Sassanians—demonstrated the capacity to attract an indigenous following among, or exercise control over, all of the peoples of the Fertile Crescent and its periphery. Ultimately, in the aftermath of a draining conflict between those two powers in the early seventh century, a rival faith-based movement emerged in the heart of the Arabian desert. It came to be known as Islam. As Lewis points out, the "early Islamic chronicles tell of a group of people known in Arabic as Hanif who, while abandoning Paganism, were not prepared to accept any of the competing religious doctrines on offer at the time. They were among the earliest converts to the new religion of Islam."[25]

Islamic Era

Islam was established by an Arabian trader named Muhammad ibn Abdullah ("son of Abdullah") in 610 on the basis of a revelation he claimed to have received from Allah ("the one true God"). Muhammad (570-632) was from Mecca, where he first revealed Allah's message. He was later forced to migrate to Medina, along with his followers (the first Muslims) in 622, before rallying to retake Mecca in 629. The subsequent expansion of the Muslim world was, in part, a product of the concept of holy war (jihad), which was conceived by Muhammad as a means to spread the Islamic faith beyond the Saudi Arabian cities of Mecca and Medina during the seventh century.

The allure of jihad was attributable both to mundane avarice and divine inspiration: territorial expansion in the mortal world and eternal rewards in the afterlife. Under the auspices of the Koran, which Muslims believe God revealed directly to Muhammad, those who perish while carrying out jihad become martyrs and are thus entitled to an afterlife of perpetual pleasures. With these worldly and otherworldly incentives to draw upon, Muhammad's descendents continued the pursuit of jihad in earnest after his death in 632, rapidly expanding the territory under Islamic control east as far as present-day India and Pakistan, north into the Byzantium, and west into North Africa and, eventually, southwestern Europe. A pair of successive Islamic imperial powers—the Umayyads of Damascus and Abbasids of Baghdad, respectively—were responsible for the maintenance and expansion of the Islamic world over the initial half-millennium following Muhammad's death.[26] The latter replaced by the former as the principal power in the Muslim world in approximately 749. That remained the case until late in the first millennium, the political fragmentation of the Abbasid caliphate left four kingdoms—the Saffarids in eastern Iran, Samanids in Khurasan, Tulinids in

Egypt and Aglabids in Tunisia—grappling for a share of control over the Greater Middle East.[27]

Broadly concurrent with the decline of the Abbasids, the Ottoman Empire established and expanded its control across the Islamic world from a base of operations in what is now the Turkish city of Istanbul. The Ottomans eventually extended their empire beyond the Greater Middle East into southeastern Europe. After gaining a foothold in the Balkans by virtue of a victory over the Serbian dynasty at the Battle of Kosovo in 1389, the Ottomans pushed steadily northward. They occupied Romania in 1504, took Belgrade—capital of communist Yugoslavia during the Cold War and the Republic of Serbia since then—in 1520, and assumed control of Hungary in 1529. Sieges of Vienna, immediately following the Hungarian conquest and again in 1574, were turned aside by the Christian defenders of Austria, who fought under the banner of the Habsburg dynasty.[28] Indeed, the relatively contentious nature of the contemporary relationship between many member states of the European Union (EU) and Turkey is, at least to an extent, a reflection of these centuries-old Christian-Ottoman confrontations. As historian Ira Lapidus contends, much "of Ottoman history was shaped by their extraordinary commitment to conquest in the name of Islam. The Ottoman wars gave them a reputation among Muslims as the greatest of Muslim states devoted to the jihad. In Europe, they left the reputation of the scourge of God and terror for centuries. The image of the ferocious Turks lives on today."[29]

Colonial Era

The Ottoman Empire reached its height prior to the ill-fated siege of Vienna in 1574. Once turned back, it continued to exercise control over much of the Greater Middle East. However, the empire's power subsequently underwent a gradual, but steady, decline as a result of uprisings among subject peoples and a struggle with the Persians for control over the Gulf. Above all, the Ottomans' decline and fall between the late seventeenth and early twentieth centuries was attributable to the rising power of the nation-states of Western Europe, and their subsequent development and expansion of colonial empires throughout the developing world. As renowned Middle Eastern historian Albert Hourani notes, by 1918, the "military control of the British and France in the Middle East and Maghrib was stronger than ever before, and, what was even more important, the great [Ottoman] imperial government under which most of the Arab countries had lived for centuries, and which had served as some kind of protection against European rule, was soon to disappear."[30]

Essentially, the negotiation of the Treaty of Versailles at the conclusion of World War I effectively signaled the end of the Ottoman Empire. The ensuing era of European colonialism in the Islamic world, in turn, had a deep impact upon modern Muslim-Christian relations, both within, and outside of, the Greater Middle East. In the contexts of the French and British colonial empires in North Africa, Palestine and the Persian Gulf, for example, Islam provided a useful foundation for the independence struggles that led to the establishment of states such as Algeria, Morocco, Tunisia, Iraq, India and Pakistan.

It was six centuries after the conduct of the last of the Medieval Crusades that the Europeans renewed their interest in the Greater Middle East. French Emperor Napoleon Bonaparte's occupation of Egypt from 1798-1801 was the first significant incursion. By the midpoint of the nineteenth century, the British had entered the picture as well, seizing the Yemeni port of Aden and bolstering their nascent presence in the Persian Gulf by establishing diplomatic and economic relationships with the rulers of Abu Dhabi, Dubai and Sharja in the subsequent years. France, for its part, was in control of much of the North African Maghrib by 1860.[31] As for the natives residing within each of these areas, Hourani notes bluntly that "[f]aced with this explosion of European energy, the Arab countries, like most of Asia and Africa, could generate no countervailing power of their own."[32]

Concurrent with the genesis and subsequent expansion of European political control over a wide swath of territory in the Persian Gulf and broader Middle East in the nineteenth and twentieth centuries, the United States also gradually developed its own interests in the region. America's first contact with the Gulf came in 1833 when a Massachusetts merchant named Edmund Roberts arrived in Muscat and negotiated a treaty of amity in commerce with the Sultan of Oman. The treaty, which remains in force today, opened a new market for US goods such as cotton textiles and furniture and also served as a harbinger of an eventual challenge to Britain's then predominant commercial and political position in the region.[33]

Over the ensuing twenty years, the United States gradually expanded its private and governmental interests in the Gulf, using the relatively secure environment guaranteed by the British presence in the region to its advantage. By the mid-1850s, American diplomats began to cultivate a relationship with the Persian Empire, one that was not formalized for more than a quarter-century and had, by 1900, embroiled Washington in the Great Game between Britain and Russia for economic and political control over the Greater Middle East from the Gulf to Central Asia. The stakes in that "game," in turn, were raised substantially as the extent of the region's vast petroleum deposits became increasingly evident in the subsequent decades, a period that coincided with a perpetual growth in demand for oil to fuel the industrialization of North America, Europe and the Far East.[34] As historian Michael Palmer notes, the

> industrial revolution changed the face of the world. By the turn of the century machine power had replaced that supplied by animals or nature. Coal had long since replaced wood, and was being displaced by petroleum, yet another fossil fuel. ... By 1900, the strategic significance of the Persian Gulf increased steadily, even at a time when the Middle East's oil production was limited and the region's known reserves were marginal. Of the world's industrial and military powers, only the United States and Czarist Russia were major producers and exporters of oil. The other powers—Germany, Japan, France and Great Britain—relied on foreign, usually American, imports, and eagerly searched abroad for new sources of oil.[35]

The prosecution of World War I, during which the allies relied almost exclusively on the United States for oil to fuel their armies, navies and nascent air forces, only enhanced the strategic importance of the petroleum-rich Persian Gulf. At the conclusion of that conflict, the allies gathered in Paris, where they fashioned a settlement—the Treaty of Versailles—that awarded Britain and France de facto control over substantial territories in the Gulf and its geographic vicinity. In particular, the treaty stipulated that those Arab territories formerly within the Ottoman Empire would be provisionally independent but also subject to the rendering of assistance and advice by a state with a "mandate" for them. Britain held the mandates for Iraq and Palestine, and France for Syria and Lebanon; as a result, those states enjoyed an advantageous strategic position in the region relative to other outside actors such as the Americans.[36]

While the United States chose to disengage itself from the affairs of the Europeans—and their colonial mandates—politically in the aftermath of World War I, private American interests continued to play an influential role in the Greater Middle East generally and the Gulf specifically. In 1933, for example, Standard Oil of California (SOCAL) secured a 60-year concession to develop Saudi Arabia's petroleum industry as a partner in the California-Arabian Standard Oil Company (CASOC).[37] SOCAL had previously secured a stake of the oil industry in neighboring Bahrain. Largely as a result of US involvement, petroleum production in the Gulf increased by 900 percent from 1920-39.[38]

During the prologue to, and conduct of, World War II, those states whose petroleum operations were primarily under the control of British corporations—most notably Iraq and Iran—exhibited substantial production declines from 1938-41 and modest increases from 1942-45.[39] By contrast, productivity remained considerably more stable in Saudi Arabia, where CASOC managed the operations.[40] These developments reflected the relative strengths of the United States in terms of technological skill in the oil fields and military power as opposed to that of Britain, particularly given that the latter faced an existential threat at home—and was thus unable to focus as much as it would probably have liked on its colonial interests—prior to America's entry into the war following the Japanese attack on Pearl Harbor in December 1941. By the end of the conflict, it was clear that Washington rather than London would play the West's leading role in the region in the future. Palmer, for instance, notes that the "American decision to take the leading role in the postwar development of the petroleum industry of the Middle East was based on a sober, but realistic assessment of British capabilities—diplomatic, economic, and political. Since the end of the First World War, Great Britain had demonstrated that it lacked the capital to develop the region, certainly to the extent that the United States now considered necessary."[41]

Ultimately, the establishment and expansion of the roles of US-based oil companies in the Gulf prior to outbreak and conduct of World War II had both short- and long-term consequences. In the short term, it led to considerable profits for the American corporations involved and also to a greater reliance by the United States and its allies on the region's petroleum deposits. Over the longer term, that reliance forced Washington to play more robust political and military roles in the Gulf in order to safeguard its economic interests therein. The American role was limited only so long as the British—and, to a lesser degree, the French—had the military capacity and political will to ensure regional stability. In the aftermath of World War II, they had neither, which left the administration of President Harry S. Truman to fill the power vacuum in order to prevent the Soviet Union from doing so as the Cold War era commenced. As Hourani concludes,

> Overshadowing Britain and France were the two powers whose potential strength had been made actual by the war. The United States and the Soviet Union had greater economic resources and manpower than any other states, and in the course of the war had established a presence in many parts of the world. Henceforth they would be in a position to claim that their interests should be taken into account everywhere, and the economic dependence of Europe upon American aid gave the United States a powerful means of pressure upon its European allies.[42]

US Foreign Policy and the Persian Gulf—Cold War Era

American presidents have employed a variety of tools in the interrelated conduct of foreign and national security policy over the past two and one-quarter centuries. In general terms, the approaches they choose to pursue are typically conditioned by the changing nature and perception of the threats they face and the contemporary domestic and foreign crises to which they must respond. Nonetheless, irrespective of the historical circumstances, three rules have consistently proven indispensable to the effective formulation and implementation of policies designed to safeguard American interests within and outside of the United States. It is essential first to define a state's national interests, second to prioritize those interests and third to take policy decisions accordingly.

More pointedly, the policies that grow out of those decisions are the product of an admixture of three elements—interests, commitments and capabilities. States develop their interests on the basis of a range of factors, including economics, politics, security, geography, history, individual leadership, culture (most notably ethnicity and religion) and the unpredictability of unfolding events. Consequently, leaders make commitments that are, in turn, contingent on the state's economic, military and political capabilities at a particular historical juncture.

During the Cold War, the United States developed and implemented foreign policies that responded primarily, if not always exclusively, to its bipolar struggle against the Soviet Union. Notwithstanding their individual particularities, the presidential administrations serving in office between the conclusion of World War II in August 1945 and the implosion of the Soviet Union in December 1991 each defined American interests relative to those pursued by the leadership in Moscow at a given point. Most such policies were based at least in part on the containment doctrine outlined by seminal Cold War strategist George F. Kennan in the aftermath of World War II. The Truman administration, for example, opened the Cold War by committing itself to the economic prosperity, political integration and military security of Western Europe (through Marshall Plan grants and the establishment of the North Atlantic Treaty Organization [NATO], respectively) in order to limit the Soviet sphere of influence to Eastern and Central Europe. The Ronald W. Reagan administration, by contrast, successfully pursued the rollback of Soviet influence at the global level by increasing US military spending during the 1980s to a level at which Moscow could no longer compete and elected to release the vice grip it had previously held on the states of the Warsaw Pact. And the George H.W. Bush administration was left to orchestrate, if not preside over, the opening act of the restoration of democracy across Eastern and Central Europe in 1989-90, which culminated in the reunification of Germany in October 1990.

While their conception was by no means unchallenging, the policies each of these leaders and their advisors crafted were a product of an all but identically structured international system. In short, they each had a familiar bipolar model to use as a point of departure in constructing and implementing their respective policies. As was the case across the globe, the American-Soviet relationship served as the primary basis for US strategy in the Persian Gulf and broader Middle East during the Cold War years. However, the ethnic, religious and geopolitical complexity of the region—and unpredictability of developments therein—also demanded subtle alterations in the approach of an administration when a crisis situation developed. The forthcoming review of the most significant such imbroglios and the resultant US responses is subdivided into five chronological contexts: the opening stage of the Cold War from 1945-49, the 1950s, the 1960s, the 1970s and the 1980s.

1945-50

As the East-West divide that characterized the half-century-long Cold War opened and rapidly solidified in the aftermath of World War II in Europe, several related developments had a direct impact on American interests in the Persian Gulf and broader Middle East. In particular, those developments grew out of three sets of issues, all of which were at least somewhat interconnected: the eruption of an Arab-Israeli conflict following Britain's abandonment of its mandate in Palestine; the deepening of economic and political linkages between the United States and Saudi Arabia; and the proverbial strategic chess match pitting Washington against Moscow for political influence—and, in some cases—territorial control over states such as Iran, Iraq and Egypt. The management of the resulting relationships and crises proved consistently challenging to American (and, for that matter, Soviet) policymakers over the ensuing four decades.

Upon assuming the League of Nations mandate for Palestine articulated in the Treaty of Versailles, Britain had to deal with a fundamental ethno-religious conflict— the struggle pitting predominantly Muslim Arabs against Zionist Jews for the right to establish states under their respective auspices—within the territory over which London exercised de facto control. It was a conflict the British proved unable to resolve and one that continues to frustrate regional peacemakers ranging from the United States and Russia to the EU and UN in the 2000s.[43]

National Socialist Germany's targeted effort to eliminate Europe's Jews resulted in substantial migration flows of Holocaust survivors to Palestine following the fall of Adolf Hitler's regime. It also led to renewed calls for the establishment of an independent Jewish state in that context. With tensions between Palestinian Arabs and

Jews escalating, Britain turned its mandate over to the UN and withdrew in May 1948. At that point, the Jews declared independence and established the state of Israel, which was immediately recognized by both the United States and the Soviet Union. Wholly unwilling to accept a Jewish state in their midst, forces from Egypt, Iraq, Jordan, Lebanon and Syria invaded Palestine and engaged in battle with the Israeli army. In what proved to be a preview of future wars between Arabs and Israelis in the region, the latter prevailed. By early 1949, the UN stepped in to negotiate an armistice that formalized Israeli control over three-fourths of Palestine. However, by that point, two-thirds of the Palestinian population had fled into the surrounding Arab states, providing one of many excuses for subsequent Arab-Israeli wars in each of the succeeding four decades.[44]

Concurrent with the eruption of the first of myriad Arab-Israeli conflicts in Palestine, the United States continued to deepen its economic and political ties with Saudi Arabia. By the late 1940s, the Truman administration had come to the realization that the domestic oil supply would not be sufficient to meet consumer, industrial or military demand in the future. That realization led to increased commercial and military linkages between the Americans and Saudis. CASOC, for example, took on two additional partners (Standard Oil of New Jersey and Standard Oil of New York) and its Saudi-based subsidiary changed its name to the Arab-American Oil Company.[45] Those commercial links, which were mutually beneficial to the Saudis and American at the economic level, also led to an increased US military presence in the Gulf for two reasons. First, the Truman administration was determined to guarantee American access to the region's natural resources. It did so by regularly dispatching naval assets to the Gulf as a precursor to the establishment of bases there.[46] Second, the head of the ruling Saudi monarchy—Abdul Aziz bin Abdul Rahman Al Saud (known to the West as Ibn Saud)—was willing to allow an increased US presence so long as Washington agreed to guarantee his own security. Ibn Saud's security concerns at that juncture grew primarily out of the disapproval of Arab regimes across the Greater Middle East (and Wahhabi Muslims within the kingdom itself) of Saudi connections to an America that supported the nascent Israeli state.[47]

The initial diplomatic confrontation between the United States and the Soviet Union in the Gulf came in 1946 in the context of Iran. In January of that year, the Iranian government lodged a complaint with the UN Security Council that the Soviets were interfering in its internal affairs. Truman responded by offering economic and political support to Tehran and warning the Soviets that he would consider the use of military force should they continue to occupy the territory they had seized in northern Iran. Although the Soviet Union backed down and withdrew in March, the dispute between the two superpowers over their respective roles in the Greater Middle East had by no means been resolved. Moscow remained a threat to Iran, as well as neighboring Turkey, over which Britain exercised perpetually fleeting influence by that point. As Palmer notes, "in Iran and Turkey as elsewhere in the region, the United States was gradually supplanting Great Britain as the preeminent external power in the diplomatic arena."[48]

1950s

The United States had to strike a prudential balance between global and regional interests in constructing and implementing its policies toward the Middle East generally and the Persian Gulf specifically throughout the Cold War years. During the 1950s in particular, that balance tilted decidedly in favor of global level considerations in the bipolar struggle with the Soviet Union. Three examples demonstrate such strategic considerations: US intervention in Iran in August 1953 to replace a left-leaning government likely to favor the Soviet Union with an authoritarian one allied with Washington; the Dwight D. Eisenhower administration's decision not to back a French, British and Israeli attack on Egypt given the potential for escalation to a global confrontation pitting the Americans against the Soviets in the context of the November 1956 Suez Crisis; and repeated American and British attempts to construct a regional alliance system in the Gulf comparable to the European-based NATO, none of which proved successful.

The outbreak of the Korean War in June 1950 demonstrated to US leaders the Soviet Union's capacity to use communist surrogates—in this case, the regime of North Korean dictator Kim Il Sung—to expand its sphere of influence beyond the confines of Central and Eastern Europe. It also strengthened Washington's determination to preclude similar Soviet-backed initiatives in the Persian Gulf. As a result, when it appeared Iranian Premier Mohammed Mossadegh was seeking closer ties to Moscow through the request for a loan in June 1953, the Eisenhower administration authorized the Central Intelligence Agency (CIA) to do what it could to bring down Mossadegh's government. Consequently, a CIA-supported coup resulted in the replacement of Mossadegh with Mohammed Reza Shah Pahlavi two months later. The Shah remained a strong US ally until he, too, was overthrown by way of the Iranian Islamic Revolution of 1979.[49]

The Suez Crisis was driven by four related geopolitical factors. First, the Soviets and Americans were each eager to undermine the other's interests in the Middle East. Second, Israel's very existence provided a constant source of fury among the leaders and peoples of the surrounding Arab states. Third, the British and French remained somewhat reluctant to admit they no longer had the economic, military or political capacity to play nearly so influential a role in the region as they had in the past. Fourth, Egyptian President Gamal Abdel Nasser was busy casting himself as the leader of a nascent Arab nationalist movement that drew much of its strength from dissatisfaction over Israel's territorial control over most of Palestine and the presence of non-Muslim actors—whether American, European or Soviet in orientation—in the Islamic world.

Each of those factors contributed to the onset, escalation and resolution of the crisis over the latter half of 1956. In July, for instance, Secretary of State John Foster Dulles announced that the United States would withdraw a previous offer to finance the construction of the Aswan High Dam in Egypt. In response, Nasser nationalized the Suez Canal, in which France and Britain held majority stakes, as a means to raise the requisite funds for the dam project. London and Paris attempted to take revenge—and flex their own political muscles in the region—by collaborating with Israel in the conduct of military operations to seize the canal. However, following Israel's 29 October assault across the Sinai Peninsula and subsequent British and French bombing raids on Egypt, the Soviet Union sensed a strategic opening and expressed its support for Nasser. Concerned that the imbroglio could escalate and spark a global level confrontation, the Eisenhower administration pressed its Western European and Israeli allies to stand down, which they did.[50]

At the broader geo-strategic level, the coup in Iran and the Suez Crisis coincided with British efforts to establish a Middle Eastern alliance system to safeguard its interests (and, to a lesser degree, those of the Americans) in the Persian Gulf. Initially, London took the lead, pressing for the creation of a formal multinational defense arrangement. It realized that goal—at least on paper—when Iraq and Turkey signed a bilateral security agreement known as the Baghdad Pact in February 1954. Britain joined the pact two months later, followed by Iran and Pakistan in 1955.[51] But Iraq withdrew in the wake of a July 1958 nationalist coup that ended the rule of the Hashimite monarchy in Baghdad, and the alliance changed its name to the Central Treaty Organization (CENTO) in 1959.[52] While the United States never formally joined CENTO, it replaced Britain as the West's most influential player in the organization given that the Suez Crisis resulted in a marked decrease in London's role in the region. Ultimately, neither the Baghdad Pact nor CENTO served to foster a substantial degree of unity, either between the Middle East's most powerful states and the West or among the Arabs themselves. In fact, in the wake of the Suez Crisis, the Baghdad Pact and, later, CENTO, served as convenient targets for Nasser to criticize in rallying support for his own pan-Arab nationalist agenda.[53]

1960s

During the 1960s, American engagement in the Middle East was limited relative to US initiatives in other regions of the developing world. In particular, that lack of interest was manifested in examples ranging from President John F. Kennedy's launch of an Alliance for Progress in Latin America to President Lyndon B. Johnson's focus on, and progressive escalation of, the Vietnam War. Concurrently, developments in the Arab world—most notably the decline of Nasserism, the conduct of the Six-Day War in June 1967, and an Iraqi coup that propelled a then little known Baathist politician named Saddam Hussein into the circle of power in Baghdad in July 1968—led to a deepening of existing (and the creation of new) problems with which subsequent policymakers in Washington would have to deal.

Nasserism reached its height in the aftermath of the Suez Crisis, as evidenced by the establishment of a United Arab Republic (UAR) of Egypt and Syria in February 1958.[54] Nasser's pan-Arab support was on the decline by the early 1960s. The UAR was dissolved in 1961, subsequent calls by the Egyptian leader for regional unity proved largely futile and, ultimately, his diplomatic provocation of Israel led to the eruption of the Six-Day War, which the Jewish state won handily. Most significantly, Israel's military victory over the combined forces of Egypt, Jordan and Syria resulted in its acquisition of the Gaza Strip, West Bank of the Jordan River, East Jerusalem and Golan Heights—parcels of territory that remain central to the Arab-Israeli peace process in the

2000s. As Hourani explains,

> The war changed the balance of forces in the Middle East. It was clear that Israel was militarily stronger than any combination of Arab states, and this changed the relationship of each of them with the outside world. What was, rightly or wrongly, regarded as a threat to the existence of Israel aroused sympathy in Europe and America, where memories of the Jewish fate during the Second World War were still strong; and the swift Israeli victory also made Israel more desirable as an ally in American eyes. For the Arab states, and in particular for Egypt, what had happened was in every sense a defeat which showed the limits of their military and political capacity; for the USSR it was also a kind of defeat, but one which made the Russians more resolute to prevent their clients from incurring another defeat of the same magnitude. At a very deep level, the war left its mark on everyone in the world who identified himself as either Jew or Arab, and what had been a local conflict became a worldwide one.[55]

Indeed, since the establishment of the Israeli state, the politics of the Greater Middle East have presented a dilemma to would-be peacemakers in Palestine. Geographically, Israel's location in the heart of the Arab world and the presence of Palestinian refugee camps in neighboring states such as Jordan and Lebanon has rendered the involvement of those states in the settlement of Israeli-Palestinian differences all but unavoidable. Yet, notwithstanding the peace treaties Israel has forged with Egypt and Jordan, the Jewish state is widely perceived as an enemy of Islam among Arabs across the region. Linkages between states such as Iran and Syria and terrorist organizations have only exacerbated matters.

Additionally, on the heels of the Six-Day War and Nasser's related fall from grace, the rise of another Arab ruler destined to destabilize the region was in progress in Baghdad. Saddam was among the Baathist Party leaders who engineered the 17 July 1958 coup that removed the regime of General Abdul Karim Qassem from power. Although Ahmad Hasan al-Bakr was named Iraqi President, Saddam exercised considerable political influence as well. Saddam consolidated his position over the ensuing decade, before replacing Bakr as president in 1979, a position he held until the liquidation of the Baathist dictatorship through the conduct of the Second Iraq War in 2003.[56]

1970s

More than anything, the events of the 1970s in the Persian Gulf and broader Middle East served to reiterate in the minds of leaders and policymakers in Washington the centrality of the region to the interests of the United States. Two such events—and their impact on the lives of Americans at home and abroad—stood out above the rest: the October 1973 Yom Kippur War pitting Israel against its Muslim neighbors and the subsequent imposition of an Arab oil embargo against the West; and the 1979 Islamic Revolution in Iran in the context of which students loyal to Shiite cleric Ayatollah Ruhollah Khomeini stormed the US Embassy in Tehran and took the diplomats working inside hostage.

The October War commenced with coordinated surprise attacks by Egyptian and Syrian forces on Israel on Yom Kippur (a Jewish holy day). The initial Arab assaults were reasonably effective; however, the tide quickly turned in Tel Aviv's favor and—as was true of the Six-Day War—the 1973 conflict illustrated the military superiority of the Jewish state. Ultimately, the United States and Soviet Union, which supported the Israelis and Arabs, respectively, exerted pressure on the two sides to accept a ceasefire, in order to ensure that war did not escalate to an extent that would spark a military confrontation between the superpowers.[57]

From the American perspective, the most significant consequence of the imbroglio was the decision by Saudi Arabia to impose an embargo on oil exports to the United States, one that remained in force until the spring of 1974. The Saudi embargo, coupled with reductions in production by several other Arab member states of the Organization of Petroleum Exporting Countries, caused marked increases in the price of gasoline in the United States and Western Europe, contributing to economic downturns across the Western world. It also demonstrated once again the centrality of the Persian Gulf to American interests, at home as well as abroad.[58]

One Middle Eastern state that did sell oil to the United State despite the Arab embargo was Iran. The Shah, who assumed power following the 1953 coup, remained a staunch US ally over the ensuing quarter-century. In the end, however, that alliance led to his February 1979 downfall by way a fundamentalist uprising that left Khomeini in control of a theocratic Islamic regime. The revolution in Iran represented a substantial step backward in the Gulf for the administration of President James E. Carter, who had mediated a peace agreement between Israel and Egypt just five months earlier at Camp David. Regrettably, from Washington's perspective, the situation in Iran only grew worse.[59]

In November 1979, Khomeini's supporters seized the American Embassy in Tehran, beginning a hostage crisis that crippled the Carter White House and did not end until his successor, Reagan, took office in January 1981. To complicate matters further, the month after the commencement of the hostage crisis, the Soviet Union invaded Afghanistan, prompting concerns in Washington that Moscow might eventually attempt to gain control over the Gulf through the use of force. Carter responded with perhaps the most resolute statement of his presidency, stressing in his January 1980 State of the Union Address, 'Let our position be absolutely clear: An attempt by any outside force to gain control of the Persian Gulf region will be regarded as an assault on the vital interests of the United States of America, and such an assault will be repelled by any means necessary, including military force.'[60] Nonetheless, as Reagan learned in the 1980s, policymaking toward the Gulf would involve a bit more strategic ambiguity than suggested by Carter's statement.

1980s

The complexity of the politics of the Greater Middle East generally and the Persian Gulf specifically contributed to the Reagan administration's development and implementation of policies toward the region that, while prudent in the short term, appear somewhat counterproductive when assessed over the long term. Its dealings with Iraq and Iran in particular, nearly all of which came as those states waged war with one another from 1980-88, were demonstrative of that point.

Reagan's principal objective during his tenure in office was to roll back Soviet influence across the globe through a massive US defense buildup at home and the provision of support for opposition groups seeking to overthrow the regimes Moscow backed in the developing world. The pursuit of those goals involved the Persian Gulf and Middle East only tangentially, with the administration concerned almost exclusively with short-term considerations vis-à-vis the bipolar confrontation as opposed to the long-term implications of its policies in that region. Two examples are illustrative of that approach: American provision of weaponry to Iraq despite the maintenance of public neutrality in the war between Baghdad and Tehran; and covert US support for the mujahedeen resistance movement against the Soviets in Afghanistan.

In the context of the Iran-Iraq War, the Reagan administration chose to supply Saddam's regime with a range of armaments. It did so both to ensure that the Soviet Union's influence in the Gulf did not increase relative to that of the United States (Moscow, too, provided the Iraqis with weaponry) and to reduce the chance that Iran would prevail and spread Khomeini's orthodox brand of Shia Islam across the region.[61] In addition to supplying Iraq with conventional weaponry, Washington acquiesced when some of its Western European allies (most notably West Germany) assisted Saddam's regime in the development of chemical weapons, nor did it object publicly to Baghdad's subsequent use of those munitions against the Iranians.[62]

In Afghanistan, the CIA funneled covert assistance through Pakistan to a coalition of Islamic holy warriors known collectively as the mujahedeen, some of whom were born and raised in the Middle East. US aid included Stinger ground to air missiles, which were first supplied to the mujahedeen in 1986 proved critical in counteracting the use of Hind helicopters in Soviet counterinsurgency operations in the ensuing years preceding Moscow's withdrawal in 1989.[63] Overall, the Soviets spent $75 billion maintaining their military presence in Afghanistan between 1980 and 1988; the cost of American aid to the mujahedeen during that period, by contrast, was a modest $3.3 billion.[64]

Each of the above policies had both costs and benefits for the United States. Most of the benefits came in the short term, while the primary costs have manifested themselves in the 1990s and 2000s. In the short term, for example, the Reagan administration's support for Iraq contributed to what amounted to a stalemate in Saddam's war with Iran. When that conflict ended, the Persian Gulf remained relatively stable and the Soviet Union's influence therein had not increased substantially. Similarly, American funding of the mujahedeen led to Moscow's withdrawal in 1989 and also contributed to the collapse of communist regimes across Central and Eastern Europe in 1989-90 and the implosion of the Soviet Union itself in 1991. Over the longer term, by contrast, US acquiescence, if not outright collusion, in Saddam's development of chemical weapons during the 1980s left subsequent administrations to deal with Iraqi WMD threats in the post-Cold War era. And, in Afghanistan, the American-backed resistance against the Soviet Union helped lay the foundation for the growth in power and influence of one individual with whom the CIA was aligned—albeit indirectly—at the time: Osama bin Laden.[65]

US Foreign Policy and the Persian Gulf—Post-Cold War Era

Any discussion of the post-Cold War era must include the role of President George H.W. Bush during the proverbial final act of the bipolar confrontation. Essentially, the Bush administration's policies in and beyond the Persian Gulf served as a bridge between the Cold War and post-Cold War years. With respect to the Gulf, Bush and his advisors had to manage the diplomatic prologue to, and subsequent conduct of, America's first significant "hot" conflict since Vietnam—the 1991 Persian Gulf War—a topic addressed in depth in Chapter 3. In short, on the heels of orchestrating the end of the Cold War in Europe in 1989-90, which culminated in the unification of Germany in October 1990, Bush's foreign policy team had to respond to Iraq's invasion and occupation of Kuwait. Bush did so in a resolute but pragmatic manner.

After building a broad-based coalition of European, Asian and Middle Eastern States under UN auspices, the United States presented Saddam with an ultimatum: either withdraw from Kuwait or face military action. When Saddam refused, an American-led coalition expelled the Iraqis. Yet, notwithstanding the achievement of its principal objective—the expulsion of Iraqi forces from Kuwait and elimination of a potential threat to the oil fields of Saudi Arabia—the Bush administration chose to allow Saddam to remain in power, a decision that proved shortsighted as the opening decade of the post-Cold War era unfolded.

In the immediate aftermath of the Cold War, Bush's successor—President William J. Clinton—and the latter's advisors (along with, for that matter, myriad scholars of international relations) struggled to develop a model to fit a system no longer conditioned by the actions of two superpowers grappling for power and influence across the world. For their part, scholars offered five general paradigms with potential applicability to the emerging post-Cold War order. The first model, of which Francis Fukuyama was the principal proponent, predicted a diminution of, if not an end to, conflict as a byproduct of the victory of the American-led West over the Soviet-sponsored East in the Cold War.[66] The second, put forward by Samuel P. Huntington, mirrored the Cold War system but replaced the ideological confrontation pitting the United States against the Soviet Union with cleavages rooted in religious, economic and cultural differences, which, he predicted, would divide the world between North and South, Christianity and Islam, and Orient and Occident.[67] The third reflected the self-help world of neo-realists such as Kenneth Waltz and John Mearsheimer, with states striving to advance their interests unilaterally in an anarchical international environment.[68] The fourth, promulgated by Zbigniew Brzezinski and Robert Kaplan among others, focused on the intensification of ethnic conflict manifested in a proliferation of failed states in regions as geographically diverse as Central Africa and the former Yugoslavia.[69]

With respect to the Persian Gulf in particular, the Clinton administration had to manage two fundamental threats to American interests at home and abroad, those posed by Iraq and a transnational terrorist organization known as Al Qaeda, respectively. Clinton and his advisors recognized that terrorism represented a growing danger to the United States. However, they were relatively cautious in confronting that threat, relying on limited cruise missile strikes on Al Qaeda leader Osama bin Laden's training camps in Afghanistan rather than a more robust military response to attacks such as the bombings of the US Embassies in Nairobi, Kenya, and Dar-es-Salaam, Tanzania, in August 1998.

Clinton's unwillingness to sanction the use of anything but token force against Al Qaeda paralleled his stance toward perhaps the most persistent US adversary of the 1990s: Saddam. His administration's only substantial—and somewhat sustained— response to Saddam's consistent unwillingness to adhere to a series of UN Security Council Resolutions to which he acceded at the conclusion of the 1990-91 Persian Gulf War (including, most notably, prohibitions against the development of WMD and sponsorship of terrorist groups) was a brief flurry of cruise missile strikes in the context of Operation Desert Fox in December 1998.[70] Those strikes, which came after Saddam's expulsion of UN weapons inspectors the previous month, did not result in the inspectors' return. Rather, once completed, they left Saddam free to defy the United States without repercussions until the George W. Bush administration expressed a renewed American willingness to take bold action against Iraq following Al Qaeda's 11 September 2001 attacks on the World Trade Center and the Pentagon.

In the immediate aftermath of, and subsequent weeks and months following those attacks, the Bush administration pursued two objectives that became increasingly interconnected over time: confronting bin Laden and his Taliban hosts in Afghanistan on one hand and putting Saddam on notice that he was also in Washington's sights on the other. The administration pursued these objectives in two stages, the central elements of which were the conduct of Operation Enduring Freedom from October-December 2001 to remove the Taliban from power and mitigate Al Qaeda's operational capacity and the articulation of the "Axis of Evil" approach in the context of Bush's January 2002 State of the Union address, respectively.

Bush's initial speeches in response to the 9/11 attacks focused primarily on Al Qaeda and secondarily on those states willing either to cooperate with, or directly harbor, members of bin Laden's organization and other terrorist groups.[71] During this period, the United States reformulated its strategy to counter threats posed by terrorists from one reliant on judicial measures and the occasional—and typically limited—use of military force (the Clinton approach) to one drawing on all available diplomatic, economic, military and political means (the Bush approach). Ultimately, once the Taliban had refused to comply with American demands to turn over bin Laden to answer for Al Qaeda's attacks, the Bush administration used Operation Enduring Freedom to demonstrate credibly to terrorist groups and their state sponsors that the United States would henceforth back its policymakers' rhetoric with resolute military action that, when necessary, would extend beyond the pinprick air strikes that had been Clinton's weapon of choice.

Although some high-level advisors within his administration (most notably Secretary of Defense Donald Rumsfeld) pressed for the inclusion of military operations against Iraq in the initial American response to the events of 9/11, Bush personally chose to deal with Al Qaeda and the Taliban in Afghanistan first, before enlarging the war on terror to include Saddam's regime and those presided over by the mullahs in Iran and Kim

Jong-il in North Korea.[72] Once the United States had sent the necessarily forceful message to bin Laden and Taliban leader Mullah Omar through Operation Enduring Freedom, he turned to the threats posed by Iraq, Iran and North Korea generally and Iraq specifically. In the aforementioned State of the Union address, he left no doubt that Washington would not hesitate to take action against any of the three but placed a particular emphasis on Saddam. Most significantly, he asserted that "Iraq continues to flaunt its hostility toward America and to support terror. The Iraqi regime has plotted to develop anthrax, and nerve gas, and nuclear weapons for over a decade" and cautioned that "all nation's should know: America will do what is necessary to ensure our nation's security."[73] Essentially, Bush's warning was the first rhetorical volley suggesting that the United States would in the future take action to preempt threats to American interests before such dangers had progressed to a stage at which they would prove difficult, if not impossible, to eliminate.

Fundamentally, the Clinton and George W. Bush administration's distinctive approaches to the Persian Gulf and Greater Middle East lead to five related observations. First, the 9/11 strikes demanded that the United States reformulate its approach to fighting terrorism such that all available economic, military and political options would be considered and, if necessary, utilized. Given the loss of life in New York and Washington those assaults entailed and the potential for even greater losses in the future, any other course of action would have been imprudent. Second, Clinton's approaches to confronting both Al Qaeda and Iraq from 1993-2001 proved ineffective in that they did not reduce appreciably the threats posed by either to US interests. Third, after reflecting on Clinton's limited use of force against bin Laden's organization and Saddam's regime during the 1990s, Bush and his advisors determined correctly that a more assertive approach was essential. The administration then used Operation Enduring Freedom as the first example of the application of that new strategic formula to what it defined as a long-term war on terrorism that it would carry out across the globe. Fourth, Bush served notice that he would extend the war against terrorist groups to their state sponsors and did so in the articulation of a sweeping new doctrine of preemption that is one of the principal topics of Chapter 5. Notwithstanding the inconclusive nature of the connections between Saddam's regime and the events of 9/11, the existence of consistent linkages between Iraq and terrorist groups since the 1970s suggest that allowing it to continue to cultivate such relationships in the future was simply a chance the United States could not afford to take.

Conclusions

At its core, this chapter was designed to review incisively the history of the Persian Gulf and role of the United States therein as a point of departure for the in-depth examinations of Americans policies toward that region and the broader Middle East that follow in the balance of the book. It did so in the contexts of three related sections. First, it touched on the trends of continuity and change that have characterized unfolding events in the Greater Middle East—and the behavior of individuals, states and empires driving those events—prior to the onset of the Cold War. Second, it summarized the history of inter- and intra-state relations in the Persian

Gulf during the Cold War. Third, it summarized US policymaking toward the region since the end of the Cold War.

In general terms, American engagement in the Persian Gulf has progressed through three stages between the nineteenth century and the present. During the initial stage, which lasted from the 1830s to the start of World War II, US interests in the region were all but exclusively economic in orientation. The first interactions between Americans and Arabs in the region were undertaken to establish trade relationships as US owned businesses sought new markets for their manufactured goods. Such linkages deepened with the discovery of petroleum deposits in the Gulf early in the twentieth century and the development of cooperative Arab-American ventures to exploit those resources (especially in Saudi Arabia) in the decades prior to the conduct of World War II.

US reliance on oil from the Gulf increased markedly as the region's production capacity increased concurrent with the prosecution of the latter years of the war and the division of the European continent into American and Soviet spheres of influence. The onset of the Cold War in the late 1940s coincided with the start of the second stage of Washington's relationship with the states of the Gulf and surrounding Middle East. US policymaking in the region during the Cold War was driven by both economic and strategic considerations. Unencumbered access to Gulf oil and the maintenance of a position of relative strength and influence vis-à-vis the Soviet Union in the region, respectively, were central to those considerations.

The end of the bipolar confrontation left the United States as the predominant external actor in the Persian Gulf, a role it locked into place by expelling Iraqis forces from Kuwait through the prosecution of Operation Desert Storm in the winter of 1990. American strategy in the Gulf over the ensuing decade was designed primarily to maintain regional stability—and thus ensure ease of access to oil—by containing Saddam's regime through UN sanctions and the limited use of military force. The third—and present stage—of US engagement in the Gulf, in turn, commenced with the events of 9/11. Al Qaeda's attacks that day altered the perception of threats to American interests posed by terrorist groups and their state sponsors, leading to the liquidation of Saddam's regime through the prosecution of Operation Iraqi Freedom in 2003 and continuing American-led efforts to democratize Iraq and, eventually, the broader Middle East as well.

Notes

1. Bernard Lewis, *The Multiple Identities of the Middle East* (New York, Schocken Books, 1998), 131.
2. Ibid.
3. Ibid, 6-7.
4. For an in-depth account on the minorities of the Greater Middle East, see Mordechai Nisan, *Minorities in the Middle East*, second edition (Jefferson, NC: McFarland & Company, Inc., Publishers, 2002).
5. Information drawn from selected country reports in the *2003 CIA World Factbook* (www.cia.gov).

6.   Nisan, *Minorities in the Middle East*, 4-5.
7.   "Iraq," *CIA World Factbook 2003* (www.cia.gov).
8.   Islam is by nature a religion that permeates all aspects of its adherents' lives, in both the public and private spheres. Fundamentally, it is based on five pillars, which Muslims must adhere to in order for consideration as strict observers of the faith. First, Muslims must profess their allegiance to Allah as the one true God and acknowledge Mohammed's role as his prophet. Second, they must pray five times daily while facing the holy city of Mecca, which is located in the Saudi Arabian desert. Third, they must abstain from the consumption of all food and beverages between sunrise and sunset during the holy month of Ramadan each year. Fourth, they must donate alms to the poor if they possess the resources to do so. Fifth, if financially able, they must make one pilgrimage (*hadj*)—to Islam's most holy shrine, the Kaba at Mecca, during their lifetime. For a more detailed explanation, see John L. Esposito, *Islam: The Straight Path* (New York: Oxford University Press, 1998), 88-114.
9.   Albert Hourani, *A History of the Arab Peoples* (Cambridge: Harvard University Press, 1991), 14-32.
10. Esposito, *Islam: The Straight Path*, 114.
11. Fred Barnes, "Uncovering Saddam's Crimes: The Legacy of a Mass Murderer," *Weekly Standard* (26 April 2004): 22-25.
12. Quoted in Ibid., 23.
13. Anthony H. Cordesman, "One Year On: Nation Building in Iraq," *Center for Strategic and International Studies* (8 April 2004), 10-11.
14. Reuel Marc Gerecht, "Democratic Anxiety," *Weekly Standard* (2 February 2004): 24.
15. Stephen Lanier, "Low Intensity Conflict and Nation-Building in Iraq: A Chronology," *Center for Strategic and International Studies* (14 April 2004).
16. "President Announces Intention to Nominate Ambassador to Iraq," *White House Office of the Press Secretary*, 19 April 2004 (www.whitehouse.gov).
17. Cordesman, "One Year On," 10-11.
18. Michael D. Coogan, "In the Beginning: The Earliest History," in *The Oxford History of the Biblical World*, ed. Michael D. Coogan (New York: Oxford University Press, 1998), 3-31; Zahi Hawass, "Rise and Fall: A Civilized Prehistory," in *History and Faith: Cradle and Crucible in the Middle East* (Washington, DC: National Geographic, 2002), 30-45.
19. Nisan, *Minorities in the Middle East*, 3.
20. Hawass, "Rise and Fall," 45.
21. Bernard Lewis, *The Middle East: A Brief History of the Last 2,000 Years* (New York: Touchstone, 1995), 27-28.
22. Andrew Wheatcroft, "Through a Glass Darkly: Alexander's Conquest Through the Crusades," in *Cradle and Crucible*, 45-53.
23. Barbara Geller, "Transitions and Trajectories: Jews and Christians in the Roman Empire," in Coogan, *Oxford History of the Biblical World*, 561-96.
24. Lewis, *Middle East*, 33-47.
25. Ibid., 47.
26. Hourani, *Arab Peoples*, 5-37; Lewis, *Middle East*, 51-110.
27. Ibid., 38.
28. Stanford Jay Shaw, *History of the Ottoman Empire and Modern Turkey* (New York: Cambridge University Press, 1976), 1-167; Halil Inalcik, *The Ottoman Empire: The Classical Age, 1300-1600* (London: Weidenfeld and Nicolson, 1973), 9-54.
29. Ira M. Lapidus, "Sultanates and Gunpowder Empires: The Middle East," in *The Oxford History of Islam*, ed. John L. Esposito (New York: Oxford University Press, 1999), 374.

30. Hourani, *Arab Peoples*, 315.
31. Hourani, *Arab Peoples*, 265-71.
32. Ibid., 267.
33. Palmer, *Guardians of the Gulf*, 4-5.
34. Ibid., 7-13.
35. Ibid., 13. Also see Leonard M. Fanning, *American Oil Operations Abroad* (New York: McGraw Hill, 1947), 256-59. Fanning notes that American companies produced between 60 and 70 percent of the world's crude oil between 1890 and 1918.
36. Hourani, *Arab Peoples*, 318.
37. Dore Gold, *Hatred's Kingdom: How Saudi Arabia Supports the New Global Terrorism* (New York: Regnery Publishing, 2003), 59-60; Palmer, *Guardians of the Gulf*, 18-19.
38. Fanning, *American Oil Operations*, 256-59. Reference made in Palmer, *Guardians of the Gulf*, 19.
39. In Iraq, annual oil production fell from 32,643,000 barrels in 1938 to 12,650,000 barrels in 1941, before rising to 32,112,000 in 1945. In neighboring Iran, annual oil production fell from 213,737 barrels in 1938 to 138,704 in 1941, before rising to 280,000 in 1944. Benjamin Shwadran, *The Middle East and the Great Powers* (New York: John Wiley and Sons, 1973), 197-98; Fanning, *American Oil Operations*, 257. Reference made in Palmer, *Guardians of the Gulf*, 21.
40. In Saudi Arabia, annual oil production increased from 580,000 barrels in 1938 to 5,075,000 barrels in 1940. It slipped to 4,310,000 in 1941, before rising again to 21,311,000 in 1945. Shwadran, *The Middle East and the Great Powers*, 349. Reference made in Palmer, *Guardians of the Gulf*, 22.
41. Palmer, *Guardians of the Gulf*, 26.
42. Hourani, *Arab Peoples*, 354-55.
43. For an in-depth study of the Arab-Israeli Conflict, see Vaughn P. Shannon, *Balancing Act: US Foreign Policy and the Arab-Israeli Conflict* (Aldershot, UK: Ashgate Publishing Limited, 2003).
44. Hourani, *Arab Peoples*, 359-60.
45. Gold, *Hatred's Kingdom*, 59-62.
46. Palmer, *Guardians of the Gulf*, 48-49.
47. While Truman was not willing to sign a formal defense treaty with Riyadh at that juncture, he expressed in an October 1950 letter to King Abdul Aziz bin Abdul Rahman Al Saud (known to the West as Ibn Saud), "U.S. interests in the preservation of the territorial integrity of Saudi Arabia." Parker T. Hart, *Saudi Arabia and the United States: Birth of a Security Partnership* (Bloomington: Indiana University Press, 1998), 58. Reference made in Gold, *Hatred's Kingdom*, 70-71.
48. Palmer, *Guardians of the Gulf*, 38-39.
49. For an in-depth account of US-Iranian relations during the Cold War, see Gary Sick, *All Fall Down: America's Tragic Encounter with Iran* (New York: Random House, 1985).
50. Hourani, *Arab Peoples*, 365-69; Thomas Parrish, *The Cold War Encyclopedia* (New York: Henry Holt and Company, 1996), 301-02.
51. Palmer, *Guardians of the Gulf*, 52-82.
52. Tripp, *A History of Iraq*, 145-47.
53. Palmer, *Guardians of the Gulf*, 52-82.
54. Hourani, *Arab Peoples*, 368.
55. Ibid., 413-14.
56. Con Coughlin, *Saddam: King of Terror* (New York: HarperCollins, 2002), 52-150.
57. Hourani, *Arab Peoples*, 416-19.

58. Gold, *Hatred's Kingdom*, 84-87; Hourani, *Arab Peoples*, 418-19.

59. Gilles Kepel, *Jihad: The Trail of Political Islam*, tr. Anthony F. Roberts (Cambridge: Harvard University Press, 2002), 103-35.

60. James E. Carter, "State of the Union Address," 23 January 1980, U.S. Department of State, *Basic Documents* (Washington, D.C.: US Government Printing Office, 1980). Reference made in Palmer, *Guardians of the Gulf*, 106.

61. Murray Waas, "What Washington Gave Saddam for Christmas," in *The Iraq War Reader: History, Documents, Opinions*, ed. Micah L. Sifry and Christopher Cerf (New York: Simon and Schuster, 2003), 30-40.

62. Joost R. Hilterman, "The Men who Helped the Man who Gassed his Own People," in *Iraq War Reader*, 41-45.

63. Mark P. Lagon, *The Reagan Doctrine: The Sources of American Conduct in the Cold War's Last Chapter* (Westport, CT: Praeger, 1994), 57.

64. Saadet Deger and Somnath Sen, *Military Expenditures: The Political Economy of International Security* (Oxford: Oxford University Press, 1990), 70, 126.

65. While there is no evidence to suggest that the CIA provided directed funding to Osama bin Laden's Aran jihadists in Afghanistan during the 1980s, his group was clearly allied with the Afghan resistance movement. Richard Miniter, *Losing Bin Laden: How Bill Clinton's Failures Unleashed Global Terror* (Washington, D.C.: Regnery Publishing, Inc., 2003), 9-13.

66. See Francis Fukuyama, *The End of History and the Last Man* (New York: Avon, 1993).

67. See Samuel P. Huntington, *The Clash of Civilizations and the Remaking of World Order* (New York: Simon & Schuster, 1996).

68. See Kenneth N. Waltz, "The Emerging Structure of International Politics," *International Security* 18 (Fall 1993): 44-79; John J. Mearsheimer, "Back to the Future: Instability in Europe After the Cold War," *International Security* 15 (Summer 1990): 5-56.

69. See Zbigniew Brzezinski, *Out of Control: Global Turmoil on the Eve of the Twenty-first Century* (New York: Touchstone Books, 1993); Robert D. Kaplan, "The Coming Anarchy," *Atlantic Monthly* 281 (Summer 1994).

70. Pollack, *Threatening Storm*, 87-94.

71. In an address to a joint session of Congress just over two weeks prior to the launch of operations against Taliban and Al Qaeda forces in Afghanistan, for example, Bush warned, "we will pursue nations that provide aid or safe haven to terrorism. Every nation, in every region, now has a decision to make. Either you are with us, or you are with the terrorists. From this day forward, any nation that continues to harbor or support terrorism will be regarded by the United States as a hostile regime." George W. Bush, "Presidential Address to a Joint Session of Congress," 23 September 2001, excerpted in *We Will Prevail*, 15.

72. Bob Woodward, *Bush at War* (New York: Random House, 2003), 49-50.

73. Bush, "State of the Union Address," 29 January 2002, excerpted in *We Will Prevail*, 108.

Chapter 3

George H.W. Bush Administration and the Persian Gulf, 1989-1993

Introduction

With respect to the conduct of foreign policy, all American presidential administrations must manage transitions upon assuming office. The challenges of such transitions are typically conditioned by changes that reflect the political affiliations and worldviews of a given president and his advisors, and the degrees of continuity and change prevalent in the international system at a particular temporal juncture. Over the course of the Cold War, most of those challenges were similar in character in that they grew out of the confrontation pitting the United States against the Soviet Union. Between 1945 and 1988, for example, those two states' relative power fluctuated regularly, but the bipolar structure of the global system remained relatively unchanged. When George H.W. Bush began his tenure as president in January 1989, however, the system itself was on the brink of a fundamental change. The geopolitical transformation that ensued was the result of the collapse of Moscow's communist empire and the implosion of the Soviet Union itself between 1989 and 1991. Those developments, in turn, left the United States as the world's lone superpower.

For its part, the Bush administration had both to preside over what proved to be the proverbial final act of the Cold War in the heart of Europe and, concomitantly, to plan and prosecute America's first major "hot" conflict in the strategically vital Persian Gulf. The former demanded the diplomatic orchestration of Moscow's surrender of political influence on the European continent in 1989-90. The latter entailed the construction of a coalition of states (including the Soviet Union) to oppose Iraqi President Saddam Hussein's invasion and occupation of neighboring Kuwait in 1990 and then support the subsequent expulsion of Baghdad's forces through the prosecution of the Persian Gulf War in 1991.

Those two sets of events were directly related. Ultimately, the manner in which Bush oversaw the conclusion of the Cold War through the collapse of communist regimes across Central and Eastern Europe in the fall and winter of 1989-90 and the unification of Germany in October 1990 set the stage for his administration's management of the Persian Gulf Crisis for two reasons.[1] First, the administration's diplomacy in orchestrating the unification process helped solidify individual and governmental relationships with states both within, and outside of, NATO, many of which joined the coalition in the war against Iraq. Second, its management of the closing stage of the Cold War provided valuable experience with respect to the ways to maintain domestic and international cohesion when handling complex—and, to a large extent, unprecedented—events.

Within months of taking office, Bush had a unique opportunity to orchestrate the end of the 45-year bipolar confrontation with the Soviet Union. The policies of the preceding Ronald W. Reagan administration (in which Bush served as vice president)—most notably a massive defense buildup, including the pursuit of a space-based anti-ballistic missile system, and support for revolutionary groups fighting to overthrow regimes backed by Moscow in the developing world—forced Soviet President Mikhail Gorbachev to recognize the innate economic and political flaws in the communist system.[2] Gorbachev responded with promises to enact domestic reforms and release the Soviet Union's iron grip on the member states of the Warsaw Pact, leaving the Bush team to formulate and pursue policies that would encourage the Kremlin to back its rhetoric with substantive action. Bush faced a daunting challenge in dealing with an economically and politically moribund but not militarily defeated Soviet state. Fortunately, he was not entirely bereft of historical guidance on how best to proceed. The post-World War I and -World War II settlements and their legacies of instability and stability, respectively, served as testaments both to the imprudence of humiliating a defeated state and the indispensability of American leadership in Europe and the world.

Sensibly, the Bush administration heeded past mistakes in responding to present realities. Bush recognized that the United States was the only state with the requisite political, economic and military power to manage the political reconfiguration of Central and Eastern Europe and subsequent German unification process in a manner that would take into account if not serve fully the interests of all the continent's major players. Consequently, Bush and his advisors followed three rules in formulating their transatlantic policies. First, they were firm yet prudent in dealing with the Soviet Union, pressing Gorbachev to accede to American demands without creating a perception that Moscow's security concerns had not been taken into account. Second, they also exhibited the requisite leadership to secure NATO support for his initiatives. While the United States had the final word, it did not act without consulting its allies first. Third, they gave primacy to the Washington-Bonn axis in 1989, calling for an end to the division of Germany and providing the necessary diplomatic support to ensure that the 1990 unification process proceeded under American auspices.

Bush convinced Gorbachev he could trust the United States by taking care not to humiliate the Soviet Union publicly when the Warsaw Pact collapsed. Less than a month after the fall of the Berlin Wall, Bush expressed unambiguous American support for German unification at the December 1989 Malta Summit, but he also promised Gorbachev not to further undermine his counterpart's tenuous domestic political position so long as the Soviet Union did not crack down militarily in the Baltics. Bush's treatment of Gorbachev was pragmatic. He was convinced he could count on cooperation from Gorbachev in achieving German unification on terms favorable to the United States. If Gorbachev was replaced by a communist hard-liner, that would no longer be the case. Thus, Bush accommodated Gorbachev when it was possible to do so without compromising American interests in Europe.

The Bush administration's construction of an inclusive framework—the "two-plus-four"—to facilitate German unification was masterful. The two-plus-four, which consisted of East and West Germany, as well as the United States, Soviet Union, United Kingdom and France, was an effective means to address the concerns of all the principals involved in the process. It also enabled the United States to retain a predominant role in global affairs in general and on the continent in particular. Essentially, the framework served at least some of the interests of each of the states it included, a design that also proved effective during the Persian Gulf crisis. First, it gave the Germans the right to address internal issues—most notably economic and political integration—without interference from outside parties. Second, it gave the British, French and Soviets seats at the negotiating table. Thus, all three had an opportunity to raise their security concerns with respect to the future course of a previously united Germany they held responsible for the death and destruction associated with World War I and World War II. Third, it allowed the United States to orchestrate the proceedings in three capacities—as the bipolar counterpart to the Soviet Union, the head of the alliance and West Germany's partner.

Through its role in the two-plus-four process, the Bush administration achieved the one objective it deemed indispensable to European stability and security: inclusion of the reunited Germany in NATO. The United States was the only actor in a position to extract the concessions from NATO and West Germany necessary to secure Soviet accession to membership for the reconstituted Germany in the alliance. Bush did so by offering Gorbachev "nine assurances" that mitigated the threats the Kremlin felt NATO and Germany posed to the Soviet Union.

Bush's assurances were a product of coordination between Washington and Bonn as well as transatlantic consultation and cooperation. The American-brokered NATO Summit declaration in June 1990 in London helped bolster Gorbachev's domestic political position at the concurrent twenty-eighth Congress of the Communist Party of the Soviet Union.[3] Chancellor Helmut Kohl's promises to limit Germany's military capacity and offers of economic incentives to the Soviet Union—coordinated with Bush—were the final pieces of the unification puzzle.[4] Acknowledging these accommodations, Gorbachev acceded to German unification on American terms. Bush's approach was instructive in two respects. First, it validated the position of the United States as an indispensable player in the European and international systems. Second, it illustrated the efficacy of cooperation as opposed to confrontation in the settlement of global conflicts. However, it did not preclude the potential for future flare-ups of military violence in other regions of the world.

As the Bush administration focused on the German unification process in the winter, spring and summer of 1990, tension was mounting between Iraq and Kuwait in the Persian Gulf. Put simply, Iraq's economy slipped rapidly into decline in the aftermath of its 1980-88 war with Iran. As a result, Saddam sought to obtain relief by pressuring Kuwait to lower its production of oil, which would help to raise the price of that commodity on the world market and thus increase revenues flowing into Iraq's coffers.[5] Chief among the means Saddam used to achieve that end was a massive troop buildup along Iraq's southwestern border with Kuwait. By 31 July 1990, Iraq had mobilized 100,000 troops, which Saddam threatened to utilize in order to force Kuwait to comply with his demands both with respect to oil production and a long-standing dispute between the two states over access to the Persian Gulf via control of two small islands—Warbah and Bubiyan—off the Kuwaiti coast. After assuring leaders throughout the Gulf region that he would not take immediate action, Saddam promptly broke his word, seizing Kuwait through an expeditious invasion on 2 August that left the Bush administration scrambling to formulate and deliver a effective response.[6]

With this introductory primer providing a necessary contextual foundation, the balance of the chapter examines and assesses the Bush administration's policies toward the Persian Gulf in the contexts of three related sections that unfold in the following manner:

- The first section opens with an examination of American interests in the Gulf as articulated by the Bush administration and the resultant development of policies toward Iraq from January 1989 to July 1990. However, it focuses primarily on the diplomatic prologue to, and conduct of, the Persian Gulf War and the aftermath of that conflict. Given the centrality of those developments to the US role in the Gulf both from 1989-93 and over the ensuing decade, this section is considerably lengthier than either of the chapter's ensuing sections.
- The second section considers the strengths and weaknesses of the Bush administration's policies toward the Persian Gulf generally and Iraq specifically at the US domestic level as well as in the contexts of the Gulf, Greater Middle East and global international system.
- The concluding section reiterates the chapter's most significant points, then closes with an assessment of the short- and long-term costs and benefits of the above policies.

US Interests and Resultant Policies in the Persian Gulf, 1989-1993

Once in power, a given president and his advisors must define and prioritize American national interests on the basis of what they perceive to be the prevalent threats to the United States and its allies at the time and then construct policies designed to mitigate, if not eliminate, those threats. The Bush administration judged correctly that orchestrating the peaceful end of the Cold War in Europe in a manner that would minimize US-Soviet and transatlantic differences therein was its top priority in 1989-90. As a result, it gave less credence to the politics of the Gulf generally and Saddam's machinations therein than would have otherwise been prudent in the 19 months preceding Iraq's invasion of Kuwait. As Bush and his National Security Advisor, Brent Scowcroft, acknowledge in their joint memoirs, the "Persian Gulf had not been among our major concerns early in the Administration. Despite a number of sometimes exasperating differences with Iraq, developments in the region had begun to return to normal following the 1980-88 Iran-Iraq conflict and occupied the attention of our specialists rather than the policy-making team."[7]

Notwithstanding the administration's understandable decision to focus primarily on managing the closing stage of the Cold War, it also recognized that the United States had vital interests in the Persian Gulf to protect in 1989-90. It defined those interests in terms of three interconnected issue areas, those pertaining to economics, politics and security. Economically, the United States remained dependent on the Gulf's vast oil resources, albeit less so than its Western European and Asian allies. Thus, avoiding a prolonged Middle Eastern crisis on the scale of those that impeded Western access to the region's petroleum resources during the 1970s was a paramount concern.[8] Politically, the instability that any such crisis would entail within the Gulf, and along its periphery, was likely to have disastrous consequences. Preventing regional destabilization, in turn, demanded the use of Washington's diplomatic and military assets to maintain a secure environment in the Gulf.[9]

Above all, the Bush administration possessed two fundamental strengths that enabled it to develop and implement foreign policies and take the necessary decisions to safeguard US interests within—and, for that matter, outside of—the Persian Gulf. First, Bush and the members of the inner circle of his foreign policy team had lengthy records of public service at the federal level. Men such as Bush, Scowcroft, Secretary of State James Baker, Secretary of Defense Richard Cheney and Chairman of the Joint Chiefs of Staff Colin Powell had served under President Ronald Reagan during the 1980s. Second, in working together in the past, they developed an excellent rapport and resultant ability to avoid the types of intra-administration disputes that have the potential to complicate policymaking during international crises.

Bush's accession to the presidency was the culmination of a distinguished career of federal government service spanning nearly two decades. Born into a politically connected family the head of which was Republican Senator Prescott Bush, he served as a naval aviator in World War II and earned an undergraduate degree from Yale in 1948. In addition to his 1981-89 stint as vice president under Reagan, he served as ambassador to the UN from 1971-73 and Director of the CIA from 1976-77. Bush gained valuable experience in each of these capacities, particularly at the global level, where he cultivated strong personal and professional relationships with a range of world leaders and a practical understanding of the workings of international politics.

In order to ensure the development of a cohesive policy-making framework, Bush constructed a close-knit circle of advisors with whom he had worked closely and developed cordial relationships in the past. His choice of Scowcroft as head of the National Security Council (NSC) and Baker as secretary of state were illustrative of this approach. Scowcroft and Bush served together in the administration of President Gerald Ford, the former in the same capacity as in the Bush administration and the latter as CIA chief. Scowcroft was knowledgeable on foreign policy matters and familiar with the workings of the executive branch. He also shared Bush's prudence in formulating policy initiatives, preferring to err on the side of caution. After his initial choice for secretary of defense, John Tower, failed to clear the Senate confirmation process, the President turned instead to Cheney, an old Washington hand then serving in the Congress as a ranking member on the House Select Committee on Intelligence. As was true of Baker and Scowcroft, Cheney had previous experience in the executive branch, having acted as chief of staff under Ford. These attributes made for an effective mix in a position that would involve considerable interaction between the White House and Congress.[10]

Bush's selection of Powell as chairman of the JCS following the retirement of Admiral William Crowe from that position in September 1989 was historic in two respects. At age 53, Powell became the youngest officer and the first African-American to serve in the position. A career military man, Powell fought in the Vietnam War and also served in the Carter and Reagan administrations. In the latter administration, he assumed the post of National Security Advisor in 1987, shortly after the Iran-Contra affair rocked the Reagan White House. Essentially, he possessed attributes equally suitable for the distinctive structures of the executive branch and those of the armed forces. Consequently, he was an excellent bridge between those entities.[11]

Assembling a team composed of members with both the intellectual and inter-personal skills to develop and implement effective policies under fire was Bush's first step in developing the capacity to manage international crises smoothly. Next, the administration had to construct a framework within which cabinet members and their staffs could interpret events and deliver the requisite policy advise to enable Bush to take informed decisions that served American interests constructively at a given juncture.

The Bush administrative devised a decision-making approach that, as political scientist Steve Yetiv notes, involved four interrelated levels of interaction during the Persian Gulf crisis. The first level consisted of bilateral discussions between Bush and his closest colleagues, most notably Scowcroft and Baker. The second level featured policy-making interactions within an inner circle of administration officials known as the "Gang of Eight." This group included Bush, Baker, Scowcroft, Cheney and Powell, as well as Vice President Dan Quayle, White House Chief of Staff John Sununu and CIA Director Robert Gates. The third layer was composed of the chief aides of the individuals in the Gang of Eight and thus known as the deputies committee. The fourth layer consisted of a smaller group drawn from the deputies committee, including officials from the Departments of State and Defense, the CIA, the JCS and NSC staffer Richard Haass, who drafted most of the entity's position papers.[12] The deputies committee handled day-to-day matters in managing crises, while the fourth-layer group concentrated on the conception of overarching policy initiatives, which it then sent up the pipeline for consideration at the two highest levels of interaction.[13]

Prelude to a Crisis in the Gulf, 1989-90

After conducting an initial review of US policy toward the Persian Gulf in the opening months of its tenure, the Bush administration chose to maintain the strategy of the Reagan administration, which had tilted toward Baghdad during the Iran-Iraq war. Bush's foreign policy team articulated its policy approach in the context of National Security Review (NSR)-10. Most significantly, NSR-10 emphasized that "[n]ormal relations between the United States and Iraq would serve our longer-term interests and promote stability in both the Gulf and the Middle East. The United States government should propose economic and political incentives for Iraq to moderate its behavior and to increase our influence with Iraq."[14] Bush accepted those recommendations and formalized the resultant American strategy by issuing National Security Directive (NSD)-26 in October 1989.[15]

The Bush administration's efforts to implement that strategy in the final eight weeks of 1989 and the early months of 1990 were limited all but exclusively to economic initiatives. In November 1989, for instance, the US Department of Agriculture moved forward with a Commodity Credit Corporation program that guaranteed $1 billion to US exporters in order to facilitate grain shipments to Iraq. Additionally, ignoring congressional opposition, Bush signed a directive authorizing an Export-Import Bank line of credit of nearly $200 million for Iraqi grain imports in January 1989.[16] Ultimately, those initiatives, which were designed in part as goodwill gestures to help convince Saddam to discontinue his nuclear, chemical and biological weapons development programs, represented what Baker described as the "high water mark of our efforts to moderate Iraqi behavior."[17]

Concurrent with American efforts to maintain stability in the Persian Gulf through the aforementioned economic inducements, Saddam spent the opening months of 1989 pressuring Kuwait and the United Arab Emirates to reduce their petroleum production quotas to avoid reductions in the price of oil that would result in further damage to the already crippled Iraqi economy. In short, the conduct of its war with Iran from 1980-88 destroyed Iraq's economy. The war left Iraq $80 billion in debt and unable to finance the $230 in reconstruction costs to repair the damage inflicted by the Iranians.[18] The principal means of recovery, in turn, was Baghdad's own oil industry; thus, from Saddam's perspective, the higher the price of that commodity, the better.

Despite Iraq's economic woes, Saddam remained determined both to maintain his conventional military forces and also to continue to develop WMD. In order to finance his military expenditures, Saddam chose to pressure neighboring Arab states, a strategy that became increasingly apparent to the Bush administration in the months preceding Iraq's August 1990 invasion of Kuwait. At a May 1990 meeting of the Arab League, for example, Saddam accused Kuwait of conducting economic warfare against Iraq and demanded that members of the Gulf Cooperation Council forgive Baghdad's war debts and provide it with $30 billion in economic aid.[19] Above all, Saddam sought to tap into Kuwait's $208 billion in financial assets through diplomatic pressure and, if necessary, the use of force. As former CIA analyst Kenneth Pollack concludes, "Saddam's solution was as simple as it was misguided: raid the treasure chest next door. ... Saddam believed that by invading Kuwait, he not only would get his hands on Kuwait's oil wealth, and so improve Iraq's economic prospects over the long term, but would be able to get his hands on Kuwait's financial assets, which he could use to solve his short-term budgetary needs."[20]

By July, repeated attempts by Saddam to exert the requisite political pressure on Kuwait to force it to reduce its production of oil had proven fruitless. Consequently, he commenced a military buildup on the Iraqi-Kuwaiti border that reached 120,000 on the eve of the invasion on 31 July. A meeting between Saddam and American Ambassador April Glaspie on 25 July in Baghdad, the particulars of which remain a point of contention between members of the Bush administration and its critics, did not lead Saddam to settle the dispute with Kuwait peacefully.[21] Instead, in the early hours of 1 August, Iraqi forces crossed the border into Kuwait, firing the proverbial opening shot in the 1990-91 Persian Gulf conflict.

Responding to the Invasion

Bush first received intelligence reports suggesting an impending Iraqi invasion from Scowcroft and Haass shortly before 8:30 p.m. on the evening of 1 August 1990. Haass suggested Bush attempt to reach Saddam by phone to try to dissuade the Iraqi leader from sending his troops across the border, but before the president could act, the White House received word from the American Embassy in Kuwait that the invasion was already underway. Despite Saddam's previous threats, the attack took Bush somewhat by surprise. As he recalled, "I found it hard to believe that Saddam would invade. For a moment I thought, or hoped, that he might withdraw, having made his point. I worried about the invasion's effect on other countries in the area, especially our vulnerable friend Saudi Arabia."[22]

Initially, Bush took two steps, which, together, set the tone for the administration's subsequent management of the crisis. First, he instructed Scowcroft both to consult with Baker, who was engaged in arms control talks with Soviet Foreign Minister Eduard Shevardnadze in Irkutsk, Siberia, and to set up a meeting of the NSC, which would convene prior to the president's departure for a previously scheduled meeting with British Prime Minister Margaret Thatcher in Aspen, Colorado. Second, Bush directed American Ambassador to the UN Thomas Pickering to request an emergency meeting of the Security Council and push for a resolution condemning Iraq's invasion. From the outset, Bush was determined to exhibit firm US leadership, while acknowledging the importance of UN support to legitimize America's actions internationally.[23]

In Washington, Bush was both resolute and pragmatic in responding to Iraq's aggression. On the morning of 2 August, he signed an executive order to freeze all Iraqi and Kuwaiti assets in the United States to ensure that Saddam recognized the seriousness of the situation and would not benefit financially prior to the imposition of UN sanctions. In addition, he expressed solidarity with Iraq's Arab neighbors, offering to dispatch a squadron of F-15s to Saudi Arabia, which was potentially Saddam's next victim. However, Bush did not want to commit the United States to a longer-term plan of action until the administration could discuss the available options in greater depth. Consequently, his comments to the press preceding the initial NSC meeting on the crisis suggested that the administration was exploring options but "not contemplating" American intervention in the Persian Gulf.[24] His rhetoric was chosen carefully. As Scowcroft pointed out, Bush's "language was picked with two thoughts in mind: First, don't say anything at this early point which would telegraph his thinking. Second, make clear that the NSC meeting was not a decision session but a discussion of the situation and options for reacting."[25]

Discussion at the ensuing NSC meeting focused primarily on three issues: oil, UN sanctions and American-Soviet cooperation. Scowcroft argued that "the most significant issue economically is oil. ... We should mount an embargo of Kuwaiti and Iraqi oil purchases."[26] Bush concurred, but also stressed the importance of imposing sanctions under UN auspices in order to cultivate broad-based international support in opposition to Iraq. In particular, he asserted that "[i]nternational sanctions will give us security cover. They will give some spine to Saudi Arabia and others to take difficult actions, like closing the pipelines [to Iraq]." In addition, Bush stressed the importance of including the Soviet Union in the process, noting that Baker was pressing Shevardnadze and Gorbachev to develop a joint statement condemning the Iraqis. Keeping Moscow in the loop was essential in order to ensure Security Council support and increase the pressure on Iraq, which had long enjoyed conciliatory relations with the Soviet Union.[27]

While Bush and Scowcroft flew to Aspen for the former's meeting with Thatcher, Pickering concentrated on rallying support at the UN and Baker aides Dennis Ross and Robert Zoellick worked with Shevardnadze deputy Sergei Tarasenko in Moscow to fashion a joint statement condemning the Iraqi invasion.[28] Pickering achieved the desired result in New York in the form of UN Security Council Resolution 660, which condemned Saddam's aggression and demanded that Iraq "withdraw immediately and unconditionally all its forces to the positions in which they were located on 1 August 1990."[29] After in-flight telephone consultations with Egyptian President Hosni Mubarak and Jordan's King Hussein, during which the former asked for and received a two-day window to attempt to devise a pan-Arab resolution of the imbroglio, the president met with Thatcher in Aspen. Predictably, Thatcher pushed for a forceful response to the Iraqi dictator's initiative.[30]

Following an evening flight back to Washington, Bush convened a second NSC meeting on the crisis on the morning of 3 August. While significant, ease of access to Gulf oil was no longer the lone critical issue under discussion. Deputy Secretary of State Lawrence Eagleburger, for example, argued that "[a]s the bipolar world is relaxed, it permits [aggression such as that of Iraq against Kuwait], giving people flexibility because they are not worried about the involvement of the superpowers. ... If [Saddam] succeeds, others may try the same thing."[31] Addressing the need to deter further Iraqi aggression, particularly with respect to Saudi Arabia, Cheney and Powell both broached the issue of American military involvement, with the latter stressing the need for a buildup of ground forces in the region. As Powell explained, "to deter further Iraqi action with Saudi Arabia would require US forces on the ground. This is the most prudent option and we need to push it with Saudi Arabia so Saddam looks south and sees an American presence."[32]

The initial UN resolution against Iraq and the shifting tone among Gang of Eight members toward the need for military action to check Saddam helped strengthen Bush's resolve as well. Although the Soviet Union had voted for Security Council Resolution 660, a joint statement condemning the Iraqi invasion remained in the works. Ultimately, Baker's team delivered. On 3 August, in the lobby at Vnukovo II Airport outside Moscow, Shevardnadze and Baker issued the statement Bush had hoped for, one that not only condemned Saddam's aggression but also called for an arms embargo against Iraq.[33] Two days later, in an impromptu statement to the press on the South Lawn of the White House, Bush issued a statement indicating his determination to reverse Iraq's gains in Kuwait. When asked by a reporter whether the United States would take action to remove Saddam's forces from Kuwait, Bush responded, "[t]his will not stand, this aggression against Kuwait."[34]

Critics have since suggested that Bush delivered his pronouncement without consulting adequately with his cabinet, Congress or world leaders. Yet, Powell—while admittedly caught off guard by the statement—insists in his memoirs that Bush's thought process was sound, noting that the president "had listened quietly to his advisors. He had consulted by phone with world leaders. And then, taking his own counsel, he had come to this momentous decision and revealed it at the first opportunity."[35] Once Bush had expressed his stance on the need for American intervention publicly, the administration was free to construct an international coalition to confront Saddam and, if necessary, forcibly expel Iraqi forces from Kuwait.

Building the Coalition

The Bush administration's development of a coalition to counter Iraq's aggression against Kuwait—initially with UN-mandated economic sanctions and, ultimately, through the conduct of the Persian Gulf War—proceeded in three stages. First, Bush and his aides consulted with Middle Eastern leaders (primarily Egypt's Mubarak, Saudi Arabia's King Fahd, Jordan's King Hussein and Syria's Hafez Assad) in order to facilitate a buildup of American military ground and air forces in Saudi Arabia in the context of Operation Desert Shield. This entailed telephone diplomacy by Bush, along with visits by Cheney to Jeddah, and Saudi Ambassador Prince Bandar bin Sultan and Saudi Foreign Minister Prince Saud to the president's vacation home in Kennebunkport, Maine. Second, the administration solidified support for the coalition, and the UN resolutions it sought to implement through consultations with Middle Eastern, Western European, Soviet and Japanese leaders. This included a mission by Baker to extract financial contributions from those states with the requisite resources to reduce the economic burden on the United States and coalition partners unable to afford the revenue strains the UN sanctions brought about. Third, Bush and Baker worked to ratchet up the pressure on Saddam by pushing for a UN-mandated use-of-force resolution against Iraq.

Essentially, Bush began constructing the coalition the day Saddam's forces crossed the Kuwaiti border. He recognized that Saudi Arabia was the key to checking Iraq's advance and thus focused the administration's diplomatic efforts on Mubarak in Cairo, Fahd and Saud in Jeddah and Bandar in Washington. Bush's first discussion with Fahd during the crisis took place following the former's meeting with Thatcher on 2 August in Aspen. Fahd was resolute in his opposition to Iraq but stopped short of approving the stationing of American forces on Saudi soil, which left Bush concerned that Saddam's neighbors were considering allowing his actions to stand rather than risk escalating the imbroglio beyond Kuwait.[36] Bush has since noted that "I began to worry that the Saudis might be considering compromise, that they might accept the new status quo on their northern border if there were guarantees from Iraq. ... There is a historical Arab propensity to try to work out 'deals'. ... We had to have our Arab allies with us, particularly those who were threatened the most—the Saudis."[37]

Bush employed a two-part strategy to convince Fahd of the indispensability of the deployment of American forces in Saudi Arabia and the administration's commitment to maintain a military presence there until the crisis was resolved. First, Bush requested that Bandar meet with Scowcroft at the White House. When Bandar expressed concerns over Washington's withdrawal of troops from the Middle East under fire in the past (most notably following the terrorist bombing of the US Marine Barracks in Beirut, Lebanon, in October 1983), Scowcroft assured the Saudi ambassador that the United States would not back down this time. He then sent Bandar to the Pentagon for a full briefing on American plans for a force buildup in Saudi Arabia.[38] The briefing helped quell Bandar's concerns enough for him to invite a senior Bush administration team to Jeddah to brief Fahd on the force buildup initiative. Prior to dispatching Cheney and General H. Norman Schwarzkopf to accomplish that task, Bush phoned Fahd with a personal assurance that "I am determined that Saddam will not get away with all this infamy. When we work out a plan, once we are there, we will stay until we are asked to leave. You have my solemn word on this."[39] Bush's diplomacy was effective, in that Fahd through Bandar acceded to the president's request prior to Cheney's departure, rendering the official decision a formality.[40]

Concurrent with the administration's efforts to obtain Fahd's support for the dispatch of American troops to Saudi Arabia, Bush pressed other world leaders in the Middle East and Europe to support a UN resolution imposing economic sanctions on Iraq. On 3 August, for example, Bush spoke first with Turkish President Turgut Ozal and later with Kohl, French President François Mitterrand and Japanese Prime Minister Toshiki Kaifu. He failed to secure a clear commitment from Ozal to close the oil pipeline between Turkey and Iraq, but did obtain consent from the latter three as to the necessity to take collective action against Saddam. Two days later, after meeting with an emissary from Baghdad who indicated that Saddam had no intention of reversing course in Kuwait, Ozal informed Bush that Turkey would accede to Washington's call to close the pipeline, but only once UN economic sanctions against Iraq were in place. Additionally, Kaifu agreed to ban Japanese imports of Iraqi oil.[41] Bush obtained the requisite inducement for Ozal in the form of Security Council Resolution 661 on 6 August. The measure imposed an economic blockade on Iraq with the exception of imports required for humanitarian and medical purposes. It was the responsibility of the United States and its coalition partners to enforce the sanctions.[42]

Cheney flew to Jeddah on 5 August and phoned Bush the next afternoon to inform the latter of Fahd's official request for an American-led military buildup in Saudi Arabia, with the caveat that Washington include Arab forces in the coalition. The buildup commenced with an alert order to the 82nd Airborne, the dispatch of a squadron of F-15s and plans in the works for the deployment of 240,000 servicemen and 1,600 sophisticated combat aircraft to the region by November. With military support from the United States formally offered and accepted, Bush spent the remainder of 6-7 August notifying American allies of the initiative before revealing his plans to the public in a nationally televised address on the evening of the eighth.[43] In that address, Bush alluded to three "simple principles" guiding the administration's policy. First, the United States sought the "immediate, unconditional, and complete withdrawal of all Iraqi forces from Kuwait." Second, "Kuwait's legitimate government must be restored to replace the puppet regime" Saddam had installed in advance of the annexation of that entity to Iraq. Third, the administration was "committed to the security and stability of the Gulf."[44]

In the initial days and weeks following the address, Bush worked to implement the second stage of the coalition-building and -strengthening process. The first step in that process entailed personal and telephone diplomacy with leaders of the members of the coalition to ensure cohesion with respect to the expulsion of Iraq from Kuwait and the political will to employ the necessary economic and military means to achieve that end. Collectively, Middle Eastern leaders responded favorably to Bush's objectives through a 12-8 Arab League vote on 10 August on a measure honoring the UN resolutions, supporting the deployment of American troops and agreeing to field an all-Arab military force in the coalition. Bush attributed at least part of the Arab support against Saddam to the emphasis he had placed on maintaining personal and governmental contacts with smaller Gulf states such as the United Arab Emirates (UAE) and Oman from the outset of his presidency. Egyptian and Moroccan troops began arriving in Saudi Arabia the day of the Arab League vote, fulfilling Fahd's request for the deployment of both Arab and Western forces within his state.[45]

Predictably, the first significant threat to cohesion inside of the Bush administration, as well as the coalition, was associated with the use of force. With Bush and Scowcroft providing the impetus over objections from Baker, the United States began pressing in the latter half of August to utilize all necessary military means to enforce the economic sanctions against Iraq through an American-led naval blockade. The issue came to a head when five Iraqi cargo ships refused to turn back from their planned course to Yemen on 18 August, providing an overt challenge to the UN-mandated embargo. Bush suggested taking unilateral military action and received earnest support from Cheney and Scowcroft as well as Thatcher. Baker, on the other hand, worried that such a move would alienate the Soviets and requested that Bush allow Moscow until 25 August to attempt to convince Saddam to relent and cease engaging in further attempts to run the blockade. Reluctantly, Bush acceded to Baker's request, acknowledging that "Jim had convinced me that the additional effort for international cooperation made sense, and I wanted the Soviets totally on our side." The Soviets failed to convince Saddam to relent and subsequently backed Security Council Resolution 665, which, on 25 August, authorized the use of military force to enforce the UN ban on trade with Iraq by any means available.[46]

The next issue for the administration to address was burden sharing among coalition members, whether military or financial, concurrent with the buildup in Saudi Arabia.

As Bush and Scowcroft explain, it was essential to develop an effective "strategy for compensating those countries most hurt by complying with the sanctions."[47] In addition, Baker notes that "diplomatic support at the United Nations, though critical, wasn't enough. From a domestic political standpoint as well as a moral one, we needed to insist upon substantial financial commitments from other countries to help underwrite the costs of the operation."[48] As a means to achieve that end, Bush dispatched Baker on a September tour of coalition states with one clear task in mind. Baker was to seek financial pledges from those allies that possessed the requisite financial capacity in order to fund the buildup and also to compensate coalition members whose opposition to Saddam entailed substantial economic and political costs.

Baker commenced his eleven-day "tin-cup" trip with a 6-7 September stop in Saudi Arabia, where he met first with Bandar and Fahd in Jeddah and second with the Emir of Kuwait (Sheik Jabir al-Ahmed al-Sabah), who had set up a de facto government-in-exile in a luxury suite at the Sheraton hotel in Taif.[49] Baker did not mince words with the Saudis, telling Fahd, "[w]e are prepared to put not just treasure but blood on the line for your country and we need you to do your fair share." Fahd acceded quickly, asking Baker to "[j]ust tell us what you want and what you need for us to do." However, upon hearing Baker's request for $15 billion, Bandar added a caveat: "[d]on't ask us for $15 billion unless you get $15 billion from the Kuwaitis. They can afford it, too. They have all these assets. What good are they if they don't have their country? So ask as much from them as you get from us. You'll find that you'll get it."[50] Bandar's observation was on the mark. The next day, Baker procured a $15 billion pledge from the Emir. These exchanges exemplified the need for some degree of reciprocity in commitments among coalition members. Sacrifices by one member necessitated equivalent sacrifices from partners with similar means.

Following a brief stopover in the UAE, Baker flew to Cairo on 8 September to meet with Mubarak, whom he had known personally since 1980.[51] Mubarak was adamant both in his incredulous reaction to Saddam's continued refusal to adhere to the UN resolutions and in his disdain for King Hussein's apparent willingness to side with the Iraqi dictator.[52] In addition to gauging Mubarak's read on the state of affairs in the region, Baker utilized the meeting to offer his interlocutor a reward for his support in building and maintaining the coalition. It came in the form of a commitment by the administration to forgive Egypt's $7.1 billion debt to the United States.[53] The initiative was indicative of Bush's firm commitment to take actions to buttress the coalition despite the potential domestic political costs those measures entailed. Thankful for the administration's inducement, Mubarak assured Baker of the continued participation of Egyptian troops in the coalition but also expressed optimism that the sanctions would produce the desired result—namely Iraq's withdrawal from Kuwait—within six weeks. Notwithstanding that optimistic forecast, Baker closed the meeting by cautioning Mubarak, "[w]e can't plan on the basis of that being true. We have to plan on the basis of it being necessary to continue to build the pressure against [Saddam]."[54]

The administration's next step in escalating the level of pressure on Iraq came in Helsinski, where Bush and Baker met with their Soviet counterparts Gorbachev and

Shevardnadze to fashion a formal joint statement on the present state of the crisis. The principal point of contention between the two sides was Saddam's attempt to link the nascent imbroglio in the Gulf to the Arab-Israeli peace process in a 12 August statement. Saddam's initiative coincided with Moscow's desire to address that issue in the context of an international conference under American-Soviet sponsorship. The United States was averse to this option, primarily because it would appear as a diplomatic triumph for Iraq in the midst of Washington's campaign to isolate Saddam. In the end, the Americans and Soviets worked out a compromise whereby the former agreed privately to work toward joint sponsorship of the aforementioned conference once the crisis was resolved and the latter acceded to the issuance of a joint communiqué stating that "[w]e are determined to see this crisis end, and if the current steps fail to end it, we are prepared to consider additional ones consistent with the UN Charter. We must demonstrate beyond any doubt that aggression cannot and will not pay."[55] Bush added a public exclamation point to the declaration by proclaiming in an 11 September address before the US Congress, "Iraq will not be permitted to annex Kuwait. That's not a threat, that's not a boast, it's just the way it's going to be."[56]

While Bush returned to Washington after the meetings in Helsinki, Baker traveled to Moscow, where he signed the documents sealing the unification of Germany and responded to Gorbachev's request for aid to shore up his state's moribund economy with a pledge to attempt to procure a $4-5 billion line of credit from Saudi Arabia to the Soviet Union.[57] Next, Baker flew to Damascus for a 14 September meeting with Assad, who harbored a long-standing grudge against Saddam but was equally determined to avoid taking a decision potentially helpful to his Israeli adversaries. Baker wasted little time broaching the critical issue, asking Assad, "[i]n the event of military action, we will need to know what you will be willing to do with your troops on the Syrian-Iraqi border?" Assad responded with a pledge of up to 100,000 troops if necessary but acknowledged his disdain for the Israelis, noting that "[w]e will do the right thing, but it is not easy to do because of our own public opinion."[58] Although Baker and Bush were hardly unaware of the political repercussions of a visit to Damascus, particularly with respect to the powerful Jewish-American lobby in Washington, they judged the potential Syrian contributions to the coalition worth the risk. The trip proved that assessment correct.

Baker completed his journey on 15 September with stops in Rome to procure a commitment from the Italians to dispatch a squadron of Tornadoes to the Gulf and Ludwigshafen, West Germany, to meet with Kohl. Given the administration's stalwart support of the unification process, Bush had high expectations for financial support from Kohl, whose state's constitution ruled out the deployment of German military forces outside of NATO territory. After reminding Kohl, "[w]e've worked very closely in the last year to meet your needs," Baker stressed that "if it looks like you're being skimpy on the money, you're getting all the benefits of this and you're not contributing. And even if I don't believe it, that's the way it's perceived." Despite the potential political repercussions in light of Germany's understandable aversion to military conflict since the conclusion of World War II, Kohl promised $2 billion in assistance to the coalition.[59] With Baker's "tin-cup" effort complete, it was left to Powell and Schwarzkopf to manage the buildup in Saudi Arabia and Bush to pave the way for an eventual use of force against Iraq if Saddam's intransigence continued.

Expelling Iraq from Kuwait

Bush's plan to develop the requisite military capacity and collective political will to engage in coalition warfare to eject Iraq from Kuwait proceeded in four stages from October 1990 to January 1991. First, Bush provided Powell and Schwarzkopf with assurances they would have the necessary resources to conduct an effective offensive campaign against Iraq. Second, the president did not flinch upon learning that Schwarzkopf was calling for a near doubling of American forces in the Persian Gulf, approving the request unilaterally and putting off a public announcement of the initiative until the completion of midterm congressional elections in early November. Third, he facilitated the passage of a Security Council resolution approving the use of all means at the coalition's disposal to force Saddam to comply with each of the UN measures passed during the crisis. Fourth, he gave diplomacy adequate time to achieve the desired results prior to authorizing the commencement of Operation Desert Storm.

In an effort to reassure the military that the administration had the political will to provide the necessary means for a successful assault on Kuwait, Bush dispatched Powell to Saudi Arabia, where the latter informed Schwarzkopf on 22 October that Bush and Cheney "will give you anything you need to get the job done. And don't worry, you won't be jumping off until you're ready. We're not going to go off half-cocked."[60] Powell respected Bush's resolve but wanted to make certain the president understood the potential ramifications of a decision to use force. At a 24 October Gang of Eight meeting at the White House, for example, Powell pressed Bush to allow more time for sanctions to take hold before committing to a full-scale war against Iraq.[61] Bush did not waver that day, nor after Powell informed the Gang of Eight on 30 October of the need to add 200,000 American servicemen to the present force of 250,000 in the Persian Gulf in order to ensure a victory over Iraq in Kuwait. As Powell noted, Scowcroft responded to the request with a gasp that was echoed by several "others" assembled at the White House that day, but Bush "had not blinked."[62] Bush acceded to the request and announced his decision publicly on 8 November.

In order to help secure coalition and congressional approval of the use of force against Iraq, the administration once again turned to the UN. In particular, Bush dispatched Baker on a month-long diplomatic mission to cultivate support for a Security Council resolution authorizing the use of all necessary means to liberate Kuwait. Baker started his trip with a 4 November visit to Manama, Bahrain, and concluded it by chairing the American delegation at the UN for the 29 November vote on the resolution. Additionally, Bush shored up transatlantic support at a series of Conference on Security and Cooperation in Europe (CSCE) meetings in Paris on 19-20 November, then continued on to the Gulf, where he consulted with Arab leaders and spent Thanksgiving with American troops in the region.[63]

In pressing for accession to the use of force resolution, Baker requested three additional assurances from Washington's coalition partners. First, they would allow all combat operations to remain under the control of American commanders. Second, they would not object to bombing Iraq. Third, they would not back out if Israel retaliated in the face of an Iraqi missile attack. The third point was particularly contentious with respect to the Arab states in the coalition, but Baker extracted the requisite commitments, the most significant of which came from Fahd, Mubarak and the Emirs of Kuwait and Bahrain.[64] During his Middle Eastern swing, Baker also met with Chinese Foreign Minister Qian Qichen at the airport in Cairo on 6 November, informing his interlocutor—in a clear reference to China's Security Council veto power—that "[w]e don't hold it against our friends that they are not joining us. But we *do* ask that they not stand in the way." Although Qian did not respond verbally, Baker noted that the former's "body language, and the tone of his opening comments led me to believe that the Chinese would not stand in the way."[65]

Following a one-day stopover in Ankara, where Ozal agreed to send Turkish armored brigades to Saudi Arabia, Baker flew to Moscow for an 8 November meeting with Gorbachev and Shevardnadze. Gorbachev pressed for two resolutions, the first setting a six-week deadline for compliance and the second authorizing the use of force once that time had expired. Baker rejected the proposal, arguing that it "would look like we were backing down from unconditional withdrawal. We'd never get a second resolution and we'd embolden Saddam to make a token withdrawal which could result in a partial solution."[66] After obtaining resolution-backing assurances from Security Council members Zaire and Angola on 16 November in Geneva, Baker returned to Washington to update Bush on his progress to date before joining the president for the CSCE meetings. Gorbachev altered the previous Soviet request in consultations with Bush on 20 November in Paris, calling for one resolution setting a withdrawal deadline after which the coalition could utilize "all necessary measures" to expel Iraq from Kuwait. Bush, who also received firm support from Thatcher and Ozal and qualified backing from Kohl and Mitterrand while in Europe, accepted Gorbachev's proposal, barring inclusion of any further qualifications.[67]

Ultimately, the Bush administration's month-long diplomatic effort proved effective, resulting in the 29 November passage of UN Security Council Resolution 678, which authorized the coalition to use "all necessary means" to eject Iraq from Kuwait if Saddam had not removed his forces by 15 January 1991. The resolution helped to lock in both international and US Congressional commitments to military action should it prove necessary. As Scowcroft explained, the resolution was "a political measure intended to seal international solidarity and strengthen domestic ... support by spelling out that we could use force and when. There could no longer be any doubt in Saddam's mind—or anyone's—that the coalition had the means and will to go to war."[68]

While the administration also remained willing to resolve the matter diplomatically if possible, the final two attempts to do so—a 9 January 1991 meeting between Bush and Iraqi Foreign Minister Tariq Aziz in Geneva and a 10 January visit by UN Secretary-General Javier Perez de Cuellar to Baghdad to consult with Saddam—proved futile. Essentially, the die was cast in Geneva. At the start of the Baker-Aziz meeting, the former handed the latter a personal letter from Bush to Saddam, in which the president indicated that "[w]hat is at issue here is not the future of Kuwait—it will be free, its government will be restored—but rather the future of Iraq. This choice is yours to make."[69] Aziz read the letter and refused to deliver it. After the meeting, Baker phoned Bush in Washington to report frankly that "[t]here's no give. [The Iraqis] did not give an inch. They're not prepared to change their position. They offered not one new thing, no single idea, and I told them that."[70] Three days later, Congress approved the use of American military forces to liberate Kuwait—the House voting 250-183 and the Senate 52-47—leaving it to Bush to make the final decision. Predictably, the 15 January deadline passed without Iraqi compliance and Bush ordered the prosecution of Operation Desert Storm, which commenced with air raids and cruise missile strikes at 3 a.m. Baghdad time on 17 January.

The Bush administration faced three fundamental political challenges during the conduct of military operations against Iraq, which lasted six weeks and included more than 100,000 air sorties over the initial month of the conflict and a 100-hour ground war at its conclusion. First, the Bush team had to preclude Israeli involvement in the wake of Iraq's launch of missile attacks on Tel Aviv two days into the operation. Second, it had to accommodate Soviet attempts to fashion a diplomatic solution prior to the opening of the ground war without allowing Saddam to avoid complying fully with the UN resolutions in place. Third, it had to determine at what point to conclude the military offensive against Iraq, bearing in mind the potential for a collapse of the coalition should the United States attempt to continue on to Baghdad to eliminate Saddam's regime.

One of the administration's primary concerns prior to the commencement of military operations was that Iraq would respond by firing Scud missiles at cities in Israel. An Israeli counterattack, should it occur, had the potential to trigger the defection of the coalition's Arab members. Indeed, Saddam employed precisely that strategy, firing eight Scud missiles into Israeli territory on 18 January and following the initial burst with additional strikes the next two days. Predictably, Israel's initial response was strident. Speaking to the press after the opening salvo, Israeli Defense Minister Moshe Arens announced that "[w]e have said publicly and to the Americans that if we were attacked, we would react; we were attacked, we will react, certainly. We have to defend ourselves."[71]

Following the initial Scud attack, the Bush administration swung quickly into action. First, Bush urged Israeli Prime Minister Ytizhak Shamir to exercise restraint rather than take action that would undermine the coalition. Second, the president dispatched Patriot missile batteries to Israel to mitigate the threat posed by the Iraqi Scuds.[72] While reluctant to remain idle in the face of the Iraqi attacks, Shamir chose not to retaliate and the coalition remained united. Powell later acknowledged the significance of Shamir's decision, noting that "[s]ometimes we fight with fury; sometimes the wisest weapon is restraint. ... Shamir showed a special brand of statesmanship in resisting heavy pressure from those around him to strike back. The forbearance of the Israelis, in the face of intense provocation, going completely against the grain ... helped keep the coalition intact."[73]

Bush also faced challenges to coalition resolve from the Soviet Union, which escalated its efforts to forge a diplomatic solution to the crisis when the United States set plans in motion to conduct a ground war in mid- to late-February. Two days into the air war, Gorbachev made his initial attempt to reduce the pressure on Iraq, stressing to Bush that a "fundamental victory has been scored" and asking, "[w]hat is the purpose of further military action?"[74] By 6 February, fearing the longer the coalition waited to commence the ground war, the greater the chances of a deterioration of its cohesion, Bush dispatched Cheney and Powell to Saudi Arabia to determine how soon Schwarzkopf's forces would be ready to conduct such an operation effectively. As a result, the administration established a go date of 21 February with a two-day window on either side.[75]

Concurrent with the return of Cheney and Powell to Washington, Gorbachev announced plans to send Soviet diplomat Yevgeny Primakov to Baghdad to attempt to convince Saddam to make a commitment to withdraw his forces from Kuwait, at which point the coalition would declare a cease-fire. To the Bush administration, the Soviet initiative was a non-starter in that the coalition demanded full compliance with UN mandates prior to a cessation of military operations. Gorbachev's proposal was understandable, particularly in light of a turbulent domestic political environment within which communist hard-liners continually pushed for a government stance favorable to the regime in Baghdad.[76] As Scowcroft asserted, "[t]hese attempts by Gorbachev to mediate were aimed primarily at salvaging some influence and building his ever-weakening political strength at home. He was fighting for his political survival and was looking for a major foreign policy coup to burnish his reputation."[77] No such breakthrough occurred.

The final flurry of political activity prior to the commencement of the ground war unfolded from 21-23 February. On 21 February, in a Gang of Eight meeting at the White House, Powell suggested that the coalition issue an ultimatum calling for Iraq to withdraw from Kuwait by noon Washington time on 23 February, after which point the ground campaign would start. As Powell pointed out, the measure would allow Gorbachev 48 hours to convince Saddam to comply and leave the impression that the administration had allowed a last window of opportunity for a diplomatic solution. Bush accepted Powell's proposal and issued the ultimatum. Predictably, the deadline expired without Baghdad's compliance. At 8 p.m. in Washington, coalition forces surged into Kuwait and southwestern Iraq.[78]

The ground war itself was over in 100 hours, resulting in a clear victory for coalition forces over an Iraqi army weakened and demoralized by the relentless air campaign to an extent that rendered further resistance both futile and undesirable. The administration's lone remaining decision to consider was when the war should end. To Bush, the answer was straightforward. Once the coalition had achieved the objectives set out during its construction—namely the UN resolutions demanding Iraq's withdrawal from Kuwait and the restoration of the Emir's government in that context—Operation Desert Storm would cease. While militarily possible, a march to Baghdad to remove Saddam from power was clearly not feasible politically at that juncture. As Bush explained, "[o]ur stated mission, as codified in the UN resolutions, was a simple one—end the aggression, knock Iraq's forces out of Kuwait, and restore Kuwait's leaders. To occupy Iraq would instantly shatter our coalition, turning the whole Arab world against us, and make a broken tyrant into a latter-day Arab hero."[79]

Aftermath of the Persian Gulf War, 1991-92

The Persian Gulf War ended with the successful prosecution of the coalition ground war, which was halted by the Bush administration on 27 February 1991. However, while Bush and his advisors elected not to continue coalition military operations to remove Saddam from power, they remained at least somewhat hopeful that the Iraqi dictator's regime would be swept aside by domestic uprisings in the conflict's wake. In fact, earlier in the month, Bush had given two speeches that were broadcast into Iraq, in which he called on "[t]he Iraqi people and the Iraqi military to take matters into their own hands and force Saddam Hussein the dictator to step aside."[80] Concomitantly, one of the many leaflets dropped by coalition airlift on Iraq during the ground war proclaimed, "O you soldier and civilian, young man and old, O you women and men, let's fill the streets and alleys and bring down Saddam Hussein and his aides."[81]

Members of two ethno-religious groups in Iraq heeded the Bush administration's calls to resist, and, perhaps overthrow, Saddam's regime: the Kurds in the north and Shiite Muslim Arabs in the south. Regrettably, because the vast majority of Saddam's elite Republican Guard military forces did not suffer substantial losses during the coalition's brief ground war in Kuwait and Iraq itself, those who chose to engage in armed opposition to the regime were at a clear disadvantage. Lacking external support, which Washington was simply not willing to provide, the Kurd and Shiite insurrections were both stillborn. Within a month, Saddam's forces had killed approximately 20,000 Kurds and sent another two million fleeing into the mountains along Iraq's border with Turkey, and also slaughtered 30,000-60,000 Shiites.[82]

Once Saddam had reasserted his power domestically by crushing the resistance movements, the Bush administration set about developing a postwar strategy to deal with Iraq. Security Council Resolution 687 represented the point of departure for that strategy, which focused on the containment of Iraq and the limitation of Saddam's potential to once again threaten the stability of the Persian Gulf. Passed by the Security Council and agreed to unconditionally by Saddam in April 1991, the resolution codified the American policy approach to the Gulf over the ensuing decade. Most significantly, that settlement stipulated that Saddam discontinue all programs designed to develop nuclear, chemical and biological WMD and the requisite medium- and long-range missile systems to use such munitions to attack his adversaries.[83] Over the remainder of his term in office, Bush relied on the UN to monitor and supervise the dismantling of Saddam's WMD programs and maintenance of economic sanctions until compliance was forthcoming. The United States also joined the United Kingdom in using aerial patrols to maintain no-fly zones in the south of Iraq to ensure that Saddam could no longer threaten either Kuwait or Saudi Arabia with invasion.[84]

Strengths and Weaknesses of the Bush Administration's Gulf Policies

All presidential administrations exhibit both strengths and weaknesses in developing and implementing their foreign and security policies, which typically become apparent in hindsight, once the consequences of those policies have manifested themselves at home as well as abroad. With respect to the Bush administration, an assessment of such strengths and weaknesses is most clearly articulated contextually through examinations of its policymaking toward Iraq as pertains to the US domestic level, Greater Middle Eastern level and global level.

US Domestic Level

Domestically, the Bush administration's principal strengths in managing the diplomatic prologue to, and prosecution of, the Persian Gulf War were threefold. First, Bush built a foreign policy team that was extraordinary in terms of the experience of its members and their ability to work together effectively. Those attributes were central to the administration's orchestration of the end of the Cold War in 1990-91 and subsequent management of the 1990-91 Gulf crisis. In particular, the relationships Bush and his advisors had established with foreign leaders contributed markedly to their ability to build a broad coalition of states to confront Saddam over his invasion of Kuwait and then expel Iraqi forces from that state. Second, Bush made a necessarily sound case in mobilizing support from the Congress and the American public for the conduct of Operations Desert Shield and Desert Storm, one that rested on the need to maintain stability in the Gulf and thus ensure continued ease of access to the region's petroleum resources. Third, by convincing its coalition partners to shoulder the majority of the financial burden the war entailed, the administration minimized the cost to US taxpayers.

Bush's only significant weakness with respect to the Persian Gulf crisis was his inability, if not unwillingness, to build on the coalition victory over Iraq by attempting to cultivate domestic approval for the launch of a more wide-ranging strategy to foster enduring political stability in the Greater Middle East. Instead, Bush chose to focus on domestic rather than foreign affairs over the balance of his term, a decision that contributed to his own defeat to then Arkansas Governor William J. Clinton in the 1992 Presidential Election. Bush's choice was understandable given the America public's reluctance to shoulder additional international burdens once the Cold War had ended and the threats posed by foreign adversaries such as the Soviet Union and Iraq no longer appeared nearly so grave as had been the case at the start of his term. However, it was one that now appears somewhat shortsighted.

Greater Middle Eastern Level

With respect to the Persian Gulf and broader Middle East, the Bush administration demonstrated five strengths in responding to—and then ending—Iraq's invasion of Kuwait. First, Bush took a firm stance in responding to Saddam's aggression from the outset of the crisis. In doing so, he left no doubt whatsoever that Iraq's occupation of Kuwait would simply not be allowed to stand. Second, Bush made a prudent choice in building the coalition under UN auspices, one that helped to secure broad international acceptance of the subsequent conduct of Operations Desert Shield and Desert Storm. Third, Baker did a masterful job in securing support for, and contributions to, the coalition from a diverse array of regional actors with distinctive economic, military and political assets. Fourth, by allowing adequate time for a diplomatic resolution of the imbroglio, the administration mitigated the perception that it was determined to use force all along. Fifth, it set a clear objective for the coalition—the expulsion of Iraqi forces from Kuwait—and brought Operation Desert Storm to a close once that goal had been achieved. Notwithstanding the long-term costs of the decision not to continue on to Baghdad and eliminate Saddam's regime, which are addressed in the chapter's concluding section, it was a prudent choice in light of the circumstances at that juncture.

The Bush administration's principal weaknesses in dealing with Saddam manifested themselves prior to Iraq's invasion of Kuwait and in the aftermath of Operation Desert Storm. They were threefold. First, the administration was understandably preoccupied with the collapse of Soviet-backed regimes across Central and Eastern Europe and the subsequent orchestration of the German unification process in 1989-90. As a result, Bush and his advisors did not spend as much time focusing on Saddam's machinations in the Gulf as would otherwise have been prudent. Consequently, they were caught at least slightly off guard when Iraq's army crossed the border into Kuwait. Second, the administration's encouragement of opposition efforts to overthrow Saddam following Operation Desert Storm—and subsequent abandonment of those who tried to do so—fostered a deep sense of distrust of the United States among Iraqi Shiites in particular. That distrust undermined American-led nation-building efforts in Iraq in 2003-04. Third, Bush and Baker made only a fleeting attempt (the October 1991 Madrid Conference) to use the coalition victory over Iraq as a point of departure to launch a broader initiative to help resolve Arab-Israeli differences and foster long-term economic prosperity and political stability in the Greater Middle East.

Global Level

The global level, the Bush administration's management of the Persian Gulf crisis was reflective of three general strengths it exhibited in dealing with both its allies and adversaries during the proverbial final act of the Cold War. First, the administration demonstrated a capacity to work constructively with a wide range of traditional allies (most notably France, Germany, the United Kingdom and Saudi Arabia) and past and present adversaries (China, the Soviet Union and Syria among others) both within and outside of the Gulf in building a UN-backed coalition to confront Saddam. Second, by expelling Saddam's forces from Kuwait, the administration sent a message to other autocratic leaders within and beyond the Greater Middle East that the United States would not tolerate action with the potential to destabilize the region. Third, while Bush was resolute in opposing Iraq, he also remained pragmatic in laying out the limited objectives the coalition would seek to achieve through the prosecution of Operation Desert Storm.

Regrettably, however, Bush's pragmatism vis-à-vis the crisis in the Gulf also limited the administration's capacity for achievement over the balance of his tenure in the White House. Rather than continue to focus primarily on global affairs after the war, Bush instead turned inward and concentrated primarily on domestic policy, one aspect of which was an imprudent tax increase that played a significant role in his loss to Clinton in the 1992 election. In doing so, he wasted an opportunity to press for the democratic transformation of the Greater Middle East in which his son—President George W. Bush—is now engaged. In the process, he focused on one of his relative weaknesses (domestic policymaking) at the expense of a clear strength (the development and implementation of foreign policy).

Conclusions

The closing stage of the Cold War in 1989-90 altered the structure of the international system from one of bipolar confrontation to one in which the United States stood alone as the predominant global power. The Bush administration demonstrated its aptitude in adapting to this geopolitical alteration through its management of the collapse of the Soviet empire in Central and Eastern Europe and orchestration of the subsequent German unification process. In each case, Bush and Baker displayed the requisite political leadership and diplomatic acumen to achieve their principle objectives—most notably the inclusion of a unified Germany in NATO—without alienating the Soviets. In responding to these events, individuals within the administration deepened their relationships with European and Soviet leaders and gained valuable experience in dealing with a wide range of state leaders and governments from the East and West during a period of unprecedented continental and global transformation. Both assets proved invaluable in meeting the challenges of the subsequent crisis in the Persian Gulf.

As was the case during the unification process, Bush responded to Iraq's invasion of Kuwait with equal measures of prudence and resolve. From the outset, he was determined not to allow Saddam's aggression to stand. However, Bush also recognized the need to avoid unilateral American action in a region generally averse to Western culture and influence. In order to achieve that end, he set about the construction of a broad coalition of Western, Eastern and Middle Eastern states that would act only under the auspices of the UN and thus mitigate the perception that the United States was acting solely in its own interest. Through the personal and professional relationships Bush and Cabinet members such as Baker, Cheney, Powell and Scowcroft had established with world leaders over the years, the administration mobilized international support against Iraq more rapidly than would likely have been the case had a set of individuals lacking those attributes been in power at the time.

Critics have suggested Bush's insistence on limiting the discussion and taking of critical decisions to a small circle of advisors—the Gang of Eight—excluded a range of potentially useful viewpoints and enabled, if not encouraged, the president to act unilaterally during the crisis. Such contentions, however, fail to recognize the utility of cohesion and personal initiative (as opposed to bureaucratic indecisiveness) in constructing and implementing policies under fire. Although Bush did take some decisions without adequate consultation with his inner circle—most notably his impromptu announcement that Iraq's occupation of Kuwait "would not stand"—he heeded Baker's advice to accommodate Soviets concerns over the blockade. He also acceded to Powell's requests to allow adequate time for the sanctions to take hold and then to provide Schwarzkopf with the requisite resources to conduct Operation Desert Storm effectively.

Throughout the crisis, the administration focused on the use of personal diplomacy, whether over the telephone or through frequent shuttles from Washington to European, Persian Gulf and Middle Eastern capitals, in order to maintain cohesion within the coalition by ensuring that each of its members' needs were met. Baker's September trip to procure financial contributions from coalition partners both to offset the costs of the military buildup and offer aid to states making significant sacrifices to enforce the economic sanctions against Iraq, and his November mission to mobilize support for the passage of the UN use-of-force resolution were two notable cases in point. Bush conducted most of his diplomacy over the phone, but also took the time to meet personally with Thatcher in Aspen and Washington, Gorbachev in Helsinki and Paris, Kohl in Ludwigshafen, Mitterrand in Paris, Hussein, Bandar and Saud in Kennebunkport, Fahd in Jeddah and the Emir of Kuwait in Taif. These consultations were effective primarily because they demonstrated Bush's personal commitment to the coalition and the objectives it sought to achieve.

Notwithstanding the importance of the administration's internal cohesion and affinity for personal diplomacy, a variety of additional factors proved indispensable to its effective management of the crisis and conduct of the war. Essentially, the leaders of states in the coalition joined primarily because it served their national and personal interests at that juncture. Their motivations included economic and political carrots from the Bush administration (Turkey, Egypt and Soviet Union), personal disdain for Saddam (Syria's Assad and Egypt's Mubarak), determination to regain sovereignty (Kuwait), a fear of direct territorial invasion (Saudi Arabia), worries over a reduction and subsequent rise in the price of oil flowing from the Persian Gulf (European states, Japan, United States) and concerns over regional instability (United States, Middle Eastern states).

Above all, the crisis demanded that the administration cobble together a coalition based on a confluence of interests. And, to his credit, Bush recognized that the coalition would remain united only so long as it was beneficial for all of its members to stay on board. As a result, he set limited objectives, all of which were codified explicitly in UN resolutions. Bush understood that once the coalition had achieved its principal objective—the ejection of Saddam's forces from Kuwait—that entity would lose its source of sustenance. Thus, he did not press for Saddam's removal from power through a sustained military offensive in Iraq. Bush and his advisors managed the crisis masterfully given the circumstances with which they had to deal. And, in the end, they displayed the requisite geopolitical prudence to retire that diplomatic creation before it collapsed under its own weight.

As is true with respect to any crisis, the Bush administration's management of the diplomatic prologue to, and subsequent prosecution and settlement of, the Persian Gulf War, entailed costs and produced benefits for the United States over both the short and long terms. Assessing those costs and benefits, in turn, is necessary to determine the extent to which one should deem the administration's actions effective or ineffective when considered in historical perspective. Consequently, this chapter closes with precisely such an assessment.

In the short term, the benefits of the Bush administration's intervention to expel Iraqi forces from Kuwait exceeded the costs markedly. The principal benefits were fourfold. First, by acting quickly to oppose and then end Iraq's occupation of Kuwait, the United States and its coalition partners prevented Saddam from achieving any permanent territorial gains. Second, in the process, the coalition reduced markedly the degree to which he could threaten regional stability in the immediate future and thus preserved the indispensable ease of American, European and Japanese access to the region's petroleum resources. Third, by striking a balance between resolve and pragmatism in managing the crisis, Bush's foreign policy team demonstrated that it would not tolerate aggression by autocratic regimes in strategically vital regions of the world, but did so without undermining its relationships with allies within and beyond the Gulf. Fourth, by seeking UN approval for Operations Desert Shield and Storm, the president minimized domestic and international criticism of the American decision to intervene. Put simply, the UN's imprimatur provided the coalition with a necessary stamp of legitimacy.

Relative to these benefits, America's short-term costs were marginal. At the military level, for example, US casualties were considerably lower than in any previous major regional conflict in American history, with deaths and injuries numbering in the hundreds rather than in the thousands or tens of thousands. Similarly, the military buildup in the Persian Gulf and subsequent prosecution of the war did not entail a marked drain on the US economy. Instead, the Bush administration's skillful diplomacy ensured that much of the financial burden was shouldered by other members of the coalition generally and Kuwait and Saudi Arabia specifically.

The longer term benefits and costs of the crisis, by contrast, were somewhat more equivalent. Above all, the American-led diplomatic and military response to Iraq's invasion of Kuwait demonstrated to Saddam that the United States would not permit him to threaten his neighbors in the Persian Gulf. It also served as a warning to dictators in other regions of the world in which America had vital economic, military and political interests. Those effects were certainly beneficial. However, because the Bush administration chose not to engage in any practically feasible pursuit of regime change in Baghdad, the United States had to continue to maintain a substantial military presence in the Gulf to contain Iraq in the future. In addition to the economic and physical costs of that presence, it contributed to the emergence of a terrorist group known as Al Qaeda under the leadership of Osama bin Laden, who opposed the stationing of American troops in Islam's most holy state—namely the Kingdom of Saudi Arabia. The dual threats posed by bin Laden and Saddam, in turn, culminated in the events of 11 September 2001 and, to at least some extent, the related conduct of the Second Iraq War in 2003.

Notes

1.	For more detailed analyses of the collapse of communist rule in Central and Eastern Europe in 1989-90 and the German unification process in 1990, see Robert L. Hutchings, *American Diplomacy and the End of the Cold War: An Insider's Account of U.S. Policy in Europe, 1989-1992* (Washington: Woodrow Wilson Center Press, 1997), Elizabeth Pond, *Beyond the Wall: Germany's Road to Unification* (Washington: Brookings Institution, 1993) and Philip Zelikow and Condoleezza Rice, *Germany Unified and Europe Transformed: A Study in Statecraft* (Cambridge: Harvard University Press, 1995).
2.	For in-depth analyses of these approaches, see Lagon, *The Reagan Doctrine* and Michael Turner, "Defence Policy and Arms Control: The Reagan Record," in John R. Lees and Turner, eds., *Reagan's First Four Years: A New Beginning?* (New York: St. Martin's Press, 1988).
3.	James A. Baker, III, with Thomas M. DeFrank, *The Politics of Diplomacy: Revolution, War and Peace, 1989-1992* (New York: G.P. Putnam's Sons, 1995), 251; Hutchings, *American Diplomacy*, 129.
4.	"London Declaration on a Transformed North Atlantic Alliance, Issued by the Heads of State and Government participating in the meeting of the North Atlantic Council in London on 5-6 July 1990," *NATO Press Service*, Communique S-I (90) 36, 6 July 1990. Reference made in Hutchings, *American Diplomacy*, 135.
5.	Michael R. Beschloss and Strobe Talbott, *At The Highest Levels: The Inside Story of the End of the Cold War* (Boston: Little, Brown and Company, 1993), 209.
6.	Oil revenues represented more than half of Iraq's GNP. Given Iraq's dependence on this commodity, Saddam criticized both Kuwait and the United Arab Emirates for raising their production levels in the spring and summer of 1990. He claimed that these actions had cost Iraq more than $14 billion in that span. George Bush and Brent Scowcroft, *A World Transformed: The Collapse of the Soviet Empire; the Unification of Germany; Tiananmen Square; the Gulf War* (New York: Alfred A. Knopf, 1998), 308-10.
7.	Bush and Scowcroft, *A World Transformed*, 305.
8.	For an in-depth analysis of American reliance on Persian Gulf oil, see Steven A. Yetiv, *Crude Awakenings: Global Oil Security and American Foreign Policy* (Ithaca, NY: Cornell University Press, 2004).
9.	Baker, *Politics of Diplomacy*, 261-64; Bush and Scowcroft, *A World Transformed*, 305-06.
10.	Bush and Scowcroft, *A World Transformed*, 16-18.
11.	Ibid., 22-24.
12.	Steve Yetiv, *The Persian Gulf Crisis* (Westport, CT: Greenwood Press, 1997), 61-62.
13.	Ibid.
14.	Bush and Scowcroft, *A World Transformed*, 305-06.
15.	Baker, *Politics of Diplomacy*, 263.
16.	Baker, *Politics of Diplomacy*, 266-67; Bush and Scowcroft, *A World Transformed*, 306.
17.	Baker, *Politics of Diplomacy*, 267.
18.	Coughlin, *Saddam: King of Terror*, 240.
19.	Amatzia Baram, "The Iraqi Invasion of Kuwait: Decision-Making in Baghdad," in *Iraq's*

Road to War, ed. Amatzia Baram and Barry Rubin (New York: St. Martin's Press, 1993), 16. Reference made in Pollack, *Threatening Storm*, 32-33.

20. Pollack, *Threatening* Storm, 33.

21. Baker, Bush and Scowcroft have all rebutted critics' assertions that American Ambassador April Glaspie left Saddam Hussein with the impression that the United States would not take any action in response to an Iraqi invasion of Kuwait in the meeting between the two on 25 July 1990 in Baghdad. Baker, *Politics of Diplomacy*, 271-73; Bush and Scowcroft, *A World Transformed*, 309-13.

22. Bush and Scowcroft, *A World Transformed*, 303.

23. Ibid., 303-04.

24. Ibid., 315.

25. Ibid.

26. Ibid., 316-17.

27. Ibid., 317.

28. Baker was taking part in a previously scheduled state visit to Ulan, Bator, Mongolia following arms control talks with Shevardnadze in Irkutsk, Siberia, and thus dispatched aides Dennis Ross and Robert Zoellick to Moscow on 2 August 1990 ahead of his own arrival there on 3 August. Baker, *Politics of Diplomacy*, 6-8.

29. *The Middle East*, 7th ed. (Washington: Congressional Quarterly, Inc., 1991), 369.

30. In acceding to Mubarak's request to attempt to negotiate an Arab solution to the crisis, Bush requested that the Egyptian President inform "Saddam Hussein that the United States is very concerned about this action. We are very concerned that other forces will be released—you know what that means, my friend. Tell Saddam that if you like." Bush and Scowcroft, *A World Transformed*, 318-19.

31. Ibid., 323.

32. Ibid., 323-34.

33. Baker, *Politics of Diplomacy*, 13-16.

34. Bush and Scowcroft, *A World Transformed*, 332-33.

35. Colin Powell, with Joseph E. Persico, *My American Journey* (New York: Random House, 1995), 480.

36. Saudi Arabia's King Fahd told Bush that "this is a matter that is extremely serious and grave. It involves a principle that can't be approved or condoned by any reasonable principle or moral. ... I hope these matters can be resolved peacefully. If not, Saddam must be taught a lesson he will not forget for the rest of his life—if he remains alive." Bush and Scowcroft, *World Transformed*, 321.

37. Ibid.

38. Ibid., 325.

39. Ibid., 330.

40. According to Scowcroft, shortly after Bush's 4 August telephone conversation with Fahd, Saudi Ambassador Prince Bandar bin Sultan first assured Scowcroft that he supported Secretary of Defense Richard Cheney's "heading the mission on the assumption that we were not talking about 'if' we were coming but 'how' and what types of units would go." Bandar then obtained Fahd's accession on this issue and informed Scowcroft, who passed the information along to Bush. Ibid.

41. Ibid., 326-32.

42. *The Middle East*, 369-70.

43. Bush and Scowcroft, *A World Transformed*, 335.

44. Ibid., 338.

45. According to Bush, in 1989, "Mubarak had offered me some advice: touch base with these

small countries whenever you can, just to acknowledge their importance to the United States, and it will make a difference with them. I had, and my wise friend Hosni had been absolutely right. We were now seeing some of the fruits of tending to these relationships. I talked to President Zayid ibn Sultan of the UAE and Sultan Qabu bin Said of Oman [on the day of the Arab League vote.] Each promised to do everything he could to support the coalition against Saddam Hussein." Ibid., 341.

46. Baker, *Politics of Diplomacy*, 285-86; Bush and Scowcroft, *A World Transformed*, 285-86.
47. Bush and Scowcroft, *A World Transformed*, 355.
48. Baker, *Politics of Diplomacy*, 287-88.
49. Ibid., 288.
50. Ibid., 290.
51. Ibid.
52. Ibid., 290-91.
53. Bush and Scowcroft, *A World Transformed*, 373-74.
54. Baker, *Politics of Diplomacy*, 291.
55. Baker, *Politics of Diplomacy*, 294; Bush and Scowcroft, *A World Transformed*, 368.
56. Bush and Scowcroft, *A World Transformed*, 371.
57. Baker, *Politics of Diplomacy*, 294-95.
58. Ibid., 298.
59. Kohl's pledge ultimately resulted in the provision of $4 billion in assistance that included millions of dollars' worth of support equipment for US forces in the Gulf, substantial increases in the amount of German economic and military aid to Turkey and the provision of German ships to transport Egyptian troops and tanks to the Gulf. Ibid., 299.
60. Powell, *My American Journey*, 487.
61. Ibid., 480.
62. Bush and Scowcroft, 392-95; Power, *My American Journey*, 44488-89.
63. Baker, *Politics of Diplomacy*, 104-05.
64. Ibid., 305-09.
65. Ibid., 309.
66. Ibid., 310-12.
67. Bush and Scowcroft, *A World Transformed*, 406-10.
68. Ibid., 416.
69. *Public Papers of the Presidents of the United States: George Bush, 1991*, Book I, 1 January-30 June 1991 (Washington: U.S. Government Printing Office, 1992), 36-37.
70. Baker, *Politics of Diplomacy*, 363-64.
71. Quoted in *The Times* (London), 19 January 1991.
72. Bush and Scowcroft, *A World Transformed*, 454-56.
73. Powell, *My American Journey*, 512.
74. Bush and Scowcroft, *A World Transformed*, 454.
75. Ibid., 466-69.
76. Ibid., 468-69.
77. Ibid., 470.
78. Powell, *My American Journey*, 517.
79. Bush and Scowcroft, *A World Transformed*, 464.
80. Andrew and Patrick Cockburn, *Out of the Ashes: The Resurrection of Saddam Hussein* (New York: HarperCollins, 1999), 12-13. Reference made in Pollack, *Threatening Storm*, 48.
81. Ofra Bengio, "Baghdad Between Shi'a and Kurds," *Policy Focus* 18-2 (February 1992): 26. Reference made in Pollack, *Threatening Storm*, 48.

82. Sarah Graham-Brown, *Sanctioning Saddam* (London: I.B. Tauris, 1999), 23; Amatzia Barram, "The Effect of Iraqi Sanctions: Statistical Pitfalls and Responsibility," *Middle East Journal* 54-2 (Spring 2000): 199. References made in Pollack, *Threatening Storm*, 50-51.
83. *The Middle East*, 369-70.
84. Coughlin, *King of Terror*, 276-89; Pollack, *Threatening Storm*, 58-64.

Chapter 4

William J. Clinton Administration and the Persian Gulf, 1993-2001

Introduction

Unlike his 10 immediate predecessors in the White House, President William J. Clinton lacked a clear, overarching national security threat with which to deal upon assuming office in January 1993. Those men faced daunting, but reasonably unambiguous, security challenges, ranging from Franklin D. Roosevelt's prosecution of World War II and Harry S. Truman's establishment and consolidation of a Western front in the emerging Cold War against the Soviet Union to Ronald W. Reagan's rollback of Moscow's global empire and George H.W. Bush's orchestration of the end of the bipolar confrontation on American terms.

Clinton, by contrast, began his first term on the heels of the end of the Cold War and the Bush administration's successful conduct of the 1991 Persian Gulf War. In particular, the expulsion of Iraqi President Saddam Hussein's forces from the neighboring state of Kuwait in February 1991 and the dissolution of the Soviet Union 10 months later left the United States bereft of a threat—actual or perceived—to US interests at home and abroad on the scale of those prevalent during the Cold War and its aftermath. These developments, in turn, engendered a sense of euphoria among academics, policy practitioners and the American public at large that allowed, if not encouraged, the Clinton administration to focus primarily on soft rather than hard security issues in articulating its initial foreign and security policies and strategies.

One of Clinton's first major foreign policy addresses, a February 1993 speech at American University in Washington, for example, was illustrative of that approach. In his address, the president noted that the

> Cold War was a draining time. We devoted trillions of dollars to it, much more than many of our more visionary leaders thought we should have. We posted our sons and daughters around the world. We lost tens thousands of them in the defense of freedom and in the pursuit of containment of communism. ... The change confronting us in the 1990s is in some ways more difficult than in previous times because it is less distinct. ... Our leadership is especially important for the world's new and emerging democracies. To grow and deepen their legitimacy, to foster a middle class and a civic culture, they need the ability to tap into a growing global economy. And our security and our prosperity will be greatly affected in the years ahead by how many of these countries can become and stay democracies.[1]

Similarly, in a September 1993 speech before the UN General Assembly, Clinton stressed that

> The momentum of the Cold War no longer propels us in our daily actions. ... The United States intends to remain engaged and to lead. We cannot solve every problem, but we must and will serve as a fulcrum for change and a pivot point for peace. In a new era of peril and opportunity, our overriding purpose must be to expand and strengthen the world's community of market-based democracies. During the Cold War we sought to contain a threat to the survival of free institutions. Now we seek to enlarge the circle of nations that live under those free institutions. For our dream is of a day when the opinions and energies of every person in the world will be given full expression, in a world of thriving democracies that cooperate with each other and live in peace.[2]

As opposed to Bush, Clinton failed to develop a clear, well-focused foreign policy blueprint. Rather than prioritize American interests consistently on the basis of an emphasis on a particular region or issue area, the Clinton administration launched and pursued a wide variety of initiatives, ranging from military intervention in the Balkans to often overbearing mediation of the Israeli-Palestinian peace process, few of which it followed through to completion. As Richard Haass, currently serving as president of the Council on Foreign Relations, has argued, "Clinton inherited a world of unprecedented American advantage and opportunity and did little with it. ... A foreign policy legacy can result either from achieving something great on the ground (defeating major rivals or building major institutions, for example) or from changing the way people at home or abroad think about international relations. Clinton did neither."[3]

There were two causes for the Clinton administration's lack of strategic clarity, neither of which was entirely the President's fault. First, Clinton's longevity in the White House detracted from his ability to maintain a foreign policy team whose members shared the same viewpoints throughout his tenure. He had two National Security Advisors (Anthony Lake and Samuel Berger), three Secretaries of Defense (Les Aspin, William Perry and William Cohen) and two Secretaries of State (Warren Christopher and Madeleine Albright) in eight years, most of whom had at least subtly different ideas of how best to define and pursue US interests. Albright and Berger, for instance, tended to have a greater affinity for the use of military force than either Lake or Christopher. Second, Clinton assumed office at the start of the post-Cold War era, a period during which the American public had no appetite for the expression of grand strategic visions or the expenditure of tax dollars abroad given that the threats previously presented by the either the Soviet behemoth or Saddam Hussein were at least perceived to have been diminished. Clinton's personal interest in domestic as opposed to foreign policy—and the primacy he often ceded to the former at the expense of the latter—only complicated matters further.

The Clinton administration's vision was both noble and understandably broad in light of the structure of the international system and position of the United States as the lone remaining superpower therein. It was also one that evolved as American policymakers were forced to respond to a variety of threats to US interests over the course of Clinton's eight years in office. Two of the most significant such threats—those posed by Saddam on one hand and Al Qaeda leader Osama bin Laden on the other—emanated from the Greater Middle East generally and the Persian Gulf specifically. Above all, the ways in which Clinton and his advisors chose to handle respond to those threats reflected their unwillingness to bear substantial economic, military and political costs in order to achieve grand strategic objectives.

While Clinton recognized that terrorism represented a growing danger to the United States, he was relatively cautious in confronting Al Qaeda, relying on limited cruise missile strikes on bin Laden's training camps in Afghanistan rather than a more robust military response to attacks such as those on the US Embassies in Nairobi, Kenya, and Dar-es-Salaam, Tanzania, in August 1998. Clinton's unwillingness to sanction the use of anything but token force against Al Qaeda paralleled his stance toward Iraq. The Clinton administration's only substantial—and somewhat sustained—response to Saddam's consistent unwillingness to adhere unambiguously to UN Security Council Resolutions prohibiting the development of nuclear, chemical and biological WMD and sponsorship of terrorist groups was a flurry of cruise missile strikes in the context of Operation Desert Fox in December 1998.[4] Those strikes, which came after Saddam's expulsion of UN weapons inspectors the previous month, did not result in the inspectors' return. Rather, once completed, they left Saddam free to defy the United States without repercussions until the George W. Bush administration expressed a renewed American willingness to take bold action against Iraq following Al Qaeda's 11 September 2001 attacks on the World Trade Center and the Pentagon.

With these observations providing a necessary contextual foundation, the balance of the chapter examines and assesses the Clinton administration's policies toward the Persian Gulf in three related sections that unfold in the following manner:

- The first section opens with an examination of American interests in the Gulf as articulated by the Clinton administration, then discusses the resultant development of policies toward that region—and, to a limited extent, the broader Middle East—from January 1993 to January 2001. Given the centrality of those developments to the US role in the Gulf both from 1993-2001 and in the years that have elapsed since then, this section is considerably lengthier than either of the chapter's ensuing sections.
- The second section considers the strengths and weaknesses of the Clinton administration's policies toward the Persian Gulf generally and Iraq specifically at the US domestic level as well as in the contexts of the Gulf, Greater Middle East and global international system.
- The concluding section reiterates the chapter's key points, then closes with an assessment of the short- and long-term costs and benefits of the above policies.

US Interests and Resultant Policies in the Persian Gulf, 1993-2001

As is true of all presidential foreign policy teams, Clinton and his advisors defined US interests on the basis of past experiences, present worldviews and the characteristics of the international system within which America interacted with its allies and adversaries. Clinton assembled one such team at the start of each of his two terms in Washington and made occasional adjustments along the way. The members of those teams (the Vice President, National Security Advisor, Secretary of State, Secretary of Defense and— albeit to a lesser degree, Director of Central Intelligence—and their staffs), in turn, were responsible for the development and implementation of policies toward the world in general and the Persian Gulf and wider Middle East in particular. Consequently, in order to better understand the foreign and security policies Clinton pursued during his first and second terms, it is first necessary to provide a primer on the individuals serving in the above positions from 1993-97 and 1997-2001, respectively.

A relative neophyte with respect to foreign affairs, Clinton entered office in January 1993 content to focus on domestic economic policy and leave US relations with external actors (especially hard core security issues) primarily to his principal advisors.[5] During Clinton's initial term, that inner circle included Vice President Albert Gore, National Security Advisor Lake and his deputy, Berger, along with Secretary of State Christopher and Secretary of Defense Aspin. The latter stepped down following the deaths of 18 US servicemen in a botched operation to secure the capture of a Somali warlord in October 1993 and was replaced by Perry. In addition, the president named Albright as American Ambassador to the United Nations and elevated her position to a Cabinet Level post.[6]

Berger, a long-time friend of Clinton, had served in the Carter administration's State Department, along with Lake and Christopher. Aspin was a former Chairman of the House Armed Services Committee and Albright a member of Carter National Security Advisor Zbigniew Brzezinski's staff. The switch from Aspin to Perry was one of two upper level security staff shifts in the first Clinton administration. CIA Director James Woolsey's resignation less than a year into his tenure and John Deutch's subsequent appointment to that position was the other. Collectively, the group was reasonably well balanced with respect to a willingness and reluctance to use force to safeguard American interests. At the White House, for instance, Berger tended to be more hawkish than Lake. And, similarly, on the diplomatic side of the equation, Christopher had much less of an affinity than Albright to resort to military tools to achieve political ends on the international stage.

For his part, Clinton was more dove than hawk, but by no means unwilling to switch course as circumstances required, most notably so during his second term. The changes the president made in his foreign policy team after defeating Republican Challenger Robert Dole in the 1996 national election was indicative of that flexibility. Berger and Albright replaced Lake and Christopher as National Security Advisor and Secretary of State, respectively, former Republican Senator William Cohen of Maine was named Secretary of Defense and former New Mexico Congressman Bill Richardson assumed Albright's Ambassadorship to the UN.[7] The elevation of Deutch's chief deputy, George Tenet to CIA Director completed a team that, overall, proved considerably less averse to military intervention generally and the limited use of force in response to current and prospective future threats to the United States and its allies in regions ranging from the

Balkans to the Persian Gulf.

On balance, the Clinton administration had a tendency to characterize its interests in broad terms that did not allow for a clear prioritization of those interests and the resultant policy developmental processes. That approach was especially evident during Clinton's first term. Consider the administration's initial National Security Strategy (NSS), a document released in July 1994. While giving minimal credence to the nascent threat of transnational terrorism, that NSS echoed Clinton's aforementioned 1993 address to the UN General Assembly, noting that the "only responsible US strategy is one that seeks to ensure US influence over and participation in collective decision making in a wide and growing range of circumstances." Further, with respect to the use of force, it stressed that while "there may be many demands for US involvement, the need to husband scarce resources suggests that we must carefully select the means and level of our participation in particular military operations."[8]

To his credit, Clinton did decide to place a greater emphasis on harder core security issues—most significantly those related to the maintenance of stability in the Balkans and Greater Middle East and the reduction of threats posed by Iraq's WMD and missile development programs and sponsorship of terrorist organizations—following his reelection in 1996. Yet, at that juncture, the president and his advisors insisted on trying to do everything rather than concentrating on one or two critical initiatives. Consider, for instance, Berger's characterization of Clinton's legacy in January 2001: "Today ... America is by any measure the world's unchallenged military, economic and political power. The world counts on us to be a catalyst of coalitions, a broker of peace [and] a guarantor of global financial stability."[9]

In general terms, the Clinton administration's final NSS, which it issued in December 1999, mirrored the above statement by Berger. In short, that document promulgated three overarching objectives. First, "to enhance America's security." Second, "to bolster America's economic prosperity. And third, "to promote democracy and human rights abroad."[10] As Yale University historian John Lewis Gaddis, perhaps the most authoritative scholar of American national security policy over the past half-century, has pointed out, the "Clinton statement seems simply to assume peace."[11]

Similar to the Clinton administration's 1994 NSS, the 1999 version failed to recognize the seriousness of the threats to the United States. In particular, that oversight was evident in the president's approach to the Persian Gulf from 1993-2001. The ensuing assessment of that approach is subdivided contextually into four parts. Those parts address the development and implementation of policies designed to mitigate threats to US interests emanating from the region in the following manner: threats posed by Iraq; threats posed by Al Qaeda; linking stability in the Gulf to that in the Greater Middle East; and connecting the dots vis-à-vis threats posed by state and non-state actors within and beyond the Greater Middle East.

Responding to Threats Posed by Iraq, 1993-2001

An examination of the Clinton administration's policies toward Iraq must begin with a caveat of sorts. Because the president was unable, if not unwilling, to identify one clear threat to US interests, he pursued a range of initiatives with variable degrees of resolve. Iraq was simply not at the top of the list. According to Kenneth M. Pollack, the point man on Iraq on Berger's staff from 1999-2001, for example, the

> Administration (especially during its first term, under the direction of Lake, the high-minded national security advisor) was seeking to create a new paradigm of international relations—a true New World Order. The goals of this new paradigm were a world of global economic development, cooperation, collective security, and the use of force only to aid the oppressed and defeat aggression. ... Actively confronting Saddam did not fit neatly into that brave new world.[12]

As a result, on Clinton's watch, the United States sought to mitigate Saddam's potential to develop nuclear, chemical and biological WMD and, perhaps, eventually transfer those munitions to terrorist organizations by relying primarily upon the UN to dispatch weapons inspectors to Iraq and oversee Baghdad's use of proceeds from the sale of its petroleum resources for essential items such as food and medicine. The president also authorized the limited use of military force against Iraq on several occasions from 1993-98, the most robust of which came in response to Saddam's expulsion of the weapons inspectors in December 1998. However, in none of those cases was an invasion of Iraq seriously considered. Instead, Clinton attempted to contain the threats posed by Iraq on the cheap in terms of both economic and political capital, domestically as well as internationally.

Given that this chapter does not focus exclusively on Saddam, the ensuing examination of Clinton's management of US policy toward Iraq from 1993-2001 is necessarily limited to a selective review of the most significant crises that defined the relationship between Washington and Baghdad during that period. Four such episodes stand out: a foiled spring 1993 plot by the Iraqi intelligence service (Mukhabbarat) to assassinate George H.W. Bush during the former president's trip to Kuwait to commemorate the coalition's victory in the 1990-91 Persian Gulf War; the brief mobilization of Iraqi forces along the Kuwaiti border in October 1994; stillborn US-backed plots to overthrow Saddam's regime in March 1995 (by Kurdish and Iraqi National Congress [INC] forces) and June 1996 (by rogue military officers); and a 1997-98 showdown between Saddam and the Clinton administration that ended with the conduct of Operation Desert Fox in December 1998.

In April 1993, Bush planned a visit to Kuwait to commemorate the American-led expulsion of Iraqi invaders from that state through the prosecution of the 1990-91 Persian Gulf War. A day before Bush's arrival, the Kuwaiti authorities announced that they had uncovered and foiled a Mukhabbarat plot to assassinate him. The Mukhabbarat had planned to detonate a bomb in the center of Kuwait City as Bush's motorcade drove through. The bomb had already been planted and was uncovered by the Kuwaitis, who passed that information along to the Clinton administration. Subsequent CIA and FBI investigations confirmed that the explosives indeed had the markings of the Mukhabbarat.[13]

Two months later, Clinton retaliated against Iraq by authorizing the launch of 23 cruise missiles into the Mukhabbarat headquarters in Baghdad, an attack that occurred in the middle of the night when the building was largely deserted and thus destroyed potentially valuable intelligence files but killed few operatives.[14] By Clinton's standards, it was a relatively forceful response, one that had been recommended by Colin Powell, who continued to serve as Chairman of the Joint Chiefs of Staff until October 1993. Clinton recalls in his memoirs that "I felt we would have been justified in hitting Iraq harder, but Powell made a persuasive case that the attack would deter further Iraqi terrorism, and that dropping bombs on more targets, including presidential palaces, would have been unlikely to kill Saddam and almost certain to kill more innocent people."[15] Notwithstanding that assessment, Saddam, who had retained power despite the Gulf War and ruthlessly crushed domestic revolts by the Kurds in the north and Shiites in the south following that conflict, likely perceived the limited missile strikes as a sign of weakness, one he would attempt to exploit with gradually but consistently increasing degrees of success in subsequent years. As Woolsey notes in one published report: after an exhaustive two-month investigation, Clinton "fired a couple of dozen cruise missiles into an empty building in the middle of the night, which is a sufficiently weak response to be almost laughable."[16]

On the other hand, while it stands to reason that the nature of Clinton's response to the assassination plot against Bush may have emboldened Saddam, the second confrontation between the two was resolved in a manner more beneficial to the United States. At the conclusion of the Persian Gulf War, Saddam agreed to abide by restrictions on WMD development and also to accept economic sanctions regulating Baghdad's income from its oil resources—both subject to UN oversight and verification—in the context of Security Council Resolution 687. Saddam challenged Clinton vis-à-vis the sanctions by amassing approximately 80,000 troops along the border between Iraq and Kuwait in the fall of 1994. The United States countered with Operation Vigilant Warrior, a reinforcement effort that quickly raised American troop strength in the Persian Gulf region from 13,000 to 60,000. Clinton's reaction, along with an explicit warning from US and British military officers that they would strike the Iraqis if they did not pull their forces back from the border region, forced Saddam to back down.[17] In this instance, Clinton's approach was effective. Unfortunately, the president did not prove nearly so resolute over the long term.

During the run-up to the 1996 Presidential Election, Clinton was willing to allow his advisors some latitude in the development of plans to weaken, if not eliminate, the Iraqi regime from within. A more direct use of US military force, however, was deemed too risky in an election year. Saddam, for his part, focused concurrently on limiting the damage the UN Special Commission for the Disarmament of Iraq (UNSCOM) could inflict on his WMD programs and maintaining firm political control at the domestic level through the ruthless repression of any individual or group that defied his regime. In addition, he used much of the money allowed through the UN-administered oil-for-food programs for military purposes, then blamed his people's hardships (most notably malnutrition among children) on the sanctions generally and the United States specifically. In particular, he skillfully manipulated international media coverage of starving children in Iraqi hospitals to generate negative publicity for Clinton at home. As Albright explains, "Saddam's goal was to foil the inspectors by gaining relief from sanctions without giving up his remaining weapons. His strategy was to publicize the hardships of Iraqi civilians in order to gain sympathy among Arabs and the West, and to an extent he succeeded. Anti-Americanism will always find a receptive audience in some circles."[18]

Against this backdrop, the Clinton administration authorized the CIA to plan two insurgency operations: one a collaborative effort with Kurdish Democratic Party head Mazud Barzani and exiled INC leader Ahmed Chalabi in 1995 and the second a coup under the leadership of an anti-Saddam faction in the upper levels of the Iraqi security services and military in 1996. Regrettably, but perhaps not unexpectedly, given Saddam's penchant for survival over the years, neither plan came to fruition. A March 1995 offensive by Kurdish forces near the northern city of Irbil appeared promising initially but the dispatch of reinforcements from the Iraqi Republican Guard in Baghdad caused the United States (which was itself unprepared to provide substantial military support should the situation sour) to caution the Kurds to stand down, which they did. The coup was also stillborn. The Mukhabbarat uncovered the plot and liquidated the conspirators in June 1996.[19] Yet, ultimately, neither operation proved particularly damaging to Clinton politically, which was probably one of the principal reasons he approved both to begin with.

Not surprisingly, Clinton proved increasingly unwilling to take any marked political risks in confronting Iraq over the final four years of his tenure in the White House. In particular, he limited himself to one relatively small-scale military operation in the face of Saddam's perpetual defiance of UNSCOM inspectors in 1997 and 1998 prior to their final departure from Iraq in the run-up to Operation Desert Fox. The start of Clinton's second term in January 1997 coincided with the commencement of a campaign by Saddam to gradually frustrate UNSCOM's efforts, while reconstituting at least some of his WMD capabilities with proceeds siphoned from the oil proceeds allowed by the UN in order to (theoretically but by no means practically) provide food and medicine to the Iraqi people. Differences within the Security Council between the United States and the United Kingdom on one hand, and France, Russia and China on the other, who favored strict and loose enforcement of the UN's resolutions, respectively, only strengthened Saddam's hand. As Pollack explains, Saddam's "goals were to impede UNSCOM's progress, exacerbate the growing differences within the Security Council, and antagonize the United States without presenting enough of a provocation to justify a major military response. However, he was also looking to fight back against the inspectors' efforts to penetrate the security of his regime."[20]

It was Iraq's repeated provocations in the latter issue area that led to an American military response—namely Operation Desert Fox. In the months preceding that operation, Saddam had repeatedly denied UNSCOM inspectors access to many of his presidential palaces, mammoth structures that had the potential for use in the concealment of WMD. In February 1998, UN Secretary General Kofi Annan traveled to Baghdad, where he negotiated a temporary compromise through which the inspectors were granted "unrestricted access" to all sites in Iraq. Yet, by November, Iraqi officials were still routinely tuning inspectors away from a variety of sensitive "presidential sites." The next month, the United States conducted four days of air and cruise missile strikes on a range of Iraqi targets, only 11 of 97 of which were directed at suspected WMD sites.[21]

According to Clinton, following the "attack we had no way to know how much of the proscribed [WMD] material had been destroyed, but Iraq's ability to produce and deploy dangerous weapons had plainly been reduced."[22] The extent to which that assessment is true remains unclear. However, one thing is clear: when the operation was complete, Iraq did not readmit the inspectors. As a result, Saddam remained free of anything but token diplomatic pressure to comply with the UN resolutions over the remainder of Clinton's second term. As journalists and public policy analysts Lawrence Kaplan and William Kristol conclude, the "whole business reflected the administration's refusal to employ measures of genuine strategic effectiveness. The Clinton policy toward Iraq may have comforted the sensibilities of its architects—but not nearly so much as it comforted Saddam Hussein, who, by the time Clinton left office, was out of the box whose confines had been mostly imaginary to begin with."[23]

Responding to Threats Posed by Al Qaeda, 1993-2001

When Clinton entered office, the principal security threats his administration would face in the future were understandably unclear. Nonetheless, Clinton's failure to mitigate one such threat emanating from the Greater Middle East—that posed by Al Qaeda—over the ensuing eight years, was one of his most significant shortcomings as president, particularly given the devastating nature of the attacks that organization staged on 9/11. Put simply, Clinton and his advisors made two sets of errors with respect to the manner in which they confronted bin Laden. First, they were late to recognize the severity of the dangers posed by Al Qaeda, choosing to treat terrorism primarily as a law enforcement issue rather than a national security concern. Second, after acknowledging the grave threats presented by bin Laden, they remained reluctant to take decisive military action against either Al Qaeda or those regimes upon which it was suspected of relying for support.

In order to assess the degree to which the Clinton administration should be faulted for its inability to weaken, if not eliminate, Al Qaeda, it is necessary to review the opportunities it had to respond to terrorist acts carried out by bin Laden and his supporters, how effectively or ineffectively it did so and why that was the case in each instance. Given that this discussion is only one component of the broader chapter and book, assessments of the following four examples are sufficient: the February 1993 bombing of the World Trade Center in New York; a foiled plot to detonate bombs aboard 11 airliners over the Pacific Ocean and subsequent failure to secure bin Laden's extradition from Sudan in 1995-96; the August 1998 bombings of the American Embassies in Nairobi, Kenya, and Dar-es-Salaam, Tanzania; and the October 2000 bombing of the USS *Cole*.[24]

The Clinton administration's first opportunity to deal with an act of terrorism directed against the United States came on 26 February 1993. That morning, a group of terrorists led by a man named Ramzi Yousef parked a rental van packed with explosives in a garage beneath the North Tower of the World Trade Center. They then lit the fuses attached to the bomb and fled. The resulting explosion caused limited damage to the infrastructure of the tower, killing six people and injuring 1,000 more.[25] Yousef, who was traveling on an Iraqi passport at the time and not apprehended until February 1995, later boasted to Federal Bureau of Investigation (FBI) agents that the objective of the operation had been to collapse the foundation of the North Tower, causing it to topple into the adjacent South Tower in hopes of killing up to 250,000, a catastrophe that would have dwarfed the losses in the 9/11 attacks.[26] The subsequent FBI investigation of the bombing uncovered considerable evidence linking Al Qaeda to the operation, a development that proved a indicator of the rising threats bin Laden was to present to US interests in the years to come.[27]

Clinton based his 1992 presidential campaign primarily on domestic rather than foreign policy issues, most notably those associated with economic and social programs. He had minimal experience in international security affairs and the initial foreign policy advisors he chose (Christopher and Lake among others) were skeptical of the robust use of military force to back diplomatic overtures. Consequently, Clinton's response to the 1993 bombing of the World Trade Center was hardly surprising. He perceived the attack as an isolated act carried out by a loosely affiliated group of individuals as opposed to a coordinated assault planned and orchestrated by a transnational terrorist organization, let alone one with state backing. As a result, the administration limited its response to a criminal investigation carried out unilaterally by the FBI, an approach that left national security institutions such as the CIA and Department of Defense largely out of the equation. This lack of collaboration reduced the potential to uncover Al Qaeda's misdeeds in an expeditious fashion, costing the administration valuable time in identifying bin Laden as a credible national security threat.[28]

Clinton did eventually recognize the pressing nature of the rising dangers presented by Al Qaeda. As he acknowledges in his memoirs, initially, "bin Laden seemed to be a financier of terrorist operations, but over time we would learn that he was the head of a highly sophisticated terrorist organization, with access to large amounts of money beyond his own fortune, and with operatives in several countries, including Chechnya, Bosnia and the Philippines."[29] Regrettably, though, Clinton remained reluctant to take decisive action to counter those threats, most emphatically so during his initial term. In January 1995, for example, a collaborative effort between US and Filipino domestic law enforcement agencies uncovered a second terrorist plot involving Yousef, an individual named Abdul Hakim Murad and an Al Qaeda member called Khalid Shaikh Mohammed. The plan was designed to facilitate the planting and detonation of bombs aboard 11 commercial airplanes bound from points in Asia to sites in the United States, with the explosions to occur over the Pacific Ocean and result in the deaths of some 4,000 Americans.[30] Fortunately, the plan never came to fruition. Instead, the Filipino police apprehended Murad in Manila in January 1995, and Yousef was taken into custody by Pakistani Special Forces and FBI agents in Islamabad, Pakistan, the next month.

Mohammed, on the other hand, remained at large.[31]

Yousef's apprehension and conviction for his role in the World Trade Center bombing in a subsequent trial in New York in 1996 contributed to the development of an increased emphasis within the Clinton administration on dealing with the bin Laden problem. Unfortunately, Clinton and his national security team proceeded to squander repeated opportunities to secure bin Laden's extradition from Sudan to the United States over the course of the 1996 election year. Bin Laden had set up a base of operations in Sudan following his expulsion from Saudi Arabia in the wake of his repeated criticisms of the political leadership in the Kingdom in 1991. Notwithstanding denials by some Clinton administration officials, published reports that have emerged in recent years indicate that Sudan offered to deliver bin Laden to the Americans—either directly or by way of a third country—on repeated occasions during 1996. Such offers were made to contacts in the CIA, the Department of State and in the US private sector.[32] Whether or not the Sudanese would actually have delivered bin Laden remains open to question. What is clear is that the political leadership in Khartoum eventually forced him to leave the country in May 1996, at which point he relocated to Afghanistan, where he reconstituted the Al Qaeda infrastructure he then used to orchestrate the events of 9/11.[33]

Had the Clinton administration elected to engage Sudan more vigorously, at least some of the attacks bin Laden carried out in subsequent years could perhaps have been prevented. One explanation as to why Clinton did not choose to pursue bin Laden any more vigorously at that juncture was that he wanted to maintain a positive focus rather than panic the public prior to the November 1996 Presidential Election, which he won handily over former Republican Senator Robert Dole. Dick Morris, one of Clinton's top domestic political advisors during his initial term, for example, notes that, "on issues of terrorism, defense and foreign affairs, generally, [Clinton] was always too wary of criticism to act decisively."[34] Unfortunately, the trend Morris points out continued throughout Clinton's final four years in the White House as well, a period during which the President had two clear opportunities to respond decisively to attacks carried out by Al Qaeda on American civilian and military targets—the August 1998 African embassy bombings and the October 2000 bombing of the USS *Cole*.

In May 1998, bin Laden called a press conference of sorts near Khost, Afghanistan in territory under the control of the Taliban. He used the occasion to publicly declare war against the United States for the fifth time since October 1996.[35] Three months later, Al Qaeda carried out bombings of the US Embassies in Nairobi, Kenya, and Dar-es-Salaam, Tanzania. The attack in Kenya killed 256 people and injured another 4,500; the strike in Tanzania left 11 dead. Among the fatalities were 12 American diplomats.[36] Clinton responded as forcefully as he had to any previous Al Qaeda assault to that point, authorizing cruise missile strikes on an alleged chemical weapons factory in Khartoum, Sudan (the government of which the administration suspected of collaboration in the embassy bombings) and Al Qaeda training camps in Afghanistan.[37]

In defending the strikes in his memoirs, Clinton recalls stressing in an address to the American people that "our attacks were not aimed against Islam, 'but against fanatics and killers,' and that we had been fighting against them on several fronts for years and would continue to do so, because 'this will be a long, ongoing struggle.'"[38] It remains unclear whether the factory in Khartoum ever actually produced chemical weapons of any sort rather than pharmaceutical supplies (as the Sudanese claimed).[39] And, regrettably, the limited missile strikes directed at the training camps in Afghanistan neither resulted in bin Laden's death nor reduced markedly Al Qaeda's capacity to threaten US interests. In short, pinprick strikes sent the wrong message to bin Laden: that Washington lacked the political will to use the full extent of its military assets against Al Qaeda. As Mike Rolince, former chief of the international terrorism division at the FBI, asserted in an interview with *National Review* editor Rich Lowry, "What you told bin Laden is that he could go and level two embassies, and in response, we're going to knock down a few huts. If you're bin Laden, that sounds like a real legitimate cost of doing business."[40]

Bin Laden continued conducting the business to which Rolince refers with tragic repercussions vis-à-vis the attack on the USS *Cole*. Al Qaeda operatives carried out the attack by guiding a small explosives-laden boat across the harbor in the port of Aden, Yemen, to the side of the *Cole*, where they detonated it. The resulting explosion ripped a hole in the side of the vessel, killing 17 American sailors and severely injuring 39 more. Clinton dispatched a team of FBI investigators to Yemen and considered a military response against Al Qaeda once reliable evidence as to its involvement in the attack was uncovered, but ultimately decided not to use force.[41] According to the President, the CIA's inability to pinpoint bin Laden's location in Afghanistan left only two other options: "a larger-scale bombing campaign of all suspected campsites or a sizable invasion. I thought neither was feasible without a [formal US legal] finding of al Qaeda responsibility for the *Cole*."[42]

Notwithstanding Clinton's explanation, there are two additional interconnected reasons why it stands to reason that he chose to act the way he did in the context of the *Cole* episode. First, he was within three months of the end of his final term and preoccupied with forging an enduring foreign policy legacy. Second, he had spent much of the previous year attempting to base that legacy upon the achievement of a lasting peace between the Israelis and Palestinians. Put simply, launching missile strikes against bin Laden—who was viewed favorably by many Palestinians and Muslims in the broader Middle East—let alone a war on terror, would have undermined his last-ditch attempts to resolve the Israeli-Palestinian conflict.

Pursuit of Peace and Stability in the Gulf and Broader Middle East, 1993-2001

The policies the Clinton administration developed in an effort to reduce the threats posed to US interests by both Iraq and Al Qaeda, in turn, affected its relationships with other states and institutions in the Greater Middle East and the resultant extent of stability (or lack thereof) across the region. In particular, three interconnected sets of relationships— those between the United States and Iran, Saudi Arabia and the principal actors in the Israeli-Palestinian peace process—stood out above the rest. Each is discussed in greater detail below.

The 1979 Islamic Revolution in Iran and maintenance of a theocratic regime in that state in the years since has rendered the development of any semblance of a constructive relationship between Washington and Tehran a perpetually daunting challenge. As was true of their predecessors, Clinton and his advisors had to strike a balance in Washington's approach toward Iran. In short, they had to acknowledge the potential for diplomatic engagement without creating the perception that the United States had any intention whatsoever of ending its criticism of Iran's sponsorship of terrorist organizations absent substantive behavioral changes on behalf of the mullahs in power in Tehran. According to Albright, "we chose a course that, though incrementally, helped us to move our relationship in the right direction, while opening the door to increased contacts."[43]

During Clinton's initial term, there was little indication of the type of diplomatic opening necessary for the development of a more constructive American-Iranian relationship. Instead, the administration placed an emphasis on its concerns over Iran's role in terrorist acts directed against the interests of the United States and its allies, most notably so in the context of the Greater Middle East. One such act was the June 1996 bombing of the Khobar Towers, a residential complex for US military forces stationed in Dharan, Saudi Arabia. The attack killed 19 American servicemen and left another 373 people injured. Ultimately, an FBI investigation uncovered evidence that the Iranian-backed terrorist group Saudi Hezbollah played a role in the planning and execution of the bombing.[44]

Concerns over Iranian involvement in the matter, irrespective of the extent of such involvement, naturally reduced the potential for a warming of relations between Washington and Tehran. On the other hand, notwithstanding those concerns, domestic political developments within Iran early in Clinton's second term suggested that a diplomatic opening might eventually come about. In particular, in May 1997, the Iranian electorate selected a reform-minded president named Muhammad Khatami. Although Khatami had only limited power (especially relative to Supreme Leader Ayatollah Ali Khamenei) over Iranian internal and external affairs, his elevation represented a window of opportunity for the Clinton administration.

For her part, Albright attempted to take advantage of that opportunity in the context of a June 1998 speech in which she welcomed "Khatami's election and the growing popular pressure in Iran for greater freedom."[45] Regrettably, albeit predictably, Khamenei was unwilling to allow Khatami much freedom to pursue even marginal democratic reforms domestically or deal with the Americans either directly or indirectly at the international level. A second US push to improve relations following further gains by Khatami's reformers in February 2000 legislative elections in Iran proved equally fruitless. In both cases, continuing US suspicion of Iran's linkages to terrorist organizations and pursuit of the development of nuclear weapons only complicated matters. Consequently, Albright concludes that

> Clinton administration policy toward Iran was calibrated appropriately. We could have achieved a breakthrough only by abandoning our principles and interests on nonproliferation, terrorism and the Middle East, far too high a price. We could have

avoided the charge that we were too soft on Iran by ignoring the reform movement entirely, but that would have left us isolated internationally and provided no incentive for Iran to change further. ... By offering an unconditional dialogue, we put the onus on Iran to explain why it was unwilling even to talk about our differences and laid the groundwork for formal discussions if and when they become possible.[46]

Managing the American-Saudi relationship proved equally challenging for the Clinton administration. Clinton had to employ a balanced approach in dealing with the Saudis. As has been the case since World War II, the United States was dependent on Saudi Arabia for a substantial proportion of the oil necessary to help fuel the growth of the American economy during the Clinton years. In addition, the United States maintained air bases in Saudi Arabia in order to maintain no-fly zones in Iraq throughout the 1990s. Thus, it was essential that Clinton and his advisors maintain a stable state of diplomatic affairs with the Saudis despite concerns over the kingdom's refusal to cooperate unequivocally in reducing the threats posed to US interests by terrorist organizations. Most significantly, the administration was frustrated over Saudi Arabia's support for Islamic charities suspected of collusion with terrorist groups—including, but not limited to, Al Qaeda.[47]

The most notable example of the Clinton administration's inability to secure Saudi cooperation in a US-administered investigation of a terrorist attack on American interests was the aforementioned Khobar Towers episode. In the aftermath of the attack, early intelligence suggested Saudi Shiite members of the Iranian-backed Hezbollah were responsible. Rather than cooperate fully with the United States, the Saudis conducted their own investigation and refused to share the documentary evidence with the FBI. As a result, the FBI failed to obtain the necessary evidence to produce any indictments before Clinton left office. As Clinton administration NSC staffers Daniel Benjamin and Steven Simon point out, the

> Saudis eventually confirmed Washington's suspicions that high-level Iranians were involved and that some of the Saudi perpetrators were thought to be living in Tehran. But the Saudis never delivered enough information, and little, if anything, that could stand up in a courtroom, where the use of intelligence as evidence is problematic in the best of circumstances. With the United States impatient to make indictments, the Saudis balked at cooperation.[48]

The connection between Iran and Saudi Arabia was particularly troubling to the Clinton administration given the traditionally cool diplomatic relationship between those two states, the vast majority of whose populations practiced Shia and Sunni Islam, respectively. It was equally alarming to Israel, as the one issue area that has typically united Muslims of differing ethnicities and Islamic stains in the past is their collective distaste for the very presence of the Jewish state in the heart of the Middle East. As *Newsweek International* editor Fareed Zakaria explains, "Israel has become the great excuse for much of the Arab world, the way for regimes to deflect attention from their own failures. Other countries have foreign policy disagreements with one another—think of Japan and China—but they do not have the sometimes poisonous quality of the Arab-Israeli divide. Israel's occupation of the West Bank and Gaza Strip has turned into the great cause of the Arab world."[49] In the end, Clinton judged that leaning too hard on the Saudis vis-à-vis the Khobar bombing or, for that matter, the kingdom's broader acceptance of and, in some cases, advocacy for Islamists' rejection of the West, would limit his ability to focus on the Middle Eastern initiative with which he was concerned the most: the Israeli-Palestinian peace process.

Throughout his presidency, Clinton remained firmly committed to resolving the confrontation that has pitted Israel against its Arab neighbors generally and the Palestinians specifically since the establishment of the Jewish state in 1948. His efforts to do so, which ranged from presiding over the signing ceremony for the Oslo Declaration of Principles at the White House in September 1993 to an ill-fated attempt to bring the Israeli-Palestinian peace process to a successful conclusion at Camp David in July 2000, were noble.[50] Yet, as was true of his predecessors over the previous half-century, and his successor, George W. Bush, Clinton was unable to bridge the long-time gaps between the two sides.

Ultimately, the sources of strive that presented the Clinton administration with what proved to be irreconcilable Israeli-Palestinian differences were fourfold. First, Israel's refusal to accept the establishment of a contiguous Palestinian state composed of the territory in the West Bank and Gaza Strip that the Israeli Defense Forces seized during the June 1967 Six-Day War and has since used for the perpetual development of settlements in areas otherwise administered by the Palestinian Authority (PA). Second, Tel Aviv's understandable reluctance to condone the return of a substantial number of the Palestinians displaced by the conduct of the 1948, 1967 and 1973 Arab-Israeli Wars and their extended families born and raised in refugee camps since—more than four million people—to Israel proper. Third, joint Israeli-Palestinian inability to resolve their differences over control of Jerusalem and the holy sites therein. Fourth, PA President Yasser Arafat's incapacity, if not unwillingness, to condemn and clamp down on the terrorist activities of Hamas, Islamic Jihad and the Al-Aqsa Martyrs Brigades.

While it is difficult to fault Clinton for focusing on an issue—the peace process—that, if resolved effectively, would likely have been quite beneficial as pertained to the stability of the broader Middle East, his efforts to produce that outcome were unsuccessful. After the Camp David talks broke up without an agreement, Clinton concluded frankly that the "parties could not reach agreement … given the historical, religious, political and emotional dimensions of the conflict."[51] Yet, because Clinton had placed such an emphasis on the peace process relative to other security challenges in the Persian Gulf and its periphery, his legacy in the region will forever be reflective of a task pursued vigorously but left undone.

Iraq, Terrorism and the Middle East: Connecting the Dots

In hindsight, perhaps the two gravest threats to US interests emanating from the Persian Gulf during Clinton's tenure in the White House were those presented by Iraq and Al Qaeda. In the years since then, journalists, policy practitioners and scholars have engaged in a debate over the extent to which such threats were connected, either directly or indirectly. This subsection examines that issue, focusing on the linkages between Iraq and terrorist organizations (most notably Al Qaeda) from 1993-2001. It opens with a primer on Saddam's long-term penchant for sponsoring terrorism, then addresses the Clinton years.

Evidence of a connection between Saddam's Iraq and terrorist organizations dates to the 1970s. In particular, Saddam first expressed an interest in supporting international terrorism in the aftermath of the October 1973 Yom Kippur War, the last of a series of Arab-Israeli Wars that left Israel in control of territory in the West Bank, Golan Heights, Gaza Strip and Suez Canal corridor abutting Jordan, Syria and Egypt, respectively. Then Palestine Liberation Organization (PLO) Chairman Arafat's refusal to openly denounce Egyptian President Anwar Sadat's subsequent willingness to pursue a peace dialogue with Israel—the first step on the road to the negotiation of the 1979 Camp David Accords—infuriated Saddam, who was not yet president of Iraq, but held considerable power in the inner circle of the political leadership in Baghdad. As a result, Saddam ordered the closure of the PLO's offices in Baghdad and began to pursue relationships with a number of other radical Palestinian groups, who were equally disgruntled over Arafat's acquiescence in the warming state of affairs between Egypt and Israel. The most well known individual associated with these groups was the Palestinian terrorist Sabri al-Banna, more commonly known as Abu Nidal.[52]

Nidal first moved to Baghdad in 1970 as a representative of Arafat's Fatah organization, but it was not until his split with the PLO that he began to rely directly on support from Saddam to fund his increasing array of terrorist activities. Those endeavors ranged from attacks on political figures inside the PLO and neighboring states (especially Syria) with which the Iraqi leadership had grievances to spectacular strikes on Western civilians such as the December 1985 bombings of the Israeli airline El Al's ticket counters at the Rome and Vienna airports that killed 18 and injured 110, including many American tourists.

In addition to Nidal, Iraq played host to Popular Front for the Liberation of Palestine (PFLP) figures including Dr. Wadi Haddad and Dr. George Habash during the 1970s and, according to one Iraqi defector, Saddam continued to harbor some 50 PFLP members into the 1990s.[53] Saddam's support for men such as Nidal, Haddad, Habash and their respective operations is the prime reason why Iraq was first placed on the US Department of State's list of state sponsors of terrorism in the late 1970s. As David Mack, who served as political officer at the American Embassy in Baghdad at the time, recalled in one published report, "we all knew precisely where Abu Nidal's house was located, although, of course, we weren't allowed to go there. Saddam liked to keep these groups there for show."[54] Saddam himself admitted as much in a July 1978 interview with *Newsweek*, acknowledging that, "regarding the Palestinians, it's no secret: Iraq is open to them and they are free to train and plan here."[55]

When Arafat engaged in negotiations with Israel in the context of the 1993 Oslo Peace Process, resulting in the establishment of the PA and subsequent ceding of limited governmental control to that entity over the administration of territory in the Gaza Strip and West Bank, Saddam did what he could to destabilize that process—and, by association—the broader Middle East by offering financial inducements for suicide attacks organized by groups such as Hamas, Islamic Jihad and the Al Aqsa Martyr's Brigade. Specifically, Saddam made a habit of paying $25,000 to the families of individuals who carried out suicide bombings against targets in Israel during the 1990s and 2000s, a bounty he eventually increased to $50,000.[56] These initiatives both improved Saddam's image in the Arab and broader Islamic worlds in the aftermath of the 1990-91 Persian Gulf War given the widespread support for the Palestinian cause that exists in those regions and also complicated the Clinton administration's attempt to resolve the Israeli-Palestinian conflict. Clinton's efforts to achieve that objective collapsed amidst the eruption of the Al Aqsa *intifada* in the fall and winter of 2000-01, an outcome Saddam can claim to have played at least a marginal role in bringing about.

Notwithstanding the relevance of the relationships Iraq built with the aforementioned terrorist groups in the 1970s and 1980s, allegations of linkages between Saddam's regime and Al Qaeda during the 1990s are considerably more germane to this book. A wide range of published reports appearing prior to—and, even more so, since—the events of 9/11 reveal evidence suggesting the existence of clear ties linking Iraq to Al Qaeda generally and to a range of terrorist operations directed against targets within, and outside of, the United States from 1993-2001. In order to assess that evidence rationally, it is considered in two interconnected clusters—those relating to Iraqi funding and training of bin Laden's operatives and the extent to which Saddam's regime was directly involved in attacks on American targets at home and abroad on the Clinton administration's watch.

The most credible evidence of linkages between Saddam Hussein's regime and Al Qaeda that has appeared in the public record to date pertains to individual contacts between the two and the funding, logistical support and training provided by officials associated with the former to members of the latter. The sources from which the evidence under consideration here is drawn range from speeches presented by Bush and his advisors and declassified intelligence reports delivered by CIA officials to Congress to a range of American and international media reports and exhaustively researched monographs addressing the relationships cultivated between Iraq and Al Qaeda prior to the events of 9/11. Collectively, these sources lay out in detail the existence of contacts between representatives of the Iraqi government and Al Qaeda that began as early as 1990 and continued over the balance of George H.W. Bush's time in office and throughout Clinton's two terms.[57] An October 2002 letter to the Senate Intelligence Committee from CIA Director Tenet is one notable case in point. In that letter, Tenet stressed that "we have solid reporting of senior level contacts between Iraq and Al Qaeda going back a decade," including "credible reporting that Al Qaeda leaders sought contacts in Iraq who could help them acquire WMD capabilities."[58] Powell's testimony before the UN Security Council in February 2003 is another. According to Powell, as far back as the "early and mid-1990s when bin Laden was based in Sudan, an al Qaeda source tells us that Saddam and bin Laden reached an understanding that al Qaeda would no longer support activities against Baghdad. Early al Qaeda ties were forged by secret high-level intelligence contacts with al Qaeda."[59]

The most comprehensive accounts of the Iraq-Al Qaeda relationship to date have appeared in a series of articles and a monograph (*The Connection: How Al Qaeda's Collaboration with Saddam Hussein has Endangered America*) by *Weekly Standard* staff writer Stephen F. Hayes. Consider, for instance, his reporting on a leaked secret memo from Bush administration officials to the Senate Intelligence Committee in October 2003. According to Hayes, the 50-point memo makes the following points: First, contacts between Saddam's regime and Al Qaeda commenced in 1990 and continued until days before the start of the Second Iraq War in March 2003, including notable bursts of activity coinciding with the showdown pitting Baghdad against Washington from February-December 1998. Second, such contacts, which were both direct and indirect in character (some within Iraq and some in other states, including Afghanistan, Pakistan, Sudan and the Czech Republic), led to the cultivation of a mutually beneficial relationship in the context of which Saddam offered financial backing to Al Qaeda, and bin Laden reciprocated by criticizing the American-backed UN sanctions on Baghdad in repeated *fatwas* declaring war on the United States. Third, while the memo is inconclusive regarding direct links connecting Saddam to Al Qaeda's attacks on US targets at home and abroad during the 1990s and 2000s, it does suggest that Iraq regularly helped Al Qaeda to train operatives to conduct of terrorist operations.[60] One such training site—Salman Pak—was situated approximately 20 miles south of Baghdad. And, as Brigadier Gen. Vincent Brooks, a spokesman for US Central Command, has asserted, Salman Pak was only one of "a number of examples" where Al Qaeda training activity occurred within Iraq.[61]

Among the contacts Hayes has cited in his reporting on the links between Saddam's regime and Al Qaeda was a 1994 meeting between an Iraqi intelligence agent named Farouk Hijazi and bin Laden in Sudan. Hijazi was captured by American troops near the Syrian border following the fall of Baghdad in April 2003.[62] Another newspaper report suggested that Hijazi had traveled to the mountains near Kandahar, Afghanistan, in December 1998 to offer bin Laden asylum in Iraq.[63] The Bush administration also believes that a senior Al Qaeda operative—Abu Musab al-Zarqawi—received medical treatment in Baghdad after he was wounded in fighting with US troops during Operation Enduring Freedom in Afghanistan, a claim the President himself made in his January 2003 State of the Union address.[64] In addition to these examples, Iraq itself identified an individual named Abd-al-Karim Muhammad Aswad as the "official in charge of the regime's contacts with [bin Laden's] group and currently the regime's representative in Pakistan" in a November 2002 article in *Babil*, a newspaper run by Saddam's late son Uday.[65]

As to Iraq's involvement in attacks carried out by Al Qaeda against American targets, perhaps the most compelling case to date has been made by scholar Laurie Mylroie, a former campaign advisor to Clinton who now publishes a weekly online newsletter entitled *Iraq News*. In a masterfully researched 2001 work entitled *Study of Revenge: The First World Trade Center Attack and Saddam Hussein's War against America*, Mylroie argued that the February 1993 bombing of the North Tower of the World Trade Center was orchestrated by Iraq and carried out by Yousef (also known as Rashid the Iraqi), who has since been linked directly to Al Qaeda as well as to Saddam's regime. In particular, Mylroie echoes an assessment she contends was the consensus among senior FBI agents who investigated that attack: that it "is best understood as a 'false flag' operation run by Iraq, leaving the Muslim extremists who participated in the conspiracy behind, to be arrested." She also contends and provides considerable documentary evidence linking Iraq to Yousef's foiled attempt to plant and detonate bombs aboard 11 airliners bound for the United States over the Pacific Ocean in 1995.[66] While perhaps not definitive, Mylroie's assertions appear all the more credible when one considers the myriad contacts between Iraq and Al Qaeda denoted by the sources cited previously.

Strengths and Weaknesses of Clinton Administration's Gulf Policies

All presidential administrations exhibit both strengths and weaknesses in developing and implementing their foreign and security policies, which typically become apparent in hindsight, once the consequences of those policies have manifested themselves at home as well as abroad. With respect to the Clinton administration, an assessment of such strengths and weaknesses is most clearly articulated contextually through examinations of its policymaking toward Iraq as pertains to the US domestic level, Greater Middle Eastern level and global level.

US Domestic Level

Domestically, the strengths of the Clinton administration's Persian Gulf policies were twofold. First, when Clinton entered office in 1993, the emerging threats to US interests were unclear. The Cold War had recently ended and most Americans were concerned primarily with economic growth at home as opposed to nascent dangers emanating from the Persian Gulf and Greater Middle East. Thus, Clinton's decision to focus on domestic rather than foreign policy was an understandable and prudent response in the short term. Second, when threats did develop and worsen—most notably those posed by Iraq and Al Qaeda— the president gradually shifted gears and eventually demonstrated a willingness to use limited military force to contain Saddam's Iraq and, if possible, eliminate bin Laden. Again, those approaches appeared reasonable at the time given that they avoided the types of risks (especially the potential for substantial military casualties) that the American public had typically proven unwilling to accept since the conclusion of the Vietnam War.

Clinton's approach also had two significant weaknesses, each of which grew increasingly evident as he neared the end of his tenure in the White House. First, one of a president's most significant responsibilities is to respond to those threats that do emerge in ways that mitigate, if not eliminate, the resulting dangers to American national interests in the future. Clinton and his advisors initially underestimated the seriousness of the threats posed by Al Qaeda in the aftermath of the February 1993 bombing of the World Trade Center. And, once the administration had recognized the extent of the security challenges Al Qaeda presented, Clinton failed to take the necessary action to reduce appreciably the capabilities of bin Laden's organization. Consequently, the United States itself remained vulnerable to terrorism to a degree that became tragically clear on 11 September 2001. Second, rather than focus on one particular set of threats or challenges (say those growing out of WMD and the state sponsorship of terrorism), Clinton chose to pursue a wide range of foreign policy initiatives but was predictably unable to follow any such initiatives through to completion. While he came reasonably close with respect to the Israeli-Palestinian peace process, the collapse of that endeavor itself produced more instability than stability in the Gulf and surrounding region.

Greater Middle Eastern Level

Notwithstanding the Clinton administration's unwillingness to take the necessary action to remove Saddam from power, his strategy of containment in the Gulf had three strengths. First, it helped to limit the threats posed by Iraq to American interests within and beyond the Greater Middle East without any significant short-term economic, military or political costs. Put simply, Saddam retained control over Iraq but his capacity to foster substantial regional instability was largely held in check. Second, it minimized differences with the Europeans on policy toward the Islamic world generally and the Middle East in particular and thus ensured cohesion in transatlantic relations concurrent with the enlargement of NATO to the East. Third, it placed an emphasis on forging a lasting settlement of the Israeli-Palestinian conflict—albeit with mixed results—rather than on confronting Iraq and Iran and alienating Muslims across the Arab world in the process.

Clinton's policies toward the Persian Gulf also had three significant weaknesses. First, although his administration did a reasonably good job in containing Iraq's military power and political influence in the Gulf, it failed to force Saddam to eliminate his WMD developmental programs in a clear and verifiable manner. The conduct of Operation Desert Fox in December 1998, while useful in illustrating America's capacity to punish Iraq militarily, did not force Iraq to readmit the UN inspectors he had expelled the previous month. Second, despite the noble efforts of Clinton and his foreign policy team, the Israeli-Palestinian conflict escalated over the course of his final four months in office. As a result, the extent of regional instability increased rather than decreased during that period. Third, the Clinton administration's failure to take military action beyond cruise military strikes against either Al Qaeda or those states suspected of supporting that organization, allowed bin Laden to enhance his capacity to inflict damage on US interests at home and abroad from 1993-2001. It also demonstrated to those regimes engaged in or considering collaboration with Al Qaeda that the costs of taking that course of action were not likely to exceed the benefits markedly.

Global Level

In general terms, there are two types of approaches to the development and implementation of foreign policy. One is reactive, the other proactive. On balance, the Clinton administration's policies toward the Persian Gulf typically reflected the former rather than the latter. With respect to its global implications, the strengths of that approach were twofold. First, because the military action the Clinton administration took against Iraq was limited and came only after Saddam had rebuffed UN efforts to maintain the inspections regime, it did not have an unbearably negative impact on the image of the United States internationally. That, in turn, allowed the administration to maintain relatively cordial relations with its allies both within, and outside of, the Gulf. Second, rather than press for revolutionary change across the Middle East in a proactive manner, Clinton chose to focus on the Israeli-Palestinian peace process and accept the status quo at the wider regional level. That strategy did not produce any drastic systemic changes such as broad-based democratization or liberalization in the Arab world, nor did it leave that potentially volatile area in considerably worse shape than was the case when Clinton took office.

On the other hand, the Clinton administration's approach also had two notable weaknesses, both of which relate to squandered opportunities. First, by failing to confront either Al Qaeda or Iraq in a more robust manner, the administration left open the potential for both to present even greater threats to the United States, its allies and the international community in the future. Al Qaeda went on to do precisely that by killing thousands of Americans and citizens from a range of other countries through the 9/11 attacks on the World Trade Center and the Pentagon. Second, it created the perception that the United States was perhaps not as likely to defend itself in the face of grave security threats as would otherwise have been assumed. That perception, for its part, increased the probability of sharper opposition if Washington was forced to take a more proactive stance vis-à-vis its adversaries in the future.

Conclusions

At its core, this chapter was designed to examine and evaluate the Clinton administration's policies toward the Persian Gulf and broader Middle East. It did so through the presentation of a three-part thematic discussion. First, it provided a necessary contextual backdrop by describing the characteristics of the international system within which Clinton and his advisors had to define and pursue the interests of the United States. That description focused primarily on the ambiguous nature of the threats to American interests in the immediate aftermath of the end of the Cold War. Second, it conducted an in-depth examination of the Clinton administration's development and implementation of foreign and security policies toward the Persian Gulf and surrounding region, one that placed an emphasis on its management of the threats posed to the United States by Al Qaeda and Iraq. Third, it evaluated the strengths and weaknesses of those policies.

As was true of his predecessor, George H.W. Bush, the policies Clinton developed and implemented in the Persian Gulf entailed costs and produced benefits for the United States over both the short and long terms. Assessing those costs and benefits, in turn, is necessary to determine the extent to which one should deem the administration's actions effective or ineffective when considered in historical perspective. Consequently, the chapter closes with precisely such an assessment.

In the short term, the benefits of the Clinton administration's policies toward the Gulf exceeded the costs, albeit to a relatively limited extent. The only significant costs were political. On those occasions that Clinton did decide to take military action against Al Qaeda and Iraq—most notably so by launching cruise missile strikes on a pharmaceutical factory in Khartoum, Sudan, and bin Laden's training camps in Afghanistan in response to the August 1998 US Embassy bombings, and prosecuting Operation Desert Fox against Saddam in December 1998 following Baghdad's expulsion of UN weapons inspectors—he did so in the face of at least some public opposition at home and abroad. The latter operation, for example, was conducted collaboratively with the United Kingdom against the wishes of the French. The fact that both operations occurred while a scandal over Clinton's relationship with White House intern Monica Lewinsky continued to unfold only complicated matters further.

The short-term benefits were twofold. First, by using force, Clinton demonstrated to Saddam and bin Laden, as well as to the US allies and the broader international community that he recognized that Iraq and Al Qaeda both posed serious threats to American interests. While more robust action would have sent an even stronger message, the strikes were commensurate with the extent of the perceived threats at the time, irrespective of the long-term accuracy of such perceptions. Second, the missile strikes in Sudan and Afghanistan and conduct of Operation Desert Fox did not result in any substantial US military casualties. That helped to minimize domestic criticism in America, particularly with respect to Operation Desert Fox. Third, the limited nature of Washington's action in both cases ensured that those concerns expressed by US allies in the Gulf and its periphery would not prove to be enduring.

Over the longer-term, however, the costs of the Clinton administration's strategic management of the Greater Middle East have exceeded the benefits markedly. Those costs were threefold. First, Clinton's decision to deal with Al Qaeda primarily, albeit not exclusively, as a law enforcement challenge rather than a threat requiring the unlimited use of military force left all but intact bin Laden's capacity to plan and prosecute terrorist acts against US interests at home and abroad. That much was evident in the aftermath of the bombing of the USS *Cole* in October 2000 and became even clearer on 9/11. Second, the limited military operations Clinton authorized American forces to conduct against Iraq were not sufficient to eliminate the potential threats Saddam posed to the interests of the United States and its allies, most notably so with respect to Baghdad's WMD developmental programs and support for terrorist organizations. As a result, it was left to Clinton's successor, George W. Bush, to eliminate those threats, a task that grew considerably more pressing in the aftermath of the events of 9/11. Third, Clinton's inability to reduce substantially Al Qaeda's operational capabilities or eliminate Saddam's regime prevented him from developing the type of revolutionary legacy the former Arkansas governor desired.

Additionally, the manner in which Clinton chose to deal with both Al Qaeda and

Iraq had one marginal long-term benefit. Because Clinton elected not to use unlimited military force in confronting either bin Laden or Saddam, it is not likely that either of the two felt the United States would take more decisive action in the future. Consequently, it is probable that neither one was as concerned with the consequences of provocative action against America as may have otherwise been the case. Thus, when the United States took decisive action following the 9/11 attacks—first against Al Qaeda and its Taliban sponsors and second against Iraq through the conduct of Operations Enduring Freedom and Iraqi Freedom—neither adversary was necessarily as prepared as it would have liked. As a result, Saddam's regime no longer exists and much of the leadership of Al Qaeda (albeit not bin Laden himself) has been either killed or captured.

In the end, although Clinton failed to respond to Saddam's infractions of UN Security Council Resolutions as effectively as George H.W. Bush managed the Persian Gulf crisis, the outcomes in each of those contexts were not related exclusively to styles of policymaking and diplomacy. The interests of the actors differed in each case, which speaks to the unpredictable nature of international affairs. The states that joined the coalition against Saddam in 1990-91 felt Iraq threatened their national interests. Many of those states held different judgments when Clinton was in office than was the case in the early 1990s, whether because of the desires to reap profits through the development of Iraqi oil resources and quell potential unrest among growing domestic Muslim communities (France), to boost the fortunes of a governmental facing a stiff reelection challenge (Germany) or a desire to retain influence as a regional and global player (Russia). Those disparate interests proved even more complicating in the context of the second Bush administration's campaign to remove Saddam from power. Ultimately, in the end, the Clinton administration responded to the complexities of the post-Cold War world by focusing on a range of different issues, but did little to mitigate the emerging threats to American interests presented by transnational terrorist networks (most notably Al Qaeda) and those states suspecting of sponsoring such groups (Iraq in particular). Those half-measures Clinton did choose to take only emboldened Saddam and allowed Al Qaeda to continue planning the 9/11 attacks that George W. Bush would have to deal with.

Notes

1. William J. Clinton, "Liberal Internationalism: America and the Global Economy," Speech at American University, Washington, D.C., 26 February 1993, excerpted in *The Clinton Foreign Policy Reader: Presidential Speeches with Commentary*, ed. Alvin Z. Rubenstein, Albina Shayevich and Boris Zlotnikov (Armonk, NY: M.E. Sharpe, 2000), 15-17.
2. William J. Clinton, "Globalism and Interdependence," Address to the United Nations General Assembly, New York, 27 September 1993, excerpted in *Clinton Foreign Policy Reader*, 15-16.
3. Richard N. Haass, "The Squandered Presidency: Demanding More from the Commander-in-Chief," *Foreign Affairs* (May/June 2000).
4. Pollack, *Threatening Storm*, 87-94.
5. In his memoirs, Clinton recalls that the "general impression among Washington observers

was that I wasn't too interested in foreign affairs and wanted to spend as little time as possible on them. It's true that the overwhelming focus of the campaign had been on domestic issues; our economic troubles demanded that. But, as I had said over and over, increasing global interdependence was erasing the divide between foreign and domestic policy. And the 'new world order' President Bush had proclaimed after the fall of the Berlin Wall was rife with chaos and big, unresolved questions." Bill Clinton, *My Life* (New York: Alfred A. Knopf, 2004), 502.

6. Warren Christopher, *Chances of a Lifetime* (New York: Scribner, 2001), 172-76; Clinton, *My Life*, 455-56.
7. Clinton, *My Life*, 737-38.
8. William J. Clinton, "Advancing Our Interests Through Engagement and Enlargement: A National Security Strategy of Enlargement and Engagement," White House, Washington, D.C. (July 1994), excerpted in *Clinton Foreign Policy Reader*, 28-29.
9. Samuel R. Berger, "A Foreign Policy for the Global Age," Remarks to the United States Institute of Peace (17 January 2001).
10. William J. Clinton, "A National Security Strategy for a New Century," *White House Office of the Press Secretary*, December 1999, iii.
11. John Lewis Gaddis, "A Grand Strategy of Transformation," *Foreign Policy* (November/December 2002): 50-51.
12. Pollack, *Threatening Storm*, 65.
13. Pollack, *Threatening Storm*, 66-67; Coughlin, *Saddam: King of Terror*, 289; Rich Lowry, *Legacy: Paying the Price for the Clinton Years* (Washington, D.C.: Regnery Publishing, Inc., 2003), 288.
14. Pollack, *Threatening Storm*, 67.
15. Clinton, *My Life*, 526.
16. Quoted in Lowry, *Legacy*, 288.
17. Pollack, *Threatening Storm*, 69-71.
18. Madeleine Albright, with Bill Woodward, *Madame Secretary: A Memoir* (New York: Miramax Books, 2003), 273-74.
19. Ibid., 72-81.
20. Ibid., 87.
21. Ibid., 87-94.
22. Clinton, *My Life*, 834.
23. Kaplan and Kristol, *The War Over Iraq*, 62.
24. The following works provide in-depth examinations of the William J. Clinton administration's handling of the threats posed by Al Qaeda to U.S. interests at home and abroad between January 1993 and January 2001: Miniter, *Losing Bin Laden: How Bill Clinton's Failures Unleashed Global Terror*; Daniel Benjamin and Steven Simon, *The Age of Sacred Terror* (New York: Random House, 2002); Peter L. Bergen, *Holy War, Inc.: Inside the Secret World of Osama bin Laden* (New York: The Free Press, 2001); and Laurie Mylroie, *Study of Revenge: The First World Trade Center Attack and Saddam Hussein's War against America* (Washington, D.C.: The AEI Press, 2001).
25. Miniter, *Losing Bin Laden*, 1-39; Mylroie, *Study of Revenge*, 78-87; Benjamin and Simon, *Age of Sacred Terror*, 7-26.
26. Mylroie, *Study of Revenge*, 48-50, Miniter, *Losing bin Laden*, 84-85.
27. Miniter, *Losing bin Laden*, 34-39.
28. Ibid., 32-34, 87-92. Complicating matters further, as Miniter notes, was the fact that Clinton never met with Director of the Central Intelligence Agency Director James

Woolsey on a one-on-one basis during Woolsey's tenure in that position from 1993-95.

29. Clinton, *My Life*, 797.
30. Miniter, *Losing Bin Laden*, 71-76; Mylroie, *Study of Revenge*, 198-207.
31. Miniter, *Losing Bin Laden*, 83-87.
32. Stephen F. Hayes, *The Connection: How Al Qaeda's Collaboration with Saddam Hussein has Endangered America* (New York: HarperCollins, 2004), 62-77; Miniter, *Losing Bin Laden*, 99-149; Lowry, *Legacy*, 314-17. For example, Miniter contends that a Pakistani-American businessman by the name of Mansour Ijaz attempted to convince several Clinton administration officials to entertain offers from Sudan to pass bin Laden along to the United States in 1996.
33. Benjamin and Simon, *Age of Sacred* Terror, 131-33.
34. Dick Morris, *Off With Their Heads: Traitors, Crooks & Obstructionists in American Politics, Media & Business* (New York: ReganBooks, 2003), 97-98.
35. Miniter, *Losing Bin Laden*, 161-64.
36. Albright, *Madam Secretary*, 366-67.
37. Albright, *Madam* Secretary, 368; Miniter, *Losing Bin Laden*, 170-86.
38. Clinton, *My Life*, 803-04.
39. Clinton himself still contends that "we did the right thing there. The CIA had soil samples taken at the plant that contained the chemical used to produce VX." Clinton, *My Life*, 805.
40. Quoted in Lowry, *Legacy*, 318.
41. Miniter, *Losing Bin Laden*, 216-29.
42. Clinton, *My Life*, 925.
43. Albright, *Madam Secretary*, 325-26.
44. Gold, *Hatred's Kingdom*, 178-80; Benjamin and Simon, *Age of Sacred Terror*, 224-25.
45. Albright, *Madam Secretary*, 320.
46. Ibid., 325-26.
47. Gold, *Hatred's Kingdom*, 176-80.
48. Benjamin and Simon, *Age of Sacred Terror*, 224-25.
49. Fareed Zakaria, *The Future of Freedom: Illiberal Democracy at Home and Abroad* (New York: W.W. Norton & Company, 2003), 152.
50. For an in-depth discussion of the Clinton administration's management of the Israeli-Palestinian peace process from 1993-2001, see Dennis Ross, *The Missing Peace: The Inside Story of the Fight for Middle East Peace* (New York: Farrar, Strauss and Giroux, 2004).
51. Clinton, *My Life*, 916.
52. Coughlin, *Saddam: King of Terror*, 140-41.
53. Ibid., 141-43.
54. Quoted in Ibid., 142.
55. Quoted in *Newsweek* (17 July 1978). Reference made in Ibid., 143.
56. Miniter, *Losing Bin Laden*, 233.
57. Sources consulted in the research and writing of the subsection of this chapter addressing the relationship between Saddam Hussein's Iraqi regime and Al Qaeda included: Coughlin, *Saddam: King of Terror*, xxv-xxxiv; Miniter, *Losing Bin Laden*, 231-41; Mylroie, *Study of Revenge*, 1-9, 106-260; Hayes, *The Connection*, 1-186; Hayes, "An Intelligent Democrat," *The Weekly Standard* (15 December 2003); Hayes, "Case Closed," *The Weekly Standard* (24 November 2003); Hayes, "Osama's Best Friend," *The Weekly Standard* (3 November 2003); Hayes, "The Al Qaeda Connection," *The Weekly Standard* (12 May 2003); Mansoor Ijaz, "Saddam and the Terrorists," *National Review* (30 June 2003).
58. Quoted in Hayes, "An Intelligent Democrat."

59. Excerpted in Hayes, *The Connection*, 22.
60. Hayes, "Case Closed"; Hayes, *The Connection*, 88-90.
61. Hayes, *The Connection*, 90-91.
62. Hayes, "The Al Qaeda Connection"; Ijaz, "Saddam and the Terrorists."
63. Julian Borger, "Saddam: 'Forging Links with bin Laden,'" *Guardian Weekly* (14 February1999). Reference made in Miniter, *Losing bin Laden*, 235.
64. Hayes, "The Al Qaeda Connection."
65. Ibid.
66. Mylroie, *Study of Revenge*, 119-26; Hayes, *The Connection*, 49-52.

Chapter 5

George W. Bush Administration and the Persian Gulf, 2001-2004

Introduction

There are few defining days in the history of any nation-state, irrespective of its internal economic, political and cultural composition. When such a day occurs, it is usually labeled in that fashion the basis of an event that delivers an unanticipated shock to a given state's political leaders and citizens, one that causes them to reevaluate their collective interests. On 11 September 2001, the United States was subjected to precisely that type of shock. That morning, 19 Al Qaeda members hijacked four American commercial airlines, which they used to launch the most devastating assault on targets in the United States since the Japanese surprise attack on Pearl Harbor on 7 December 1941. Two of the planes struck the North and South towers of the World Trade Center in New York, resulting in the collapse of both structures as millions of Americans watched on live television. A third plane flew into the Pentagon on the outskirts of Washington, D.C., and a fourth crashed in a field in Western Pennsylvania after a struggle between the hijackers and a courageous group of passengers on board. Ultimately, the attacks resulted in the loss of nearly 3,000 lives, most but not all of which were those of Americans.

The events of 9/11 raised two immediate questions in the minds of President George W. Bush and the members of his national security team. First, who was responsible for the attacks? And second, how should the United States respond—in terms of both means (diplomatic, economic, judicial, military and political) and timing? Each question demanded both short- and longer-term consideration, followed by the articulation of public statements and the subsequent planning and application of substantive action, including, if necessary, the use of military force. Bush's initial responses, delivered the day of the attacks, focused in general terms on both queries. At midday, for example, he pledged that the United States "will hunt down and punish those responsible for these cowardly acts."[1] Later, in an evening address to the nation, he reiterated that point, then added another that would foreshadow the nature of the American-led war on terrorism that has unfolded in the months and years since then, noting that "we will make no distinction between the terrorists who committed these acts and those who harbor them."[2]

Over the ensuing days, evidence implicating Al Qaeda, a transnational terrorist organization based in Afghanistan under the leadership of Osama bin Laden and harbored by the ultra-orthodox Islamic regime of the Taliban, mounted quickly. That evidence suggested that bin Laden had planned and orchestrated the attacks from Afghanistan, where he trained and then dispatched the hijackers responsible for carrying out the operation on 9/11.[3] The United States, in turn, responded by building an international "coalition of the willing" to confront Al Qaeda and its Taliban hosts. After Taliban leader Mullah Muhammad Omar refused to hand bin Laden over to Bush administration to answer for the attacks, the United States launched Operation Enduring Freedom in October 2001. With limited logistical and combat assistance from allies such as France, Germany and the United Kingdom, along with somewhat more substantial support from the opposition Afghan Northern Alliance, American forces removed the Taliban from power and reduced markedly bin Laden's capacity to organize and direct future terrorist operations on the scale of the 9/11 assaults. It did so over a period of less than two months that was followed by ongoing nation-building operations to establish liberal democratic institutions in Afghanistan.[4]

Operation Enduring Freedom demonstrated that the United States was willing to carry out the promise Bush made just hours after the events of 9/11: namely that it would seek to punish not only the terrorists responsible for the attacks but also those states or regimes willing to cooperate with or harbor bin Laden and his ilk. In reiterating that pledge in an address to Congress just over two weeks prior to the launch of operations against Taliban and Al Qaeda forces in Afghanistan, Bush had warned, "we will pursue nations that provide aid or safe haven to terrorism. Every nation, in every region, now has a decision to make. Either you are with us, or you are with the terrorists. From this day forward, any nation that continues to harbor or support terrorism will be regarded by the United States as a hostile regime."[5] At its core, Bush's stance grew out of a changing perception among the members of the administration's inner circle (and, arguably, within the American populace) of the nature of the threats to US interests posed by terrorism generally and Al Qaeda specifically, and a corresponding willingness to use all available means to eliminate those dangers. As Yale University historian John Lewis Gaddis notes, the events of 9/11 …

> certainly did shake a society. No previous act of terrorism had come anywhere close in lives lost and damage inflicted: indeed it would be difficult to think of any conventional military operation in which the results produced were so disproportionate to the resources expended. … We seemed to be back to a level of personal insecurity unknown since our ancestors were staking out a society along an advancing frontier, with the protections afforded by government trailing along behind them.[6]

One year after Al Qaeda's attacks on the World Trade Center and the Pentagon, the Bush administration unveiled a preemptive NSS equally reflective of that changing perception. Above all, the NSS was designed to eliminate threats to the United States before they become eminent and thus unavoidable. Its release coincided with Bush's then ongoing rhetorical efforts to confront Iraqi President Saddam Hussein over Baghdad's WMD developmental programs and sponsorship of terrorist organizations. Those efforts, in turn, were part of a dozen-year diplomatic, economic—and, at times, military—struggle pitting America against Iraq, one that commenced after the United States and its allies negotiated a UN sponsored cease-fire with Baghdad at the conclusion of the 1990-91 Persian Gulf War. Most significantly, that settlement stipulated that Saddam discontinue the acquisition and production of WMD and the requisite medium- and long-range missile systems to use such munitions to attack his adversaries and refrain from supporting terrorist groups, agreements that he violated repeatedly between 1991 and 2002.[7]

Iraq's record of defiance prompted Bush to issue a firm set of dictates to Saddam in a speech before the UN General Assembly in New York on 12 September 2002. In that address, which was delivered symbolically just over 12 months to the day of the 9/11 attacks, the President made three fundamental points. First, he demanded that Iraq comply immediately with all of the promises it made to the international community at the end of the Persian Gulf War, noting that Saddam had ignored 16 separate UN Security Council resolutions over the previous decade.[8] Specifically, the President emphasized that because it was continuing to pursue the acquisition of WMD and missile delivery systems, Iraq represented "a grave and gathering danger" to international security.[9] Second, he challenged the UN to carry out its responsibilities by impressing upon Saddam the need to disarm in an internationally-verifiable manner, asking members of that body's General Assembly: "Will the United Nations serve the purpose of its founding, or will it be irrelevant?"[10] Third, he pledged that the United States would take action to eliminate the threats Iraq posed to American interests— with the UN's help if possible, but also unilaterally if necessary—noting that "we cannot stand by and do nothing while dangers gather."[11]

With these observations providing a necessary contextual foundation, the balance of this chapter examines and assesses the Bush administration's policies toward the Persian Gulf through the presentation of three related sections that unfold in the following manner:

- The first section opens with an examination of American interests in the Gulf as articulated by the Bush administration, then discusses the resultant development of policies toward Iraq from January 2001 to September 2004. However, it focuses primarily on the diplomatic prologue to, and conduct of, the Second Iraq War and subsequent US-led nation-building operations in Iraq in 2003-04. Given the centrality of those developments to the US role in the Gulf from 2001 to the present, this section is considerably lengthier than either of the chapter's ensuing sections.
- The second section considers the strengths and weaknesses of the Bush administration's policies toward the Persian Gulf generally and Iraq specifically at the US domestic level as well as in the contexts of the Gulf, Greater Middle East and global international system.
- The concluding section reiterates the chapter's most significant points, then closes with an assessment of the short- and long-term costs and benefits of the above policies.

US Interests and Resultant Policies in the Persian Gulf, 2001-2004

As was true of the George H.W. Bush administration, the George W. Bush administration employed a one-plus-a-few approach to foreign policymaking in general, and in confronting and then rebuilding Iraq in particular from 2002-04. Unlike his father, but similar to Clinton, Bush opened his tenure in the White House as a neophyte with respect to international politics. Consequently, he assembled a team of advisors whose collective federal governmental experience bridged several decades, administrations and crises. Three of the four most influential members of the Bush foreign policy team—Vice President Richard Cheney, Secretary of State Colin Powell and National Security Advisor Condoleezza Rice—also served in prominent positions in the administration of the President's father. A fourth, Secretary of Defense Donald Rumsfeld, had served under Republican Presidents Richard Nixon and Gerald Ford, and in a range of advisory positions in the 1980s and 1990s.

Cheney, Powell, Rice and Rumsfeld are all members of a group of Bush advisors known as the Vulcans, a moniker that first surfaced during the 2000 Presidential Campaign. The group, which also includes Paul Wolfowitz and Richard Armitage—top deputies to Rumsfeld and Powell, respectively—was named after Vulcan, the Roman god of fire, forge and metalwork. The principal reason is one that has since become quite appropriate in light of the Bush administration's willingness to safeguard American interests through the unlimited use of military power. As James Mann, a Washington-based journalist and author of a recent book on the Vulcans explains, the word "captured perfectly the image the Bush foreign policy team sought to convey, a sense of power, toughness, resilience and durability."[12]

The Vulcans' arrival in Washington as Bush assumed office represented what Mann described as "a class reunion," given that "[m]ost of them had already worked closely alongside one another in previous administrations, and the ties among them were close, intricate and overlapping."[13] Above all, the members of the group shared similar—albeit by no means identical—viewpoints on the need to use all available measures to minimize threats to the United States and do so in a selectively multilateral fashion in those cases that one or more of America's traditional allies disagreed with Washington's views on a particular issue or policy stance. Cheney, Rumsfeld and Wolfowitz, for example, tended to be more hawkish than Powell and Armitage vis-à-vis the willingness to use force. Yet, as Mann notes, "within the broad spectrum of American foreign policy over the past three decades, [Powell and Armitage] were hardly doves and in fact shared much in common with the other Vulcans. Their relationship with hawks like Cheney, Rumsfeld and Wolfowitz was akin to that of a feuding family. They bickered; but they all seemed to need each other, and they all kept on coming back to the dinner table."[14]

As is true of any family, or, for that matter, American national security team, disagreements must eventually be settled in one fashion or another. With respect to the Bush administration, the final decision on all significant issues and policies has naturally rested with the president. However, in Bush's case, Rice has also played a critical role. When hawks and doves clash on a given issue—say the timetable for the use of force against an adversary such as Al Qaeda or Iraq—it is Rice's job to bridge the gap between the two sides and thus help Bush to arrive at a prudent decision. As Mann concludes,

> Bush's national security advisor was outweighed in the administration's inner circles by the older, more experienced figures of Cheney, Powell and Rumsfeld. Yet she was of critical importance in several ways. Of all the top-level officials, she was by far the closest to Bush. When the Defense and State Departments were divided, or when Rumsfeld and Cheney advised one course of action and Powell a different one, it was Rice who helped the president reach a decision.[15]

On balance, Bush and his advisors proved adept in responding to the events of 9/11, removing Saddam from power and laying the foundation for the development of liberal democratic institutions in Iraq and the broader Middle East. With the aforementioned description of the backgrounds and working relationships of the members of the Bush's national security team as a point of departure, the balance of this section examines the means they used to achieve those ends. It unfolds in four parts, which discuss the following issues and events: the doctrine of preemption; the diplomatic run-up to, and prosecution of, Operation Iraqi Freedom; the democratization of Iraq and the Greater Middle East; and the linkages between the Bush administration's policies toward the Persian Gulf and its conduct of the war on terrorism.

A Doctrine of Preemption

Five days after Bush's UN speech on Iraq, his administration released its first NSS since assuming office, the timing of which was, by no means, coincidental. Designed to warn American adversaries in general and Iraq in particular that the United States would not tolerate the development and proliferation of WMD or the state sponsorship of terrorism, Bush's NSS is built around three pledges. First, the United States "will defend the peace by fighting terrorists and tyrants." Second, it "will preserve the peace by building good relations among the great powers." And third, it "will extend the peace by encouraging free and open societies on every continent."[16] At its core, the NSS represents a shift in strategic thinking from an emphasis on the deterrent containment doctrine of the Cold War to a willingness to use preemptive policy-making to safeguard American national interests. It is a shift necessitated by the changing nature—and severity—of the threats posed to those interests as evidenced by the events of 9/11. As Rice, one of the principal architects of the strategy, has asserted, "some threats are so potentially catastrophic—and can arrive with so little warning, by means that are untraceable—that they cannot be contained. ... So as a matter of common sense, the United States must be prepared to take action, when necessary, before threats have fully materialized."[17]

Domestic and foreign opponents of the Bush administration, along with some of America's European allies (France and Germany in particular), have since criticized its NSS as one based all but exclusively on the preemptive use of military force, whether employed unilaterally or multilaterally. Yet, even a cursory reading of the document reveals such criticism to be misguided. It is 40 pages in length and the discussion of preemption encompasses just two sentences in one of its eight sections. Granted, Bush and his advisors stressed the use of preemptive measures in light of the dire threats posed by terrorist groups and their state sponsors and heightened public sensitivities to those dangers after the 9/11 attacks, but when taken as a whole, the NSS represents a vastly more wide ranging strategy. As Powell has pointed out,

> The NSS made the concept of preemption explicit in the heady aftermath of September 11, and it did so for obvious reasons. One reason was to reassure the American people that the government possessed common sense. As President Bush has said—and as any sensible person understands—if you recognize a clear and present threat that is undeterrable by the means you have at hand, then you must deal with it. You do not wait for it to strike; you do not allow future attacks to happen before you take action. A second reason for including the notion of preemption in the NSS was to convey to our adversaries that they were in big trouble. ... Sensible as these reasons were, some observers have exaggerated both the scope of preemption in foreign policy and the centrality of preemption in US strategy as a whole.[18]

Justifiably, in the context of the NSS, Bush cedes primacy to hard-core security issues. However, he does so by laying out the White House's strategy in terms of the proactive pursuit of eight separate goals, five of which pertain to hard-core security issues and three to the pursuit of foster economic growth and construction of enduring liberal democratic institutions in the developing world in general and the Greater Middle East in particular. Specifically, the administration pledges that the United States will:

- Champion aspirations for human dignity.
- Strengthen alliances to defeat global terrorism and work to prevent attacks against us and our friends.
- Work with others to defuse regional conflicts.
- Prevent our enemies from threatening us, our allies, and our friends, with weapons of mass destruction.
- Ignite a new era of global economic growth through free markets and free trade.
- Expand the circle of development by opening societies and building the infrastructure of democracy.
- Develop agendas for cooperative action with other main centers of global power.
- Transform America's national security institutions to meet the challenges and opportunities of the twenty-first century.[19]

Given this broad range of objectives, Bush's strategy appears not as a rash reaction to the 9/11 assaults, but as a comprehensive blueprint that takes into account the successes and failures of his predecessors in the White House over the past half-century. One of the means the United States used to weaken the Soviet Union's grip over the members of the Warsaw Pact, for instance, was by "opening societies and building the infrastructure of democracy" throughout Central and Eastern Europe. Most significantly, President Ronald Reagan's willingness to push the Soviets to loosen and then release their control over the Warsaw Pact once the arms buildup of the early 1980s put Washington in a position of relative strength vis-à-vis Moscow, triggered the subsequent collapse of Communist regimes from Bucharest to East Berlin in the fall and winter of 1989-90. The Bush NSS is designed to produce comparably revolutionary changes in the Arab world. In that sense, it is both flexible and visionary rather than ill conceived and illogical. As Powell concludes, "Together, [its eight] parts add up to a strategy that is broad and deep, far ranging and forward looking, attuned as much to opportunities for the United States as to the dangers it faces."[20]

What is most instructive about the Bush administration's NSS is the extent to which it takes a selectively multilateral stance in discussing the economic, political and military means the United States is prepared to use to preempt threats to American national interests.[21] The NSS suggests that such threats—most notably the acquisition, production and proliferation of WMD by dictatorial regimes—are best dealt with multilaterally through the organization of "coalitions—as broad as practicable—of states able and willing to promote a balance of power that favors freedom."[22] Furthermore, it renders critics' characterizations of the Bush administration's aversion to working with the UN under any circumstances less credible by justifying its doctrine of preemption in globally acceptable legal terms pertaining to a state's right to defend itself.[23]

Much of the criticism of Bush's foreign policy before, as well as during and after, the prosecution of the Second Iraq War, rests primarily on the premise that he has acted unilaterally more often than not. Responding to that criticism demands that one first defines the term unilateralism. The narrowest definition of the term would suggest that a given state is acting alone—that is without the support of any allies whatsoever, let alone the blessing of the UN Security Council or wider international community. A broader definition, by contrast, might indicate a coalition of less than 10 states acting without the authority of a formal Security Council resolution. Neither of these definitions applies to US action in the context of either Operation Enduring Freedom or Operation Iraqi Freedom. In each case, the United States acted with the direct or indirect military, logistical or political support of no less than 50 states. As Powell explains, "Partnership is the watchword of US strategy in this administration. Partnership is not about deferring to others; it is about working with them."[24]

Moving beyond its general and specific characterizations of the potential security threats the United States must confront (most notably the arming of terrorist organizations with WMD by tyrannical regimes) and the means to use in preempting those threats (collective diplomacy if possible; the multilateral or unilateral use of force if necessary), the NSS also prioritizes American interests regionally. Not unexpectedly, that prioritization places an emphasis on Greater Middle Eastern and South Asian security affairs generally and such long-standing imbroglios as the Israeli-Palestinian conflict and troubled Indian-Pakistani relationship in particular. In addressing each of these contentious relationships, the NSS acknowledges the need for the United States to strike a balance between the interests of the disparate ethnic and religious groups involved.[25] One reason why is that in order to avoid deepening the anti-American sentiments that have in the past—and continue at present—to make members of the lower classes of the Islamic world susceptible to the recruitment efforts of regional and global terrorist organizations. Rice, for example, notes that the Bush administration "rejects the condescending view that freedom will not grow in the soil of the Middle East—or that Muslims somehow do not share in the desire to be free."[26]

Diplomatic Prologue to, and Conduct of, the Second Iraq War

Bush's address to the UN General Assembly and his subsequent release of the NSS set the stage for concurrent, and equally vigorous, domestic and international debates regarding the need to disarm Iraq. Those debates eventually resulted in the passage of two measures: a US Congressional Resolution authorizing the use of force against Iraq[27] and a UN Security Council Resolution demanding that Saddam readmit and grant unrestricted investigative access to UN inspectors charged with determining the extent to which his regime has disarmed.[28] Ultimately, the construction of a coalition to disarm Iraq through the conduct of the Second Iraq War served as a practical test of the doctrine of preemption articulated in the NSS. The purpose of this section is to examine the process through which the United States applied Bush's NSS to the case of Iraq. It does so by discussing briefly the diplomatic prologue to, and prosecution of, Operation Iraqi Freedom between September 2002 and April 2003.[29]

In the contexts of Security Council Resolution 687 and 16 subsequent Security Council resolutions—the last of which (Resolution 4112) was passed unanimously on 8 November 2002—the UN demanded that Iraq make a range of behavioral modifications to ensure its re-acceptance as a productive member of the international community.[30] Saddam's regime failed to comply fully with all of these resolutions. In particular, Iraq defied UN mandates by declining to: eliminate its biological, chemical and nuclear WMD developmental programs in an unambiguously verifiable manner; cease its attempts to acquire ballistic missiles with ranges greater than 150 kilometers; renounce all terrorist organizations and refuse to harbor any members of such groups within its borders; return all foreign prisoners seized during its 1990 invasion of Kuwait and the subsequent Persian Gulf War; and refrain from repressing its domestic population.[31]

To its credit, the Bush administration applied a variety of economic, diplomatic and politico-military tools to the liquidation of Saddam's regime. The initial stage of the process was rhetorical in nature. It commenced with Bush's address to the UN General Assembly in September 2002 and continued with his nationally televised speech to the American people from Cincinnati a month later.[32] In each case, the President issued stern demands for Iraq to disarm in order to impress upon Saddam and the international community how seriously Washington viewed the matter. However, Bush was also careful to express his willingness to afford the UN an opportunity to achieve that objective peacefully before the United States would consider either the multilateral or unilateral use of force against Iraq. Furthermore, key members of the administration's national security team—most notably Rice, Powell and Rumsfeld—and also British Prime Minister Tony Blair struck similar tones in reiterating the administration's demands between September 2002 and March 2003.

Next, the Bush administration focused on the development of American and international legal measures to justify diplomatic and military action against Iraq. Domestically, Bush worked diligently to secure Congressional authorization of the use of force to disarm Iraq should such action become necessary, which he achieved through the resounding passage of a joint resolution to that end by the House and Senate.[33] Internationally, Powell collaborated with his British, French, Russian and Chinese counterparts on the Security Council to fashion Resolution 4112, which called for Saddam to readmit and cooperate unconditionally with weapons inspectors under the auspices of the UN Monitoring, Verification and Inspection Commission (UNMOVIC) or face "serious consequences."[34] The resolution passed by a 15-0 vote in the Security Council on 8 November 2002 and was agreed to by Iraq six days later.

Throughout the diplomatic process, French President Jacques Chirac was the most vociferous of several foreign leaders to express their unambiguous opposition to the use of military force to disarm Iraq and employed all diplomatic measures at his disposal to block that course of action. For example, although France voted for Resolution 4112, it did so only because that measure did not explicitly sanction the use of force against Iraq. Ultimately, when the United States, the United Kingdom and Spain indicated they would seek a second resolution condoning military action to disarm Saddam's regime, Chirac responded that "whatever the circumstances, France will vote no," ensuring that the campaign for any such resolution was stillborn.[35]

Chirac's behavior raises a simple question, albeit one that demands a relatively complex answer: why was he so insistent that the United States not remove Saddam from power? In short, there are three reasons, each of which includes both domestic and international components that require more detailed independent explanations. First, France had close public and private economic ties with Saddam's regime, which it was understandably eager to preserve. Second, France plays host to a growing Muslim population, one whose members were unequivocally opposed to US military action against Iraq and by no means averse to expressing their opposition in violent—and thus socially destabilizing—ways. Third, Chirac perceived the Iraq crisis as an opportunity to revitalize flagging French prestige—both within and outside of Europe—in opposition to American predominance in the post-Cold War international system.

Economically, France had much to lose as a result of the liquidation of Saddam's regime. At the governmental level, Baghdad is in debt to Paris to the tune of approximately $8 billion.[36] While the sum itself is not substantial, it suggests the potential existence of linkages between Chirac's administration and the regime in Baghdad that may extend at least peripherally to collusion on the development of WMD. In theory, economic connections between France and Iraq are perhaps even more relevant with respect to the private sector. Most significantly, French oil companies such as TotalFinaElf (TFE) are suspected of negotiating contracts to develop Iraqi oil resources that would enter into force concurrent with the removal of UN economic sanctions against Iraq. While TFE Chairman Thierry Demarest denies signing any such contracts, published reports indicated that the finalization of a deal for TFE to "exploit the huge Majnoon field, with 20 billion barrels of oil, in southern

Iraq, as well as the smaller Nahr Umr field nearby" was all but a formality prior to the outbreak of hostilities.[37] Given French opposition to the war, the nascent democratic Iraq is unlikely to treat TFE nearly so favorably as was true of Saddam.

In addition to these economic considerations, Chirac faced equally pressing domestic political concerns over the potentially volatile reaction of Franco-Muslim communities to any governmental support whatsoever for the American-led use of force against Iraq. As a result, Chirac was justifiably concerned over the likelihood if not certainty of domestic instability emanating from the urban housing projects in which most Franco-Islamic communities are situated given past acts of Franco-Muslim defiance ranging from public demonstrations to the commission of terrorist attacks. Yet, while Chirac's anti-war strategy mollified France's Muslims in the short term, deeper ethnic and religious divisions are likely to prevail without the development of a more effective governmental strategy to integrate Islamic communities within the societal mainstream over the long term.

Notwithstanding Chirac's domestic economic and political motivations, his opposition to and attempted obstruction of the Bush administration's preemptive strategy toward Iraq was, at its core, a product of the traditional French aversion to the expression of American power in the world. During the Cold War, France consistently sought to create independent roles for itself as a hub of opposition to US leadership within Europe and across the developing world. Manifestations of this trend included President Charles de Gaulle's acquisition of a nuclear *force de frappe* and subsequent withdrawal of France from NATO's military command structure in 1966. It is not unreasonable to characterize Chirac's behavior of late in similar terms to that of de Gaulle. Lacking the economic vitality or military capacity to portray France as a legitimate rival to the United States, Chirac attempted to achieve that objective by using the one body in which Paris possesses power relatively equivalent to that wielded by Washington: the UN Security Council. Regrettably, in the process, he may well have damaged the Franco-American relationship to an extent that will require months—and perhaps—years to repair.

Predictably, in the end, Saddam refused to cooperate unambiguously with the weapons inspectors. As a result, the United States collaborated with the United Kingdom—and, to a lesser degree, a range of other allies including Australia and several Eastern and Central European states—to forcibly remove the Iraqi regime from power over objections from the French, as well as the Russians, Chinese and several members of the Arab League. The Americans and British did so by orchestrating a campaign that took just over a month to remove Saddam's regime between March and April 2003.

The conduct of Operation Iraqi Freedom itself was relatively painless militarily and politically. The immediate aftermath of the fall of Baghdad, by contrast, was somewhat more problematic. The initial security challenges faced by coalition forces in the aftermath of the fall of Baghdad in April 2003 grew primarily out of the desire of many Iraqis to strike out against members of Saddam's Baath Party by looting the dictator's palaces and the government ministries formerly administered by his minions. And, regrettably, the subsequent inability or unwillingness of the United States and its coalition partners to take decisive action to prevent the looting contributed to a sense that the liberators had lost control of the situation. The resulting instability led to widespread criticism of the Bush administration such as that expressed by Peter Galbraith, a former American Ambassador to Croatia in testimony before Congress in June 2003: "When the United States entered Baghdad on April 9, it entered a city largely undamaged by a carefully executed military campaign. However, in the three weeks following the US takeover, unchecked looting effectively gutted every important public institution in the city—with the notable exception of the oil ministry."[38]

A Strategy to Transform the Greater Middle East

During the Cold War, most dangers the United States had to counter grew out of its adversarial relationship with the Soviet Union. Since the end of that bipolar struggle, by contrast, American presidents have had to respond to challenges related to the emergence of "failing" and "failed states" that threaten military security, economic vitality and political stability in regions deemed vital to the interests of the United States and its allies. These entities have been of particular concern to American policymakers in the 1990s and 2000s. The Clinton and Bush administrations both intervened militarily in states that could be defined as either "failing" or "failed" in terms of governmental maintenance of, control over, or humane treatment of, their populations. The former took action in Bosnia in 1995 and Kosovo in 1999 and the latter in Afghanistan in 2001 and Iraq in 2003. In each case, the use of force was followed by the conduct of post-conflict operations that have since been defined as "nation building" endeavors.

Nation building is, by no means, a new concept. It was, for example, employed effectively in the transformation of Germany and Japan from dictatorships to democracies in the aftermath of World War II. However, both the frequency of the application of nation building operations and the threats such projects are designed to counter have changed markedly over the past decade. The primary purpose of the Clinton administration's participation in nation building operations in the Balkans was to ensure political stability in a region adjacent to the borders of member states of the NATO and EU. The Bush administration, on the other hand, has supported the reconstruction and democratization of Afghanistan and played the lead role in nation-building operations in Iraq as a means to reduce the threats posed to US interests by terrorists and their sponsors in two ways: first, by replacing regimes that supported Al Qaeda either directly or indirectly; and, second, by improving the standard of living of, and affording political freedom to, the people of the Greater Middle East.

Above all, the physical and economic reconstruction and political liberalization of Iraq is absolutely indispensable to the broader transformation of the Islamic world. That much Bush and his advisors have emphasized repeatedly since the elimination of Saddam's regime in April 2003 and commencement of reconstruction operations the ensuing month. In April 2004, for instance, Bush stressed that "a free Iraq will stand as an example to reformers across the Middle East. A free Iraq will show that America is on the side of Muslims who wish to live in peace, as we have already shown in Kuwait [by way of the conduct of the 1990-91 Persian Gulf War] and Kosovo, Bosnia and Afghanistan. A free Iraq will confirm to a watching world that America's word, once given, can be relied upon, even in the toughest of times."[39]

Bush's remarks opened a nationally televised press conference addressing the many challenges associated with nation building in Iraq. The president's comments were demonstrative of two underlying points. First, Bush recognized at that juncture that the transformation of Iraq continued to present economic, military and political roadblocks that would take years, rather than weeks or months to overcome. Second, he emphasized the importance of seeing the Iraqi nation-building project through to completion, implying that subsequent administrations should maintain the commitment to the broader liberalization and democratization of the Greater Middle East over the long term. In particular, he concluded that

> America's commitment to freedom in Iraq is consistent with our ideals, and required by our interests. Iraq will either be a peaceful, democratic country, or it will again be a source of violence, a haven for terror and a threat to America and to the world. By helping to secure a free Iraq, Americans serving in that country are protecting their fellow citizens. Our nation is grateful to them all and to their families. ... Above all, the defeat of violence and terror in Iraq is vital to the defeat of violence and terror elsewhere; and vital, therefore, to the safety of the American people. Now is the time and Iraq is the place, in which the enemies of the civilized world are testing the will of the civilized world. We must not waver.[40]

At the core of insurgent efforts to undermine nation-building operations in Iraq is the fear that the United States will establish an enduring free market economy and representative government there. That outcome could eventually lead to two developments that dictatorial regimes and terrorist groups alike would abhor: an improved standard of living for members of the lower classes of society; and the creation of a political atmosphere in which individuals are free to elect and, if they choose, criticize those in power. With Iraq as a model, other countries possessing comparably autocratic characteristics to those of Saddam's former regime (examples range from Islamic states such as Saudi Arabia and Iran to more secular oriented states like Egypt and Syria) could be the next candidates for economic and political transformation.

Of those states, Iran in particular has the potential to pose significant threats to US interests in the Persian Gulf in the future. There were, for example, a variety of factors behind Bush characterization of Iran as a member of the "axis of evil" in his 2002 State of the Union address.[41] First, Tehran is in the process of acquiring and refining WMD and the means to deliver them to targets throughout the Greater Middle East. Notwithstanding its status as a signatory to the Non-Proliferation Treaty, Iran is developing a series of nominal civilian reactors that could provide the fissile materials necessary to construct atomic weaponry. In addition, Washington suspects Iran has broken its obligations under the provisions of the Chemical Weapons Convention and Biological Weapons Convention and may have the capacity to deliver missiles armed with WMD to the continental United States by 2015.[42] Second, while Iran has not been linked directly to the events of 9/11, it remains on the Department of State's list of sponsors of terrorism and is suspected of complicity in the June 1996 bombing of the Khobar Towers.[43] Third, Tehran continues to undermine the fleeting Israeli-Palestinian peace process by providing economic, military and political support to terrorist organizations such as Hamas, Hezbollah and Islamic Jihad.[44] As Rice has asserted, "Iranian behavior puts it squarely in the 'axis of evil'—whether it is weapons of mass destruction or terrorism or any of those things. It's a complicated situation, but I think the behavior speaks for itself."[45]

American efforts to promote democratic change in Iraq scare not only the Iranians, but also the leaders of terrorist organizations including, but not limited to, Al Qaeda. There are two reasons why. First, those groups thrive on discontent, if not outright desperation, to recruit members willing to sacrifice their lives to battle the adversaries they blame for the dearth of economic growth and political freedom prevalent across much of the Arab world. One such adversary (the United States) is perceived by many Muslims to be responsible for the majority of these shortcomings. Should Bush—or, for that matter, any other American president—manage to use a successful transformation of Iraq to start the engine of reform at the broader regional level, the pool of terrorist recruits would decrease substantially. Second, while bin Laden and his ilk also seek the elimination of the present governments in control of states throughout the Middle East, they would prefer that those changes come under their auspices. That would, of course, allow them to take control and install equally repressive regimes, which they could then administer in a style similar to that of the Taliban in Afghanistan. The establishment of representative democracies, by contrast, would encourage the free expression of dissent to prevent the development of any type of autocracy, whether Islamic or secular in character.

Assuming that the democratization of the Greater Middle East is a realistic long-term objective, a topic on which there is considerable debate, the Bush administration deserves credit for taking the initial step toward its achievement. However, it is also essential to recognize that the pursuit of such a revolutionary transformation will entail substantial costs and require a commitment that lasts for decades rather than years. Most significantly, those costs will grow out of the myriad challenges associated with the transformation Bush has suggested the United States should pursue. Such challenges are primarily ethnic and religious in orientation, each set of which is addressed briefly below.

Broadly articulated ethnic differences between groups tend to complicate reconstruction efforts at the national level, most notably as pertains to the creation and subsequent administration of economic and financial institutions in a given domestic environment. When individuals of one ethnic persuasion are appointed to leadership positions in such institutions, their counterparts from other groups understandably demand equitable treatment that, while morally just in theory, may slow the recovery process in practice. The reluctance of members of a particular ethnic group to accept advice from, and thus place their trust in, foreigners, is equally problematic. When those foreigners represent institutions perceived to be in business simply to do the bidding to the United States, earning that trust can be exceedingly difficult within the developing world generally and the Greater Middle East specifically.

Challenges related to linguistic differences and intra-ethnic familial and tribal rivalries typically prove especially daunting at the local level. Even if, for instance, one ethnic group is represented on a transitional economic or political body at the national level, it is by no means certain that decisions taken by that entity will be accepted by the leaders of tribes or villages thousands of miles from the capital. And, in those cases where local leaders agree to help administer humanitarian aid in an area under their control, communications are not always smooth between starving civilians and the foreign soldiers or Non-Governmental Organization (NGO) workers distributing foodstuffs.

Similarly, religious impediments to the economic and financial aspects of nation building manifest themselves in interactions among individuals, states and institutions at several different levels. Inter- and intra-denominational differences, for instance, are often evident locally and nationally, as well as regionally and globally. Domestically, inter- and intra-denominational religious disputes have the potential to undermine both the political and economic aspects of reconstruction projects. Some international religious impediments to nation building grow out of global issues (support from a small but violent minority of Muslims for transnational terrorist organizations, as evidenced by efforts to sabotage reconstruction efforts in Afghanistan and Iraq, is one such example). Others are the result of the use of NGOs to spread one faith (most often Christianity or Islam) in a state or region where the vast majority of the inhabitants already adhere to another.

Putting forward the effort to overcome these hurdles—and accepting the requisite economic, military and political costs that accumulate along the way—will provide an opportunity to alter the broader relationship between Islam and the West in an equally favorable manner. The United States has embraced comparably daunting challenges in the past, most notably its commitment in the aftermath of World War II to the idea of a Europe whole and free. That project is now nearly 60 years old and gradually nearing completion with the EU and NATO both moving forward with their most recent enlargement processes in 2004. Lacking the economic, military and political sacrifices the Americans and Western Europeans made during the Cold War, the European continent, too, might still lack the freedoms the Bush administration now hopes to spread to the Greater Middle East.

Connecting the Dots: Iraq, Al Qaeda and the War on Terrorism

When Bush took office, he was left to build on the mixed results recorded by the Clinton administration vis-à-vis its policies toward Al Qaeda and that group's state sponsors. Rather than pressure the Taliban, which harbored bin Laden in Afghanistan from 1996-2001, diplomatically or consider the deployment of military forces in that context, Clinton chose to pursue bin Laden primarily through domestic law enforcement bodies and weaken Al Qaeda to the limited extent possible through a single flurry of cruise missile strikes.[46] As former Clinton aide Dick Morris contends, "All our [present] terrorist problems were born during the Clinton years. It was during his eight years in office that [Al] Qaeda began its campaign of bombing and destruction aimed at the United States. ... Bill Clinton and his advisors were alerted to the group's power and intentions by these attacks. But they did nothing to stop [Al] Qaeda from building up its resources for the big blow on 9/11."[47]

Regrettably, the Bush administration's initial approach to the issue of Al Qaeda proved no more robust than Clinton's as the President and his advisors worked to craft an effective foreign and security policy blueprint in the weeks and months preceding the events of 9/11. Prior to assuming office, Bush joined Cheney and Rice at a briefing conducted by Clinton's third Director of Central Intelligence, George Tenet. During the briefing, Tenet warned all three that bin Laden represented a "tremendous threat" to American interests at home and abroad, one that was "immediate."[48] Over the ensuing months, the CIA issued several more warnings, including 34 communications intercepts in the summer of 2001 indicating that Al Qaeda was planning a major operation against the United States by issuing subtly coded statements such as "Zero hour is tomorrow" or "Something spectacular is coming."[49]

The CIA's warnings stirred the Bush administration to action, albeit of a sort that had not extended beyond the planning stage when Al Qaeda launched its attacks on the World Trade Center and Pentagon. Rice, for example, was in the process of preparing a National Security Directive on the issue on September 10, one that built on lower-level National Security Council discussions on the construction of a strategy to eliminate Al Qaeda.[50] That planning, of course, shifted rapidly into concrete military action against both Al Qaeda and the Taliban in the aftermath of 9/11. And the conduct of Operation Enduring Freedom turned out to be just the initial battle in the Bush administration's conduct of a broader war against transnational terrorist groups and their state sponsors. Ultimately, that war resulted in the elimination of Saddam's regime as well.

While no member of the Bush administration has ever argued publicly that Iraq was directly involved in either the planning or conduct of the 9/11 attacks on the World Trade Center and Pentagon, it is possible to construct a circumstantial case that suggests the existence of precisely such a linkage.[51] It is perhaps most appropriate to begin articulating that case with an examination of Saddam's own behavior the morning of the attacks and over the ensuing days. In the hours prior to Al Qaeda's strikes in New York and Washington, Iraq placed its military forces on their highest level of alert since the outbreak of the 1990-91 Persian Gulf War. Saddam himself retreated into the depths of one of his fortified bunkers in Tikrit, the northern Iraqi city from which he first emerged as a powerful figure in the Baath Party.[52] Nor did Saddam's regime indicate any sign of even token disapproval of the attacks. To the contrary, it issued a statement claiming that the United States deserved the attacks.[53]

There are, of course, at least two contrasting explanations for Iraq's behavior concurrent with, and in the aftermath of, the events of 9/11. One, the most conservative of the two, is that Saddam approved of, but was not involved in, the attacks and nonetheless figured he would be a convenient target for retaliatory strikes by the United States given the consistently adversarial nature of the relationship between Washington and Baghdad from 1990-2001. Another, for which there is limited—albeit by no means definitive—evidence, is that Iraq was directly involved in the planning of the assaults and training of at least some of those Al Qaeda operatives who carried them out. Con Coughlin, who has written one of the more comprehensive recent biographies on Saddam, sums up these alternate explanations nicely, noting that the "intense secrecy and security that surrounded Saddam's every move meant it was impossible to say for sure why the Iraqi leader had placed his country on high alert and retreated to a bombproof shelter, but the timing alone was sufficient to raise suspicions."[54]

Three pieces of evidence in particular indicate that Iraq may indeed have played a role in the 9/11 attacks. First, two Iraqi defectors who were debriefed by Western intelligence officials in late 2001 claimed that Iraq had established a terrorist training camp at the Salman Pak military base south of Baghdad for use in training groups of Islamic fighters from Saudi Arabia, Yemen and Egypt. Furthermore, the camp's features included an old Boeing 707, which was employed to "teach the recruits how to hijack a plane using only their bare hands or knives, techniques similar to those used by the September 11 hijackers."[55] Second, the transitory Iraqi coalition government established after the elimination of Saddam's regime in the context of the Second Iraq War has produced a memo it claims documents a visit by 9/11 ring leader Mohammed Atta to that Salman Pak training camp in July 2001.[56] Third, Czech officials have asserted repeatedly that Atta met with Iraqi intelligence agent Ahmed al-Ani in Prague several times in 2000 and 2001.[57] While these pieces of evidence are circumstantial at best and have never been cited publicly by Bush administration officials, they certainly raise suspicions worthy of at least some consideration, particularly considering both Saddam's enmity toward the United States and his long history of support for terrorist organizations over the years.

Strengths and Weaknesses of Bush Administration's Gulf Policies

All presidential administrations exhibit both strengths and weaknesses in developing and implementing their foreign and security policies, which typically become apparent in hindsight, once the consequences of those policies have manifested themselves at home as well as abroad. With respect to the Bush administration, an assessment of such strengths and weaknesses is best articulated contextually through examinations of its policymaking toward Iraq as pertains to the US domestic, Greater Middle Eastern and global levels.

US Domestic Level

When assessed in terms of their implications at the domestic level, the strengths of the Bush administration's policies toward the Gulf are threefold. First, by using all available means to confront both Iraq and Al Qaeda, the administration has reduced appreciably the collective threats they pose to the United States. In particular, irrespective of the extent of Iraq's WMD programs in the past,[58] the liquidation of Saddam's regime has mitigated the potential for the use of such munitions against American citizens in the future. While terrorists generally and Al Qaeda members specifically continue to stage attacks designed to destabilize the new Iraq, bin Laden has failed to orchestrate an effective assault on US soil since the events of 9/11. For that alone, Bush is to be commended. Second, the prosecution of Operation Iraqi Freedom demonstrated to the American public that the United States continues to possess the world's most powerful military forces and thus retains the capacity to back its rhetorical warnings to adversaries with the decisive use of force when necessary. Third, to his credit, Bush was willing to take a political risk in confronting Saddam, one that, while enhancing American security at home, has also resulted in a significant drop in his public approval ratings as a result of the casualties suffered by US servicemen in 2003 and 2004 in Iraq. Regrettably, a substantial bloc of the American electorate simply does not recognize that reducing the threat to the US population overall often entails sacrifices by many of its members.

Bush's Gulf policies also have two weaknesses at the domestic level. First, the administration underestimated the challenges associated with stabilizing Iraq in the immediate aftermath of the fall of Saddam's regime and maintaining a secure environment therein over the ensuing weeks and months of military occupation. As a result, Bush has faced greater criticism from the American public than would have otherwise been the case. Second, complicating matters further, a postwar investigation by the US Senate Intelligence Committee determined that the CIA overestimated the extent of Saddam's biological, chemical and nuclear weapons developmental programs prior to the conduct of the war against Iraq. Specifically, the committee found that most of the "judgments in the [CIA's October 2002 National Intelligence Estimate] either overstated, or were not supported by, the underlying intelligence reporting."[59] That assessment appears sound given that American forces have yet to uncover any substantial WMD stockpiles in Iraq. And, although Bush did not base the case for war against Saddam solely on the WMD issue, the failure to find any such munitions has certainly hurt the president politically—and deservedly so.

Greater Middle Eastern Level

As pertains to the Greater Middle East, the fundamental strengths of the Bush administration's policies toward the Persian Gulf are threefold. First, the elimination of Saddam's regime represented a useful a point of departure for the eventual liberalization and democratization of Iraq, an outcome that, if achieved, will demonstrate the potential for a broader regional transformation. Any systemic transformation must begin somewhere. In light of Saddam's history of aggression and repression of his people, Iraq was clearly an appropriate place to begin this one. Second, Saddam's fall and subsequent capture served as a lesson to other Arab leaders—namely that absent behavioral changes vis-à-vis the development of WMD and sponsorship of terrorist organizations, they could be next in line for regime change. Third, in launching nation-building operations in Iraq, the American-led coalition presented a challenge to those opposed to the liberal democratic values the West represents. Terrorist groups including, but not limited to, Al Qaeda, responded to that challenge by traveling to Iraq to wage war against coalition forces and their allies. Consequently, the front in the war on terrorism is now in Iraq rather than the United States or elsewhere in the West. That is advantageous to America, albeit only so long as it maintains an unambiguous commitment to the security and stability of the nascent new Iraq.

However, there are also two weaknesses in the Bush administration's approach. First, while the administration did an excellent job prosecuting Operation Enduring Freedom, it did not plan thoroughly enough for the occupation of Iraq and conduct of nation-building operations in that context. Most significantly, the United States did not initially anticipate the difficulty of creating and maintaining a secure environment in Iraq. Consequently, progress in the reconstruction and democratization of that state has not proceeded as quickly as either the coalition, or the Iraqis themselves, would have liked. Second, the difficulty in achieving such progress has led to criticism of the United States and its coalition partners both within, and outside of, Iraq. The criticism, in turn, has already—and will likely continue to—undermine other American policies toward the Greater Middle East, most notably so with respect to the troubled Israeli-Palestinian peace process.

Global Level

The most effective means to assess the ramifications of the Bush administration's policies at the global level is to focus on the most wide-ranging statement articulating its strategic vision: the September 2002 NSS. That strategy has six strengths. First, Bush's NSS articulates an innovative approach in an incisive manner, avoiding the myriad diplomatic ambiguities of the 1999 Clinton NSS and is thus intelligible to a considerably broader American audience. In particular, the latter leaves no doubt that the war on terrorism is central to American national security, but specifies a range of interconnected economic, military and political tools it intends to use in waging that conflict over the short, medium and long terms. Second, Bush's NSS emphasizes that the United States will act to preempt threats to its interests rather than react to such dangers after the fact. This is an extraordinarily necessary adjustment in light of the events of 9/11. To deem the attacks a law enforcement matter, conduct an investigation and try those perpetrators eventually captured in a domestic court as the Clinton administration did following the February 1993 World Trade Center bombing would have been politically untenable and practically counterproductive after the 2001 strikes. Such a process would have done little to weaken Al Qaeda's capacity to plan and carry out an equally, if not more, devastating attack in the future.

Third, Bush's NSS expresses the administration's prudential willingness to strike a balance between multilateral and unilateral action in confronting terrorists and their state sponsors. In particular, Bush notes pledges in the NSS that the United States will act multilaterally whenever possible and unilaterally only if absolutely necessary. In its efforts to limit—and eventually eliminate—the threats posed to American interests by Al Qaeda, the United States has received support from its European, Middle Eastern and Central, South and Far East Asian allies that includes intelligence sharing, law enforcement cooperation, the deployment of military forces and leadership of nation-building operations in states ranging geographically from Iraq to the Philippines. In addition, although the Bush administration did not secure a clear UN mandate to eliminate Saddam's regime through the conduct of the Second Iraq War, it attempted to acquire Security Council support repeatedly and lobbied successfully for the passage of Resolution 1441.

Fourth, Bush's NSS addresses soft as well as hard security issues and justifies its doctrine of preemption in accordance with established international legal norms. It explains, for example, that "for centuries, international law recognized that nations need not suffer an attack before they can lawfully take action to defend themselves against forces that present an imminent danger of attack." It then adds a necessary caveat that relates to the changing nature of the dangers presented by non-state actors in the 2000s, arguing that "the greater the threat, the greater is the risk of inaction—and the more compelling the case for taking anticipatory action to defend ourselves, even if uncertainty remains as to the time and place of the enemy's attack."[60]

Fifth, Bush's NSS prioritizes American security interests geographically, placing an emphasis on the Greater Middle East relative to other regions of the world—one that parallels America's commitment to the war on terrorist groups and their state sponsors broadly, and Iraqi and broader Greater Middle Eastern stabilization and democratization in particular. That commitment is evident in initiatives including, but not limited to, ongoing reconstruction operations in Afghanistan and Iraq as well as the promulgation of a "Road Map" designed to achieve the eventual resolution of the Israeli-Palestinian conflict. What is perhaps most significant of each of these initiatives is their multilateral nature. The United States, for example, has successfully lobbied its NATO allies to take the lead in the reconstruction of Afghanistan while it continues to focus on the search for bin Laden and liquidation of Al Qaeda and Taliban loyalists who remain entrenched in the hinterlands of that state. Similarly, the "Road Map" was drafted by a state/institutional quartet composed of the United States, Russia, the UN and the EU.

Sixth, Bush's NSS touches on the need for political reforms that would favor citizens at the expense of the repressive regimes—some aligned with the United States—that are the rule rather than the exception across the Arab world. More pointedly, since releasing its strategy, the Bush administration has asserted consistently that the Greater Middle East is both suitable for, and deserving of, the development of institutions based on free market economic and liberal democratic political principles.

In addition to its many strengths, Bush's NSS has two significant weaknesses. First, it appears to make a somewhat ethnocentric—and not necessarily accurate—assumption that its allies will acquiesce in, if not welcome, the Bush administration's attempts to defend, preserve and extend peace under American auspices. That assumption was at least somewhat inaccurate, as evidenced by the difficulty Bush had in building a diverse coalition to confront Saddam via the conduct of the Second Iraq War. The principal reason why is that, along with a sense of angst over their inability to prevent the United States from taking whatever action it deems appropriate to safeguard its national interests, those very interests, in some cases, conflict with the aims of American allies and adversaries alike. In the Middle East, for example, it should have come as less of a surprise to the Bush administration than was the case that authoritarian leaders in places such as Saudi Arabia and Egypt would frown on a vision of long-term democratization that would ultimately reduce their own power at best and cause their regimes to fall at worst.

Second, Bush's NSS does not fully acknowledge the extent to which concomitantly de-emphasizing the low politics of the environment (still a high-priority issue in many Western European capitals) and pressing for the forcible disarmament of states such as Iraq, Iran and North Korea will foster serious discord in transatlantic relations. In short, the Bush administration did not strike a particularly conciliatory tone in the transatlantic relationship broadly or in Franco-American and German-American relations specifically during the months preceding the 9/11 attacks. While the resultant conduct of Operation Enduring Freedom restored a measure of solidarity in the transatlantic relationship, that goodwill quickly dissipated in the wake of Bush's unveiling of the NSS. The subsequent diplomatic prologue to, and prosecution of, Operation Iraqi Freedom deepened existing divisions across the Atlantic and opened new ones within Europe between the anti-war French and Germans on one hand and the pro-war British, Spanish, Italian and Polish governments on the other. Many of those differences would still have existed even had the Bush administration struck a more conciliatory tone with the French and Germans among others over the first eight months of 2001. However, that course of action may have muted their public expression to an extent during the diplomatic encounters that preceded the US-led invasion of Iraq.

Conclusions

All leaders face a variety of crises and challenges during their tenures. Ultimately, the differences in the gravity of such developments and the manner in which a given leader responds determine how history will judge that individual. The most significant crisis Bush has had to confront to date—the 9/11 attacks—was as grave as any single challenge faced by any of his predecessors in the White House. The president's leadership in the aftermath of that crisis and his management of the subsequent war against Al Qaeda and Taliban forces within and beyond Afghanistan were laudable. The Bush administration's NSS represented a logical continuation of its response to the events of 9/11, one that acknowledged the need to preempt threats to American interests at home and abroad by confronting terrorist organizations and their state sponsors. The rationale for the administration's security strategy remains sound, and its legal basis—that of self-defense—just under established principles of international behavior. The failure to take action while threats to the security of the United States mount, on the other hand, would be indefensible.

The greatest danger to American interests at present is that posed by the potential acquisition of nuclear, biological or chemical WMD by terrorist groups and the subsequent use of such munitions against targets within and beyond the continental United States. Iraq clearly had the potential to present precisely that type of threat by transferring WMD to regional and global terrorist groups. In particular, Saddam's repeated violations of UN resolutions designed to curtail his WMD developmental programs, his proven willingness to use such munitions against his domestic and international adversaries, and his support for terrorist organizations rendered Iraq a legitimate target for regime change. Consequently, Bush chose correctly to demand that Iraq disarm and attempted to do so under the multilateral auspices of the UN rather than on an unambiguously unilateral basis.

In the end, notwithstanding the UN's noble intentions to eliminate Iraq's WMD programs by way of weapons inspections carried out by the UNMOVIC, the United States had no choice but to remove Saddam from power through the use of military force in order to ensure that he fully dismantle his WMD programs and cease supporting terrorist organizations. However, the benefits of that action will clearly exceed its costs, but only so long as Washington maintains a long-term commitment to democratic and economic progress in Iraq and the Greater Middle East. That commitment should be characterized by a continued American willingness to strike a balance between Western secular governmental principles and Islamic theology in facilitating the development of a representative Iraqi government that serves the political and religious interests of all of its citizens.

As was true of George H.W. Bush and Clinton, the policies George W. Bush has developed and implemented in the Persian Gulf entail costs and benefits for the United States over both the short and long terms. Assessing those costs and benefits, in turn, is necessary to determine the extent to which one should deem the administration's actions effective or ineffective when considered in historical perspective. As a result, the chapter closes with precisely such an assessment.

The short-term costs of the Bush administration's policies toward the Gulf are fourfold. First, the financial and military burdens associated with the prosecution of Operation Iraqi Freedom and the subsequent conduct of nation-building operations in Iraq have been substantial. Collectively, in excess of 1,000 US servicemen had died and more than 6,000 had been wounded in operations in Iraq by mid-September 2004, with the vast majority of those casualties occurring since 1 May 2003.[61] In addition, the administration's commitments in Iraq have entailed significant economic losses. This is the case in large part because the United States failed to secure either political support—or financial contributions—from nearly so wide a range of coalition partners in the run-up to the Second Iraq War as was the case with respect to the 1990-91 Persian Gulf War. Thus far, Washington has already spent, or allocated, in excess of $100 billion on the reconstruction and democratization of Iraq. And the tab is likely to continue to rise considerably in the future.

Second, politically, the credibility of the United States is at stake on two levels. Bush has consistently promised to replace Saddam's autocratic regime with enduring democratic institutions, irrespective of the economic and physical costs (in dollars and lives, respectively). He has also pledged to achieve that objective with—or without—economic and military assistance from US allies and the broader international community. Breaking either of those promises would undermine Washington's credibility at home and abroad—and, perhaps, appear as a sign of weakness in the war against terrorism. The realization of any, if not all, of the above benefits demands the maintenance of a reasonably stable security environment in Iraq. Regrettably, the pursuit of that objective will continue to result in the loss of lives of individuals participating in nation-building operations in the new Iraq.

Third, the Bush administration's decision to invade Iraq without the passage of a UN Security Council resolution explicitly authorizing the use of force against Saddam, caused serious discord in America's relations with its allies in Europe and the Middle East. In particular, the rift between the United States and the United Kingdom on one hand, and France and Germany on the other, represented the most serious break in the transatlantic relationship since Paris withdrew from NATO's military command structure in 1966. Fourth, that discord carried significant political repercussions for Bush at home, where his public approval ratings have slipped concurrent with perpetually rising international disapproval of what many perceive as an American penchant for unilateralism.

The short-term benefits, by contrast, are threefold. First, the United States and its coalition partners removed Saddam from power and did so through a well-executed military operation that was completed in less than one month. Despite the failure to uncover substantial WMD stockpiles in Iraq, the region is clearly better off without Saddam. During his time in power, he killed hundreds of thousands of his own people, repeatedly invaded neighboring states and consistently supported terrorist organizations. Those facts alone were more than enough to justify his regime's liquidation. Second, by removing Saddam from the scene and characterizing Iraq as the frontline in the war on terrorism, Bush reduced the direct threats posed by Al Qaeda and its sponsors to America itself. Third, Washington's resolve in confronting Saddam provided a lesson that has led at least one other Arab dictator (Libya's Moammar Ghadafi) to change his behavior. In December 2003, Ghadafi agreed to dismantle all of Libya's WMD programs.[62]

The probable long-term costs of the Bush administration's policies toward the Gulf and broader Arab world are twofold. First, as discussed previously, American credibility is at stake in Iraq, particularly in light of the CIA's exaggeration of the extent of Saddam's WMD programs in the months preceding the war. In order to justify its actions internationally, the United States must maintain an unequivocal commitment to the economic and political transformation of Iraq. Achieving that objective demands the maintenance of security in Iraq, which is sure to continue to result in the loss of the lives of American servicemen for an indeterminate period of time. Second, those casualties are sure to have political repercussions at home, irrespective of which party is in control of the White House and Congress. Should a given president, whether a Republican or a Democrat, yield to popular pressure for a premature withdrawal from Iraq, the region would likely collapse into chaos. Such chaos would provide new havens for bin Laden and his ilk and thus raise the terrorist threats to the US interests both at home and abroad.

The likely long-term benefits of Bush's policies in the Gulf generally and in Iraq specifically, by contrast, are fourfold. First, so long as America and its coalition partners maintain their collective commitment to see the liberal democratization of Iraq through to completion, the prospects for the eventual transformation of the Greater Middle East will remain promising. That is why staying the course despite the financial and physical costs of doing is absolutely essential. Second, despite the instability prevalent in Iraq in the short-term, that state still possesses the world's second largest petroleum reserves. The emergence of a stable democracy in Iraq, one aligned with Washington, will eventually produce greater ease of US access to the oil that helps to fuel the American economy and those of its European allies. Third, in light of Saddam's past behavior, it is not likely that he would ever have refrained permanently from the pursuit of biological, chemical and nuclear WMD. Thus, his removal simply preempted a problem that otherwise would have threatened the stability of the region again in the future. Fourth, leaving Saddam in place would also have allowed him to continue to cooperate with terrorist organizations, which he did consistently despite perpetually increasing scrutiny from the United States and the international community between 1991 and 2003. That outcome would simply not have been acceptable in the post-9/11 era.

Ultimately, four related conclusions grow out of this cost-benefit analysis. First, the Bush administration has acknowledged the indispensability of nation building to the war on terrorism as evidenced by the commitment it has made to the establishment of an enduring democracy in Iraq since the elimination of Saddam's regime. In short, the administration has recognized that following the reconstruction of Iraq through to completion is its only prudent course of action, particularly given the potential for that state to develop into a base for terrorist organizations should nation building fail. Second, it is clear that providing the necessary security safeguards to allow for the emergence of a vibrant economy and stable representative political system over the medium term and the maintenance of both over the long term will be difficult. The strength of the insurgency in 2004 has been particularly illustrative of that point. Third, Bush's resolute commitment to nation building in Iraq has already entailed— and will undoubtedly continue to generate—substantial economic and physical costs. The more those costs (especially the loss of American lives and funds to maintain the military presence) rise, the greater the pressure to reduce the US commitment will grow. Nonetheless, irrespective of who occupies the White House from 2005-09, Bush or Democratic challenger John Kerry, abandoning Iraq is simply not a realistic option given that American credibility and security are on the line. Fourth, so long as the United States maintains its commitment, the situation is likely to improve rather than deteriorate over the long term. The aforementioned projections for economic growth suggest as much. Fifth, should nation building in Iraq succeed, it certainly has the potential to serve as a foundation for the broader democratization of the Greater Middle East, albeit over a period of decades rather than years.

Notes

1. George W. Bush, "Remarks by the President upon Arrival at Barksdale Air Force Base," 11 September 2001, excerpted in *We Will Prevail*, 2.
2. George W. Bush, "Presidential Address to the Nation," 11 September 2001, excerpted in Ibid., 2.
3. Bob Woodward, *Bush at War*, 42-57.

4. For an in-depth examination of the organization and conduct of Operation Enduring Freedom, see Tom Lansford, *All for One: Terrorism, NATO and the United States* (Aldershot, UK: Ashgate Publishing Limited, 2002).
5. George W. Bush, "Presidential Address to a Joint Session of Congress," 23 September 2001, excerpted in *We Will Prevail*, 15.
6. John Lewis Gaddis, *Surprise, Security and the American Experience* (Cambridge: Harvard University Press, 2004), 72-73.
7. Yetiv, *Persian Gulf Crisis*, 184-85. These requirements are set forth explicitly in United Nations (UN) Security Council Resolution 687, which was approved on 3 April 1991.
8. George W. Bush, "Remarks at the United Nations General Assembly," *White House Office of the Press Secretary* (12 September 2002); National Security Council (NSC), "A Decade of Deception and Defiance: Saddam Hussein's Defiance of the United Nations," Background Paper for President Bush's UN Address, *White House Office of the Press Secretary* (12 September 2002): 4-7.
9. Bush, "Remarks at the UN."
10. Ibid.
11. Ibid.
12. James Mann, *Rise of the Vulcans: The History of Bush's War Cabinet* (New York: Viking, 2004), ix-x.
13. Ibid., x.
14. Ibid., xvii.
15. Ibid., 315.
16. George W. Bush, "National Security Strategy of the United States of America," *White House Office of the Press Secretary* (17 September 2002): i.
17. Condoleezza Rice, "2002 Wriston Lecture at the Manhattan Institute," *White House Office of the Press Secretary* (1 October 2002).
18. Colin L. Powell, "A Strategy of Partnerships," *Foreign Affairs* (January/February 2004): 24.
19. Bush, "National Security Strategy."
20. Powell, "A Strategy of Partnerships," 23.
21. In particular, the NSS states that "[w]e must be prepared to stop rogue states and their terrorist clients before they are able to threaten or use weapons of mass destruction against the United States and our allies and friends." Bush, "National Security Strategy," 8.
22. Ibid., 15.
23. Ibid., 9.
24. Powell, "A Strategy of Partnerships," 25-26.
25. Bush, "National Security Strategy," 5-9.
26. Rice, "Wriston Lecture."
27. United States Congress, "Joint Resolution Granting Authorization for the Use of Military Force Against Iraq," *United States Congress* (10 October 2002).
28. UN Security Council, "UN Security Council Resolution 1441," *United Nations Press Office* (8 November 2002).
29. For an in-depth account of the diplomatic prologue to, and conduct of, Operation Iraqi Freedom, see Lansford and Pauly, *Strategic Preemption: US Foreign Policy and the Second Iraq War*.
30. NSC, "A Decade of Deception and Defiance," 4-7; UN Security Council, "Resolution 4112."

31. NSC, "A Decade of Deception and Defiance," 4-7.

32. Bush, "Remarks on Iraq at Cincinnati Museum Center," 7 October 2002, excerpted in *We Will Prevail*, 192-200; Bush, "Remarks at UN General Assembly."

33. United States Congress, "Joint Resolution for the Use of Military Force Against Iraq." The House approved the resolution by a 296-133 vote on 10 October 2002; the Senate approved it by a 77-23 vote on 11 October 2002.

34. UN Security Council, "Security Council Resolution 1441."

35. "It's Not Easy being French," *Economist* (3 April 2003).

36. Powell, "A Strategy of Partnerships," 25-26.

37. Robert Kagan, "America's Crisis of Legitimacy," *Foreign Affairs* (March/April 2004): 83.

38. Quoted in James Fallows, "Blind Into Baghdad," *Atlantic Monthly* (January/February 2004): 73.

39. George W. Bush, "Address to the Nation in Prime Time Press Conference," *White House Office of the Press Secretary* (13 April 2004).

40. Ibid.

41. George W. Bush, "State of the Union Address," *White House Office of the Press Secretary*, 29 January 2002.

42. "Blowing your Chances," *Economist* (22 August 2002); "Know Thine Enemy," *Economist* (31 January 2002).

43. "Background Note: Iran," *US. Department of State*, December 2001.

44. "The Spectre of being Next in Line," *Economist* (11 April 2002).

45. Condoleezza Rice, "Remarks on Terrorism and Foreign Policy at Paul H. Nitze School of Advanced International Relations," *White House Office of the Press Secretary* (29 April 2002).

46. For an in-depth assessment of the Clinton and Bush administrations' respective efforts to counter the threats posed by Al Qaeda, see Thomas H. Kean, Lee H. Hamilton, Richard Ben-Veniste, Fred F. Fielding, Jamie S. Gorelick, Slade Gorton, Bob Kerrey, John F. Lehman, Timothy and James R. Thompson, *The 9/11 Commission Report: Final Report of the National Commission on Terrorist Attacks Upon the United States* (New York: W.W. Norton & Company, 2004). The report does not fully apportion blame for the events of 9/11 on either administration.

47. Morris, *Off With Their Heads*, 70.

48. Woodward, *Bush at War*, 34-35.

49. Ibid., 4.

50. Ibid., 34-36.

51. In depth-investigations by both the 9/11 Commission and the US Senate Intelligence Committee uncovered linkages between Iraq and Al Qaeda, but neither found unambiguous evidence that Saddam played a direct role in the planning and execution of the 11 September 2001 attacks on the World Trade Center and the Pentagon. Kean, et al., *9/11 Commission Report*, 145-266; US Senate Select Committee on Intelligence, "Report on the U.S. Intelligence Community's Prewar Intelligence Assessment on Iraq," *US Senate Select Committee on Intelligence* (July 2004): 304-40.

52. Coughlin, *Saddam: King of Terror*, xxv-xxvi.

53. Miniter, *Losing Bin Laden*, 239-40.

54. Coughlin, *Saddam: King of Terror*, xxv.

55. Ibid., xxvii.

56. Con Coughlin, "Does This Link Saddam to 9/11," *Daily Telegraph* [London] (14

57. Coughlin, *Saddam: King of Terror*, xxvi.
58. The US Senate Intelligence Committee has determined that the CIA overestimated the extent of Iraq's chemical, biological and nuclear weapons programs prior to the prosecution of Operation Iraqi Freedom. US Senate Select Committee on Intelligence, "Prewar Intelligence Assessment on Iraq," 8-14, 84-211.
59. Ibid., 14.
60. Bush, "National Security Strategy," 11.
61. "Iraqi Coalition Casualty Count," <http: //icasualties.org/oif> (18 September 2004).
62. George W. Bush, "President's Remarks on Libya's Pledge to Dismantle WMD Programs," *White House Office of the Press Secretary* (19 December 2003).

Chapter 6

Safeguarding US Interests in the Persian Gulf: Policy Prescriptions for the Future

Introduction

Interactions between states are central to the conduct of international relations. That has been the case throughout history. On a daily basis, events unfold that involve, and are influenced to varying degrees by, leaders and their advisors, and the states they serve. That is indisputable. However, the reasons why states and the individuals in control of the governments of those entities behave in a particular manner serve as perpetual sources of debate for scholars and policy practitioners, who base their observations and analyses on a variety of historical and political scientific approaches. Reviewing the most basic of such points of contention, in turn, is a useful means to begin any policymaking discussion.

Historians, for example, emphasize the importance of individual behavior in conditioning international interactions, suggesting that one leader—whether a politician, diplomat or general—may react to a given situation in a different manner from another under similar, if not identical, circumstances. In particular, they typically argue that while the past provides many instructive lessons for application in the present, the complexity of human behavior still renders unfolding events largely unpredictable. As Yale University's John Lewis Gaddis notes, "We know the future only by the past we project into it. History, in this sense, is all we have. But the past, in another sense, is something we can never have. For by the time we've become aware of what has happened it's already inaccessible to us: we cannot relive, retrieve, or rerun it as we might some laboratory experiment or computer simulation. We can only *represent* it."[1]

Political scientists, by contrast, believe that it is indeed possible—and, in most cases, preferable—to paint an accurate picture of the future through the use of predictive models based upon past and present human behavior. More pointedly, according to the University of Chicago's John J. Mearsheimer, "none of us could understand the world we live in or make intelligent decisions without theories. Indeed, all students and practitioners of international politics rely on theories to comprehend their surroundings. Some are aware of it and some are not, some admit it and some do not; but there is no escaping the fact that we could not make sense of the complexity of the world around us without simplifying theories."[2]

In general terms, contemporary political scientists are split primarily between two theoretical schools—realism/neo-realism and liberalism/neo-liberal institutionalism. As promulgated by Hans Morgenthau in his 1948 book *Politics Among Nations*, realism emphasizes the self-serving nature of human behavior and the role of the state as the central actor in international relations. Most significantly, realists contend that states seek to maximize power relative to their neighbors in order to ensure their own survival.[3] Kenneth Waltz, the first—and still most well known neo-realist—promulgated the fundamental precepts of this paradigm in his 1979 work *Theory of International Politics*. Waltz assumes the structure of the international system—unipolar, bipolar or multipolar—determines the behavior of the states interacting therein. Irrespective of historical time frame and contextual characteristics, he describes the nature of that system as anarchic, in that it lacks an effective government, a uniform set of laws above states, a credible police force to enforce any such strictures, or a common sense of community. Additionally, he discounts the relevance of the internal characteristics of states—political and economic ideology, ethnicity, language, culture and religion—in the ordering of the system.[4]

Neo-liberals and other critics of neo-realism acknowledge the existence of anarchy but contend that institutions have the potential to facilitate cooperation rather than conflict among states in the international system. They are also less averse than Waltz and his adherents to the notion that individuals often drive interactions among both states and institutions. P. Terrence Hopmann and David Dessler, for instance, are critical of Waltz's parsimony regarding the exclusivity of the international system as a motivator of state behavior. Hopmann asserts that a comprehensive model of negotiating processes and the roles of individuals therein is essential in order to enable diplomats to cope with an increasingly interdependent world.[5] Dessler proposes a transformational paradigm based on a hybrid of neo-realist and neo-liberal precepts. He links states and the systemic constructs within which they act and interact in the following manner. First, the structure of a system both enables and constrains actions. Second, states' actions can alter the underlying structure of the system.[6]

The principle weakness of neo-realist theory is its rigidity and resultant inability to explain or forecast accurately alterations in the international system and the management of crises therein. Historians and political scientists critical of neo-realism focus more on the roles of individuals, states and institutions in given scenarios, whether unfolding events involve politics, economics, military conflict, diplomacy or an admixture of those elements. While neo-realism was generally effective in explaining events during the Cold War, it failed to anticipate either the conclusion of that global struggle in 1989-90 or the increasing complexity of the international system in the 1990s and 2000s. Collectively, on the other hand, realism, neo-realism, liberalism and neo-liberal institutionalism and their many theoretical offshoots do provide useful analytical frameworks through which to consider policymaking and decision taking strategies.

Ultimately, given the relative strengths and weaknesses of history and political science, it stands to reason that US policymakers would be wise to draw on each of these approaches in developing strategies designed to safeguard American interests at present in the years to come. This is of particular importance with respect to the regions of the world most critical to the conduct of US foreign policy in the post-9/11 era—the Greater Middle East generally and the Persian Gulf specifically. Consequently, an incisive review of several such approaches will provide a necessary contextual foundation for the subsequent articulation of effective American policies toward the Gulf and wider Arab and Islamic worlds in the future.

One of the most provocative paradigms related to the Greater Middle East is the one offered by Samuel P. Huntington in his 1996 book *The Clash of Civilizations and the Remaking of World Order.*[7] In contrast to the Cold War era, during which states struggled for power on the basis of disparate political and economic philosophies, Huntington contends that contemporary international relations are conditioned primarily by common cultural identities transcending state boundaries in regions across the globe. He asserts that "culture and cultural identities, which at the broadest level are civilizational identities, are shaping the patterns of cohesion, disintegration and conflict in the post-Cold War world," noting that individuals residing within these civilizations define themselves in terms of "ancestry, religion, language, history, values, customs and institutions," identifying culturally with "tribes, ethnic groups, religious communities, nations and, at the broader level, civilizations."[8]

Huntington describes the emerging civilizational system as one divided between groups of Western and non-Western states, which are categorized into eight major civilizations—Western, Sinic, Islamic, Orthodox, Japanese, Hindu, Buddhist and Latin American. He acknowledges that states will remain the central actors in international affairs, but also contends that interactions among those states are "increasingly shaped by civilizational factors."[9] The major civilizational players in the new system are those defined as Western, Sinic and Islamic, with the United States and China heading the first two and the third lacking any one predominant state actor. Above all, his approach vis-à-vis the Islamic civilization has attracted widespread public interest since the events of 9/11.

Huntington developed his paradigm as a means to help make sense of four general post-Cold War models of order he classifies in the following terms: One World: Euphorias and Harmonies; Two Worlds: Us and Them; 184 States; and Sheer Chaos.[10] The first model, of which Francis Fukuyama is the principal advocate, suggests a reduction of, if not an end to, conflict as a result of the victory of the American-led West over the Soviet-sponsored East in the Cold War.[11] The second mirrors the Cold War system but replaces the ideological confrontation pitting the United States against the Soviet Union with cleavages rooted in religious, economic and cultural differences, which divide the world between North and South, Christianity and Islam, and Orient and Occident. The third reflects the self-help world of neo-realists such as Waltz and Mearsheimer, with states striving to advance their interests unilaterally in an anarchical international environment.[12] The fourth, proposed by Zbigniew Brzezinski and Robert Kaplan among others, focuses on the intensification of ethnic conflict manifested in a proliferation of failed states in regions as geographically diverse as Central Africa and the former Yugoslavia.[13]

Huntington contends that his civilizational model serves as a useful lens through which to synthesize the most relevant aspects of each of these approaches, pointing out that "[v]iewing the world in terms of seven or eight civilizations ... does not sacrifice reality to parsimony as do the one- and two-world paradigms; yet it also does not sacrifice parsimony to reality as the statist and chaos paradigms do."[14] Huntington's model has both strengths and weaknesses, the collective identification of which serves as a useful means to gain the deeper understanding of the Persian Gulf and broader Arab and Muslim worlds necessary to develop effective policies toward the states situated therein in the post-9/11 era.

While the world standard of living was highest among Western states during the twentieth century, Huntington suggests that overall power levels are presently shifting in favor of the Sinic and Islamic civilizations, with both entities demonstrating an ability to modernize without abandoning their distinctive cultural and religious identities. With respect to Islam in particular, he cites Maxine Rodinson's contention that "there is nothing to indicate in a compelling way that the Muslim religion [has] prevented the Muslim world from developing along the road to modern capitalism."[15] Additionally, Huntington argues that Western primacy is likely to diminish as the relative demographic, economic, military and political power of the Sinic and Islamic civilizations increases over the long term.[16]

In comparing the relative power resources of the Western and Islamic civilizations, Huntington points both to rising population levels throughout the Islamic world and increases in the number of Muslims residing in the West (most notably in the United States and Europe). He cites, for example, statistical estimates indicating that the percentage of the global population adhering to Islamic religious precepts rose from 12.4 in 1900 to nearly 20 percent at present, increases that have enabled Islam to establish itself as the second most practiced religion in the world behind Christianity with approximately 1.2 billion followers.[17] In light of these demographic trends and the increasing emphasis on distinctive cultural characteristics in the post-Cold War era, Huntington asserts that the potential for clashes among the most powerful civilizations is in a perpetual state of growth, predicting that future clashes are most likely to occur between the American-led West and the Sinic or Islamic civilizations—if not both— arising from a volatile "interaction of Western arrogance, Islamic intolerance and Sinic assertiveness."[18]

In focusing on the rising popularity of political Islam from the late 1970s into the early 1990s, he fails to acknowledge explicitly the possibility that such dynamism was a transitory phenomenon rather than the harbinger of a permanent reconstitution of politico-religious philosophy. His approach is somewhat ignorant of the complexity of change—past, present and future—in the Islamic world. As Shireen Hunter, director of the Islam Program at the Center for Strategic and International Studies, argues, "Islamic civilization is a hybrid and a syncretic phenomenon that developed from early Islamic encounters with other regions and civilizations in the course of its historical expansion; the notion of Islamic civilization as a unique and coherent phenomenon does not reflect reality. Like all civilizations, Islamic civilization is a living, evolving organism, constantly responding to new realities and circumstances."[19]

Scholars also clash over the role and relevance of the state in modern Muslim societies. Bernard Lewis and Bassam Tibi, for example, emphasize an augmentation and a diminution, respectively, of the power of states in the Middle East, North Africa, Central Asia and other Islamically oriented regions. Lewis contends that "present-day states in the Islamic world, even those claiming to be progressive and democratic, are—in their domestic affairs, at least—vastly stronger than the so-called tyrannies of the past."[20] By contrast, Tibi argues that "resurgent Islamic fundamentalism is serving to undermine state power in the Greater Middle East and thus exacerbating the instability of the region."[21]

Huntington's suggestion that in the aftermath of the Cold War, the United States lacked clearly defined threats on the basis of which to prioritize its interests and develop policies to further those interests accordingly is reasonable. However, his references to Iran and Turkey as candidates to develop roles as core states of the Islamic civilization are problematic.[22] Iran is a majority Shiite state and would likely have difficulty mobilizing support among the Sunni Muslims who compose the vast majority of the population of the Muslim world. Turkey, on the other hand, is secular in political orientation and has greater potential to serve as a bridge between Islam and the West than as a leader of an emerging Islamic civilization, as evidenced by its membership in the NATO, aspirations to join the EU and collaborative military relationship with Israel.

Huntington's forecast of an impending clash between the Western and Islamic civilizations is his most controversial assertion, albeit one that appears somewhat more credible in light of the events of 9/11. However, selective cooperation among states in the Western and Islamic worlds remains possible. As Georgetown University's John L. Esposito argues, "Islamic neo-modernists do not reject the West in its entirety; rather, they choose to be selective in approach. They wish to appropriate the best of science, technology, medicine and intellectual thought but to resist acculturation or the assimilation of Western culture and mores, from secularism and radical individualism to the breakdown of the family and sexual permissiveness."[23]

With these observations as a point of departure, the balance of the chapter draws broadly on the strengths and weaknesses of the George H.W. Bush, William J. Clinton and George W. Bush administrations' respective policies toward the Persian Gulf and Greater Middle East in assessing the prospects for America's role in those regions in the future. It does so through the presentation of three related sections that are structured in the following manner:

- The first section defines American interests in the Gulf and broader Arab world and examines the most significant potential threats to those interests in the post-9/11 era.
- The second section lays out a pragmatic, selectively multilateral, policymaking framework designed to safeguard US interests in the above contexts in the forthcoming years.
- The concluding section articulates a series of policy prescriptions that will prove helpful in implementing that policymaking framework successfully.

Threat-Based Definition of US Interests in the Persian Gulf

Upon assuming office, any American presidential administration faces two fundamental challenges in formulating and implementing its national security policy. First, a given president and his advisors must define and prioritize the nation's interests at that historical juncture. Second, they must determine the present and potential future dangers most likely to threaten those interests. What, in turn, renders each of these challenges extraordinarily daunting, relatively easy to overcome or somewhere in between these two extremes, is the extent to which unanticipated events alter an administration's initial interest and threat calculations over the balance of its tenure in Washington.

While generally reflective of the above definition, the private formulation and public articulation of American national security policy—or, in some cases, lack of one or both—has varied from administration to administration over the course of the history of the United States generally and since the end of World War II specifically. During the Cold War, for example, most administrations built their security policies toward the Soviet Union around the strategy of containment originally conceived by American diplomat George F. Kennan in the aftermath of World War II. Although some US Presidents were more forceful than others in dealing with Moscow both rhetorically and practically, each focused primarily on ensuring that the Soviet Union did not extend the physical presence of its military forces far beyond its sphere of influence in Eastern and Central Europe. Only one—Ronald Reagan—elected to shift from a strategy of containment to one that sought to "roll back" Soviet influence across the globe, a move that helped to convince political leaders in Moscow (President Mikhail Gorbachev in particular) that they could no longer compete with the United States economically and, ultimately, politically or militarily either. In the end, that realization led to the conclusion of the Cold War by way of the collapse of Communist regimes throughout the Warsaw Pact in 1989-90, the reunification of Germany in October 1990 and the implosion of the Soviet Union itself in December 1991.

Since the end of the Cold War, the Greater Middle East broadly and the Persian Gulf in particular have grown ever more central to US interests. The past three Americans presidents all authorized the use of military force in the Gulf in an effort to safeguard those interests, each acting on the basis of what they perceived to be the most serious threats to the United States. George H.W. Bush, for instance, viewed the maintenance of stability in the Gulf as paramount, most notably so because of American dependence on the petroleum resources situated therein. Thus, when Saddam invaded Kuwait, the President took the necessary action to force an Iraqi withdrawal and restore the regional status quo. Clinton attempted to contain Iraq through UN sanctions and the limited use of force, discouraging Saddam from aggression against his neighbors and retaining the status quo in the process. Yet, despite the increasing threats of terrorism emanating from the Gulf and wider Muslim world, he was unwilling to respond with larger scale military operations given domestic concerns over casualties and the likely electoral costs such losses would entail. George W. Bush, by contrast, unveiled a preemptive NSS as a result of the events of 9/11. He applied that strategy to the case of Iraq, liquidating

Saddam's regime through the prosecution of Operation Iraqi Freedom, then launching nation-building operations in Iraq as the initial step toward the liberal democratic transformation of the Greater Middle East.

It is essential to consider history, whether distant or more recent, in defining one's interests. This is certainly true with respect to the Gulf and the wider Arab world, especially in light of the impact of the Bush I, Clinton and Bush II administrations' respective policies on those regions in the 1990s and 2000s. Three such sets of present and future American interests—those based on security, economics and politics—demand, and receive, closer attention here.

US Security Interests in the Gulf

The 9/11 attacks demonstrated to all Americans the seriousness of the threats posed by terrorist organizations. In light of the backgrounds of the Al Qaeda members who carried out those assaults (15 of the 19 were Saudi Arabian in origin), the Persian Gulf is a necessary focal point for the prosecution of the war on terrorism, albeit not the only one. There are two interconnected reasons this is true now and will likely remain so for an indeterminate period moving forward. First, the Bush administration's elimination of Saddam's regime and subsequent push for the democratization of Iraq represents a direct challenge to Al Qaeda and those Muslims who favor Osama bin Laden's radical vision of Islam. As a result, substantial numbers of terrorists have flooded into Iraq since Saddam's fall in April 2003 in an effort to recast the Iraqi state under their auspices rather than those of the United States. Second, should the Americans succeed in liberalizing Iraq and thus opening new economic and political opportunities for its people, Arabs beyond the Gulf are likely to prove considerably more receptive to a broader systemic transformation over the long term. That outcome would all but certainly reduce the terrorists' own base of support.

While there is no way to guarantee that Al Qaeda will not carry out another devastating attack on US soil in the future, it is clearly in Washington's interest to eliminate as many of bin Laden's ilk in Iraq as possible so long as that option is available. Staying the course is essential both in order to reduce the threats to Americans at home and provide the security and stability necessary for the new Iraq to redefine itself politically and thrive economically. As demonstrated by Al Qaeda and its Taliban hosts in Afghanistan, failed states serve as ideal operational bases for terrorist groups to plan attacks on Western targets. Seeing the Iraqi nation-building project through to completion is thus an indispensable US foreign policy objective, one that should not change appreciably no matter which political party controls the White House in the years to come.

US Economic Interests in the Gulf

Economically, the United States has two sets of interests in the Persian Gulf at present. The first is a reliance on oil from the region, one that has been evident for at least the past half-century and especially so since the 1973-74 Arab oil embargo. The second is more recent—the need to help facilitate the development of a prosperous free market economy in the new Iraq. Neither is likely to disappear, or even change appreciably, in the immediate future.

Put simply, American economic growth—or lack thereof—is conditioned in part on ease of access to oil from the Persian Gulf. Saudi Arabia and Iraq possess the world's two largest reserves of petroleum. Consequently, a reduction, if not a stoppage, of the flow of Gulf oil tends to increase markedly the price of that commodity on global markets. Ultimately, the cost of such shifts is borne by the consumers whose spending helps to drive the US economy, which is why American presidents have consistently tried to maintain good relations with the Saudis. George H.W. Bush's decision to confront Saddam militarily in 1990, for example, was based primarily on his concern that Iraq would follow its seizure of Kuwait with an invasion of Saudi Arabia.

The elimination of Saddam's regime and occupation of Iraq have increased the potential for that state to contribute substantially to the Gulf's production of oil. However, in order for that to occur, the United States must create a secure environment, one at least relatively free of the violence that has plagued Iraq since Saddam's fall in April 2003. Above all, security is critical to Iraqi economic growth. In the short term, such growth will hinge primarily on Baghdad's ability to further develop its petroleum fields and keep the oil flowing consistently. Deeper reforms and economic diversification are longer-term goals with the potential prove beneficial both within Iraq and as pertains to the broader regional transformation in which America is presently engaged.

US Political Interests in the Gulf

The United States also has two related sets of political interests in the Persian Gulf. Each involves Iraq, although in slightly different ways. First, the development of enduring representative governmental institutions will be indispensable to the stability of Iraq over both the near and long terms. It is also critical at the regional level. Should the terrorists succeed in preventing the emergence of a democratic Iraq, an anarchic environment would probably develop instead, one with the potential to destabilize the broader Arab world. That is, of course, an outcome that Washington simply cannot accept as it would render the Gulf more threatening to America than when Saddam was in power.

Second, at the international level, the United States has staked its credibility on the successful completion of the liberal democratization of Iraq. Whether one agrees or disagrees with George W. Bush's decision to remove Saddam's regime without the support of the UN Security Council, America now has an opportunity to change both Iraq and the Greater Middle East for the better. Anything less than the maintenance of an unequivocal commitment to the transformation of Iraq would further diminish the standing of the United States in the world. It would also cost the Iraqis and, perhaps, Arabs across the Gulf and its periphery the chance to improve their standards of living and engage freely in political debate in the future. Ultimately, neither outcome would serve the interests of the United States or those of its allies that believe in the freedom of expression as opposed to the repressive means of governance espoused by Saddam, bin Laden and their supporters.

Threats to US Interests in the Gulf

Understandably, given the emphasis the latter Bush administration has placed on its doctrine of preemption generally and the removal of Saddam's regime specifically, current and probable future threats to American economic, political and security interests in the Persian Gulf are all related primarily to the conduct of US-led nation-building operations in Iraq. Those threats are best articulated contextually as pertains to the prospects for economic growth, the installation of liberal democratic institutions and enduring domestic security within Iraq.

The initial security threats faced by coalition forces in the aftermath of the fall of Baghdad in April 2003 grew primarily out of the desire of many Iraqis to seek revenge against members of Saddam's Baath Party by looting the dictator's palaces and the government ministries formerly administered by his minions. Unfortunately, the subsequent failure of the United States and its coalition partners to take decisive action to prevent the looting contributed to a sense that the liberators had lost control of the situation. Yet, in the end, looting proved to be just the first of many obstacles to the stabilization of Iraq under the auspices of the American-led coalition and nascent Iraqi domestic police and military forces.

The most daunting of those obstacles have been erected by two sets of insurgents, those with internal and external roots. Internal opponents of the interim Iraqi government led by Prime Minister Iyad Allawi since late June 2004 are composed of former Baath Party members still loyal to Saddam, nearly all of whom practice the Sunni strain of Islam, and dissatisfied Shiites willing to support radical clerics such as Moqtada al-Sadr, a 30-year-old firebrand with ties to the theocratic regime in neighboring Iran. External foes include a range of terrorist operatives, some of whom are aligned with Al Qaeda and have entered Iraq since the end of major combat operations as a result of lax controls along the Iranian, Saudi Arabian and Syrian borders.[24] Allowing either to succeed in preventing the democratization of Iraq would have disastrous implications for that state as well as the United States vis-à-vis its war on terror.

Regrettably, the problem of terrorist violence has had a tendency to grow progressively worse as positive developments in the economic and political situations in Iraq (the subjects of the ensuing two sections) have convinced insurgents to escalate their attacks in an effort to derail the reform process while they still can. In April 2004, for instance, simultaneous eruptions of violence in the Sunni Baathist stronghold of Fallujah and among al-Sadr loyalists in Najaf and Kufa led to the deaths of more than 100 coalition soldiers. It was the single most violent month since the start of nation-building operations.[25] Should more direct collusion develop among Sunni and Shiite insurgents and foreign fighters—especially those loyal to Ansar al-Islam, a terrorist organization linked to Al Qaeda associate Abu Musab al-Zarqawi[26]—on a wider scale, it would likely create serious problems for the coalition as it attempts to pass on more security responsibilities to Allawi's government over the balance of 2004. Concerns over that probability prompted US Secretary of Defense Donald Rumsfeld to postpone for three months a planned June 2004 draw down of American forces in Iraq from 135,000-115,000.[27]

The challenge over the medium term is for the US-led coalition to collaborate with the Iraqis in improving their security forces' collective capacity to deal with the insurgents and also to develop more effective border controls. Both these steps will be indispensable to preventing an escalation of the terrorist threat to Iraq. As Amir Taheri, an Iranian-born journalist and scholar of Middle Eastern politics, asserts, terrorism in Iraq "is, in fact, a security problem, which must be combated with policing methods."[28] The problem is that terrorist strikes have the potential to reduce the will of the police to remain at their posts on a consistent basis. Once a permanent Iraqi government has assumed power, it will eventually need to acquire armed forces of a sufficient strength to safeguard its interests against external threats, whether those dangers are presented by neighboring countries, transnational terrorist groups, or—as is perhaps the most probable scenario—a combination of the two.

Economically, providing for the needs of Iraqis requires a secure environment, one in which there is a sense that threats to life and property are declining rather than increasing on a daily basis. Put simply, the development of that type of environment will carry a steep price tag. That much became evident when, in September 2003, the Bush administration submitted a request to Congress for supplemental funding of $87 billion ($67 billion for the American military and $20 billion for the reconstruction of Iraq), one that was approved a month later.[29] The military segment of the request equated to more than $4 billion a month to maintain US forces in Iraq through the end of 2004. Beyond that, additional appropriation requests are all but a certainty, as indicated by Gen. Richard Myers, Chairman of the Joint Chiefs of Staff, in April 2004.[30]

Understandably, redressing the excesses of the past is an objective that will require years, if not decades, rather than months to achieve. Initial infusions of cash in the first stage of that process were earmarked for humanitarian aid and the reconstruction of infrastructure in the fields of oil production and electricity generation. Subsequent injections of funds have been reserved primarily for the training and payment of salaries for members of the Iraqi security forces and government ministries as well as for the refurbishment of schools and payment of teachers. The logic behind these measures is two-pronged: invest in infrastructure (especially the oil industry) that will enhance Iraq's capacity to generate greater revenues in the future, while putting its citizens to work with money drawn from external sources in the short term.

The sources from which the US-led Coalition Provisional Authority (CPA) drew funds during its year administering Iraq included the aforementioned infusion to help meet reconstruction needs, in addition to pledges of some $18 billion from other states and institutions (most notably the IMF and World Bank), and $13 billion from Iraqi oil revenues and seizures of the assets of Saddam's regime.[31] The problem is that the vast majority of these monies had yet to enter the economy prior to the transition from CPA to Iraqi interim governmental control in June 2004. As a result, progress has been limited with respect to electricity generation in particular. For example, a year after the end of Operation Iraqi Freedom, the level of electricity available across Iraq had yet to surpass pre-war levels.[32]

The prospects for growth in the medium term, by contrast, are considerably more encouraging. One positive indicator pertains to the issue of job creation. Between April 2003 and March 2004, the unemployment rate in Iraq dropped from 50-60 percent to 25-35 percent.[33] In addition, those numbers are likely to fall further as reconstruction aid enters the economy over the balance of 2004 and Iraq's capacity for generation of autonomous revenues increases. More precisely, Bill Block, a US Treasury Department economist working for the CPA, has predicted that the GDP of Iraq will reach $24-25 billion by the end of 2004.[34] Collectively, these indicators—positive and negative alike—demonstrate that while all has certainly not proceeded smoothly in the economic context, there is reason for at least a measured degree of optimism.

Once Saddam's regime had been eliminated, it was left to the CPA (and, as of May 2003, its Chairman, L. Paul Bremer in particular) to establish the basis for an enduring representative democracy in Iraq. He spent his year at the head of the CPA working on two major political projects. First, he orchestrated a process through which an initial Iraqi Governing Council (IGC) composed of members from each of Iraq's principal ethnic and religious groups (the Shiites, Sunnis and Kurds) drafted an interim constitution to serve as the foundation for long-term political transformation. Second, he developed a plan for the progression from an interim Iraqi governing body in June 2003 to a transitional government by January 2005 to a permanent elected government by the end of December 2005.[35]

Upon assuming power, Bremer correctly insisted that no one with even marginal ties to Saddam's regime would be allowed to hold a politically influential position, most notably so on the 25-member IGC, which held its initial meeting in July 2003 and was charged with drafting an interim constitution. Conceived as an interim body with an indeterminate tenure, the IGC had two fundamental weaknesses, both of which reflected deeper threats to the democratization process within Iraq. First, while broadly representative of Iraq's diverse ethnic and religious composition, the IGC lacked any leader capable of commanding widespread support among Shiites, Sunnis and Kurds. The one figure capable of generating such respect among majority Shiites, for instance, was (and remains) the Grand Ayatollah Ali Sistani. Yet, as is the case with most mainstream Shiite clerics, he prefers to focus on religion and play a more indirect role at the political level within Iraq. According to Reuel Marc Gerecht, a fellow at the American Enterprise Institute and expert on Shiism, "clerics like Sistani ... understand that clerics cannot become politicians without compromising their religious missions."[36] Second, the divergent interests of its members—and their respective constituencies—complicated the interim constitution drafting process. Initially opposed by the IGC's five Shiite members, the constitution was eventually approved by way of a negotiated compromises to include one provision on minority rights for the Kurds, Sunnis and women, and another recognizing Islam as the central source of Iraqi law in March 2004, the constitution's long-term viability remains very much in doubt.[37]

The constitutional dilemma is one of the more problematic issues that John Negroponte, who Bush appointed as the first post-Saddam US Ambassador to Iraq, will have to help Allawi's interim Iraqi government to address effectively.[38] Others include the timetable for the progression from interim to transitional to permanent governance in Iraq between June 2004 and December 2005 and what role, if any, the UN will play in that process. Allawi is scheduled to serve from 30 June 2004 through the establishment of a transitional National Assembly and executive and judicial governing councils by 31 January 2005. The executive will be composed of a three-member Presidency Council to include a prime minister responsible for the day-to-day management of governmental affairs. The Presidency Council will appoint both the prime minister and a nine-member Supreme Court.

Ultimately, the 275-member National Assembly will be responsible for drafting a permanent constitution, which must be approved in a national referendum no later than 15 October 2005. Assuming that deadline is met, elections for a permanent government will follow, with the members of that body scheduled to assume office by 31 December 2005 and manage the future of the new Iraq thereafter. Whether that timeline is followed to the letter remains open to question and will likely be a product of both the security environment in Iraq and economic progress—or lack thereof—in that context in 2005.[39] What is clear, however, is that the character of the political entity that emerges in Iraq and its maintenance over the long term will be conditioned primarily by the relationships among, and decisions made by, the Iraqis themselves.

A Framework for US Policymaking in the Persian Gulf

Given the centrality of the Second Iraq War and its aftermath to the present US role in the Persian Gulf, it is logical to begin the process of building a framework for the development and implementation of policies toward that region in the future with an examination of the extent to which the George W. Bush administration's doctrine of preemption represents a divergence from the past. Yet, prior to engaging in a discussion of the merits of any strategy based primarily on preemptive relative to reactive measures, it is first necessary to define the terms upon which that debate focuses. In short, policymakers use preemptive tools to prevent the emergence of a threat to the interests of a distinct actor or actors before it becomes imminent and thus exceedingly difficult, if not impossible, to eliminate without bearing unacceptable costs.

At its core, the word preemptive is, at least some cases, interchangeable with preventative, as are policies and strategies articulated through the use of such rhetorical devices. In addition, there are a variety of different means through which to achieve preemptive and preventative objectives. For the purposes of this book, those means are best defined as military and non-military in nature. The former include both the limited and unlimited use of military force by one or more states, whether acting with or without the imprimatur of an international organization such as the UN, NATO or EU. The latter range from the issuance of rhetorical warnings to the imposition of economic, judicial and political sanctions.

Historical examples of states taking preemptive action, whether military or non-military in character, are myriad and include ancient as well as contemporary cases drawn from every corner of the globe. However, since the principal issues under consideration here involve modern rather than more historically distant events, examples drawn from the pre-Cold War, Cold War, post-Cold War era and post-9/11 eras will suffice.

Notwithstanding the devastating nature of World War II, which cost more lives than any other conflict in the world's history, its conclusion was ensured by an unprecedented use of military technology that could certainly be described as preventative, if not unambiguously preemptive, in character. As the war in the Pacific proceeded through its final months in the spring and summer of 1945, it became increasing apparent to the Harry S. Truman administration that the Japanese were not likely to surrender without organizing and staging a stalwart defense of their home islands. More pointedly, US military leaders viewed Tokyo's defense of Okinawa from April-June 1945, in the context of which 100,000 Japanese and 7,000 Americans perished, as a preview of what they anticipated would be a considerably more brutal struggle for the home islands.[40] At least in part as a result of that assessment, Truman elected to force the Japanese into submission by dropping atomic bombs on Hiroshima and Nagasaki on 6 and 9 August, respectively, which led to Tokyo's decision to surrender on 10 August. While those bombings killed nearly 200,000 civilians, they also rendered unnecessary a conventional invasion that would likely have produced the deaths of millions of Americans and Japanese. The bombings were thus preemptive, as they prevented an extraordinary loss of life that would, in all probability, otherwise have occurred.

During the Cold War, American presidents used a variety of preventative military and non-military means to further US interests relative to those of the Soviet Union. Examinations of the preventative efforts of the administrations headed by two particularly charismatic leaders—John F. Kennedy and Ronald W. Reagan—will prove especially useful in illustrating that point. The firm yet prudential management of the Cuban Missile Crisis in October 1962 by the former and the rollback of Soviet global influence by the latter were each demonstrative of the utility of the employment of proactive rather than strictly reactive policymaking tools in eliminating threats to the United States posed by a dangerous adversary.

The stiffest test Kennedy faced during his presidency came in October 1962 when American reconnaissance photos revealed an ongoing Soviet initiative to install nuclear-tipped missiles on the island of Cuba. After considering a range of options that included a preemptive military invasion of Cuba to remove those missiles that had already arrived, Kennedy decided to impose a naval blockade of the island, which could technically be deemed an act of war under international law. Ultimately, Soviet leader Nikita Khrushchev backed down and removed the missiles from Cuba.[41] At its core, Kennedy's action was preemptive in that it prevented the Soviet Union from increasing markedly the threats it already posed to the continental United States and did so before the missiles were fully operational and the potential for their use was *imminent*.

Similar to Kennedy, Reagan took a proactive stance in US-Soviet relations and he did so in the aftermath of Moscow's most aggressive foreign policy initiative since the 1962 episode in Cuba—its invasion of Afghanistan on the eve of the start of the 1980 Presidential race in December 1979. After defeating President Jimmy Carter in the ensuing election, Reagan crafted and implemented a strategy that sought to confront the Soviet Union and "roll back" its global influence through two means. First, the Reagan administration engaged in a massive military buildup that included the proposed development of a Strategic Defense Initiative to safeguard the United States against the threat of Soviet intercontinental missiles via space-based lasers. Second, it challenged Moscow by supporting insurgencies fighting Soviet-backed regimes in developing world states ranging from Afghanistan to Nicaragua and spent much less money that the Soviet Union in the process. Collectively, these initiatives helped to convince Gorbachev the Soviets could no longer compete with the United States in terms of either economic vitality—and related conventional military reach—or political influence. As a result, Moscow gradually reduced its control over the Warsaw Pact, which led to the proverbial closing act of the Cold War, one that was managed by the George H.W. Bush administration from 1989-1992 and left the Clinton administration facing a new set of threats over the balance of the 1990s.[42]

Put simply, Reagan recognized that he could prevent unnecessary American—and, for that matter, Central and Eastern European—sacrifices, whether in terms of military outlays or the limitation of economic opportunity and political freedom over the long term through the implementation of a range of proactive (and, to some extent, preemptive) policies in the short term. As Max Boot, a senior fellow at the Council on Foreign Relations, suggests, "Ronald Reagan waged political, economic, and moral warfare on the 'evil empire,' and even sponsored proxy wars, but he prudently refrained from direct military attacks. His is a preemptive strategy we can and should apply around the world today."[43]

As argued previously, the Clinton administration failed to reduce significantly the threats posed to American interests by either Al Qaeda or Iraq. However, it did learn a valuable lesson with respect to the utility of preemptive action in the region of the world upon which it focused most of its foreign policy attention—the Balkans. After standing by as Bosnian Serb leaders Radovan Karadzic and Ratko Mladic (both of whom have been charged with war crimes by the International Criminal Tribunal for the Former Yugoslavia [ICTY] but remained at large as of September 2004) presided over the slaughter of thousands of Muslim and Croat civilians during the 1992-95 civil war in Bosnia-Herzegovina, Clinton chose to act when a similar threat of genocide emerged in Kosovo in 1999. Instead, Clinton acted preemptively to prevent then Serbian President Slobodan Milosevic from eliminating the ethnic Albanian population of Kosovo, pressing successfully for NATO intervention without a UN Security Mandate.[44]

For their part, the Western Europeans (France and Germany included) accepted Clinton's leadership and, by association, the preemptive use of military force wholeheartedly. Consequently, Milosevic was left with no choice but to cease his ethnic cleansing campaign and is presently being tried for war crimes and crimes against humanity by the ICTY in The Hague. In short, preemption worked for the

Clinton administration long before its formal articulation as US policy by Bush in the 2002 NSS. As Gen. Wesley Clark, who served as NATO's Supreme Allied Commander in Europe during its operations against Serbia and subsequently conducted an unsuccessful run for the Democratic Presidential Nomination in 2003-04, has written, "Nations and alliances should move early to deal with crises while they are still ambiguous and can be dealt with more easily, for delay raises both the costs and risks. Early action is the objective to which statesmen and military leaders should resort."[45]

Regrettably, neither Clinton nor George W. Bush acted either early or proactively enough to prevent the occurrence of the events of 9/11. The attacks on the World Trade Center and Pentagon did, however, impress upon the Bush administration and the American public at large that the United States was not nearly so invulnerable to the sudden infliction of massive civilian casualties by an external adversary as was previously believed. That realization led correctly to a fundamental reassessment not only of American national security strategy but also of the way in which it should be articulated publicly. To treat the attacks as a criminal matter and leave the subsequent investigation and response to the Justice Department—Clinton's method choice after the February 1993 bombing of the garage of the North Tower of the World Trade Center—would have been inconceivable morally as well as politically. Yet, drafting and issuing a new NSS in the short term, would have been equally impractical and thus imprudent.

Instead, the Bush administration began by defining the fundamental challenges the United States would face in waging a war against terrorism of indeterminate length, one generally comparable in its global scope, if not in the monolithic nature of the adversary, to the five decade long Cold War. It then planned and conducted Operation Enduring Freedom against Al Qaeda and its Taliban sponsors in Afghanistan from October-December 2001 as a means both to weaken bin Laden's network and serve notice to those regimes that chose to support terrorist groups that their actions would have serious consequences. Next, it used much of 2002 to identify and issue overt warnings to those states it perceived as the most stalwart and, consequently, the most threatening, pursuers of WMD and sponsors of terrorism—most notably Iraq, Iran and North Korea. Lastly, it incorporated a range of military and non-military preemptive and preventative means to safeguard US interests at home and abroad into the NSS Bush promulgated that September, then applied that doctrine of preemption to the case of Iraq.

Given the dangers to American interests represented by bin Laden and his ilk—state-based or otherwise—in the post-9/11 world, it is essential that the United States continue to take a proactive approach to the conduct of the war on terrorism, most notably so as pertains to the Persian Gulf and Greater Middle East. However, that approach should incorporate elements of Bush's NSS as well as the strategies of past administrations discussed above. Additionally, as is true of any strategy, American policy practitioners must consider its impact on three different sets of actors: the domestic population all presidents are sworn to protect; the allies of the United States; and its adversaries.

Protecting for the Security of the American Populace

Above all, any American president must use the requisite means to protect the citizens of the United States from threats to their security, whether such dangers are internal or external in origin. That duty has taken on added significance since the events of 9/11. Al Qaeda's attacks demonstrated that the relative freedom from external threats Americans enjoyed at home in the past no longer exists. As a result, it is essential that the United States continue to employ all of the tools at its disposal in combating both terrorists and those regimes that choose to support them. Regrettably, confronting terrorist groups and their sponsors will always entail costs, especially when it is deemed necessary to deploy a substantial number of American servicemen to fight abroad. The elimination of Saddam's regime and conduct of nation-building operations in Iraq have demonstrated as much in terms of the rising economic price tag and casualty count. Yet, it is also important to recognize that failing to act against tyrants and terrorists such as bin Laden and Saddam would likely leave the United States more vulnerable to assaults on the scale of those on 9/11 in the future. Put bluntly, while it is tragic that American soldiers must die to reduce the likelihood of a second 9/11, that is also the nature of warfare.

With the respect to the Persian Gulf and broader Middle East, there are a variety of general means through which the United States can and should seek to reduce, if not eliminate, the threats to American interests posed by terrorists and their state sponsors. As illustrated by the actions of the past three presidential administrations, those means range from rhetorical warnings and economic sanctions to limited and unlimited military operations and nation-building projects. The challenge is to choose options that are commensurate with the threats a given group or regime represents at a particular historical juncture. In the case of Iraq, Saddam's past suggested that nothing short of a march on Baghdad was likely to result in his removal. With Saddam no longer in power and the economic and political transformation of Iraq underway, diplomatic and economic sanctions, or, perhaps, inducements may be sufficient to produce gradual liberal democratic reforms in other states in the Gulf. The prospects for such changes, in turn, will hinge on the manner in which the United States deals with its allies within, and outside of, the Gulf in the years to come.

Dealing with US Allies

When it comes to inter-state relations, political scientists from the realist and neo-realist schools have at least one thing right. States typically seek to further their own interests first and expect even their staunchest allies to do the same. When those interests coincide, states have a greater tendency to act in an unambiguously multilateral manner. When they do not, unilateralism is the more probable course of action. While allies' interests are understandably not always alike, it stands to reason that those interests are more often similar than dissimilar. Otherwise, engaging in such a relationship would be impractical. Consequently, it is usually best to conduct relations with one's allies in a selectively multilateral fashion. This was the rule rather than the exception throughout the Cold War and during the aftermath of that global standoff and it remains the case in the post-9/11 world. The United States, for example, acted in a selectively multilateral manner when prosecuting Operation Desert Fox in 1998 (the British joined in and the French opted out) and also in prosecuting Operation Iraqi Freedom in 2003 (again, London was on board, while the French joined the Germans in opposing the war).

In pursuing its policies toward the Persian Gulf in particular, the United States will have to continue to engage in relationships with two clusters of allies, those within the region and along its periphery on one hand, and its fellow NATO members on the other. Policymakers in Washington would be wise to continue to act in a selectively multilateral fashion in managing both sets of relationships. Inside the Gulf, that means encouraging an enhanced NATO role—albeit on American rather the UN, French or German terms—in the context of nation-building operations in the new Iraq. It also means pressing for political reforms in states such as Saudi Arabia and Egypt concurrent with renewed diplomatic efforts to achieve progress in the troubled Israeli-Palestinian peace process. Outside of the Gulf, the United States should focus on bridging the transatlantic and inter-European governmental gaps that opened during the diplomatic prologue to, and prosecution of, the Second Iraq War. Myriad US administrations were forced to close similar gaps during the Cold War and it is by no means unreasonable to believe the same is possible in the post-9/11 era.

Confronting US Adversaries

Not all adversaries of the United States pose comparable threats to American interests. States suspected of possessing active nuclear, chemical and biological WMD developmental programs and supporting terrorist organizations, for instance, are considerably more threatening to the United States than those that oppose Washington's vision of the world but lack the operational capacity or political will to move beyond a verbal articulation of such differences. That is why characterizing the war on terror in the Manichean terms the latter Bush administration has chosen is useful rhetorically but not as effective in practical terms. The administration acknowledges as much in its NSS by laying out a range of diplomatic, economic and military tools for confronting its adversaries, especially with respect to the Greater Middle East. The American-led coalition eliminated what it perceived as the region's most dangerous state through the conduct of Operation Iraqi Freedom. But, to date, its actions against other regional troublemakers such as Iran and Syria have been limited to diplomatic warnings and economic sanctions.

In the future, it would be wise to categorize potential dangers to the United States emanating from the Persian Gulf on the basis of two related levels of threats. Those levels, in turn, could be characterized in the following terms. The first level features two types of actors: adversaries with active WMD programs and links to terrorist organizations that have remained intact since the events of 9/11; and terrorist groups that have demonstrated the capacity and will to carry out attacks on Americans across the globe. The most notable examples of such actors in the Gulf region are Iran, Syria and Al Qaeda. The second level also features two types of actors: states that have pursued WMD and sponsored terrorists in the past, but since indicated a willingness to change their behavior; and those terrorist groups that lack either the logistical capacity or the desire to threaten US interests beyond the Middle East. Libya is a case in point. The potential for American military action would, of course, be greater with respect to level-one actors relative to level-two actors. American policymakers could then identify the dangers to the United States by way of that threat matrix and decide what, if any, action to take.

Recommendations for the Implementation of US Policies Toward the Gulf

The framework outlined above is designed—and should be viewed—as a general model for use in the development of policies toward both the Persian Gulf and broader Arab and Islamic worlds over the short, medium and long terms. However, it will not be effective without the provision of more specific guidance on the challenges US leaders will face and the options they would be wise to choose in pursuing America's interests in those regions in the future. This section provides a series of such policy prescriptions that pertain to the contexts of Iraq, the Gulf and the Greater Middle East.

Policy Prescriptions for Iraq

In addition to the discord the Bush administration's selectively multilateral action against Iraq helped to generate between Washington and traditional American allies such as France and Germany, it has also forced the United States to shoulder nearly all of the military and economic burdens associated with the ongoing Iraqi nation-building project. The purpose of that project is both noble and revolutionary: the development of an economically prosperous and politically free Iraq as the first step in the transformation of the Greater Middle East. However, achieving these objectives in Iraq, let alone at the broader regional level, will entail a long-term commitment that has already resulted in a substantial loss of American lives and growing financial burden on US taxpayers.

Irrespective of the party affiliation of the leadership of the executive and legislative branches in Washington, it is essential that the United States maintain its economic, military and political commitments to Iraq in the years to come. Economically, patience and persistence will prove indispensable to the achievement of Iraqi self-sufficiency and, eventually, prosperity. Understandably, it will take time for the tens of billions of dollars in aid pledged by America and other donors to the reconstruction of Iraq. The United States must work with officials in the nascent Iraqi government to ensure that assistance funds are appropriated expeditiously and transparently. Washington should also continue to encourage private investment in the new Iraq that extends beyond transitory contracting projects and the extraction of petroleum to the development and modernization of the manufacturing and service sectors of the economy. Although security and stability are necessarily predominant short- and medium-term concerns, the extent to which the Iraqi standard of living improves will determine whether transformation of Iraq succeeds over the long term.

Militarily, one thing is clear. The United States will have to maintain its current force levels in Iraq at least until a permanent representative government in Iraq has been established there, an outcome that is expected by the end of 2005. Beyond that point, a less substantial presence may be deemed acceptable. Ultimately, however, it is not the number of American servicemen in Iraq, but the manner in which they are utilized that matters most. The United States should employ overwhelming force when necessary to prevent the breakdown of order in a given city or region of Iraq. However, even in those cases, American commanders should include the Iraqi security forces in the process to whatever extent possible in order to facilitate the eventual full turnover of such responsibilities to the government in Baghdad. Under no circumstances should the United States create the impression that it is there to police the Iraqis themselves on a daily basis. To the extent possible, American military action should be directed primarily toward foreign terrorists who have crossed the border into Iraq rather than homegrown insurgents such as those loyal to Saddam or Sadr. That will allow the Iraqis security forces to focus more attention on the latter group of troublemakers.

Politically, the United States must keep three things in mind as it attempts to contribute to the development of lasting liberal democratic institutions in Iraq. First, it will take time to heal past wounds inflicted by Saddam on Iraq's majority Shiite and minority Kurdish ethnic groups. It is only natural that the members of those groups remain suspicious of Iraq's Sunnis, who are themselves concerned that they will now be repressed if the government is controlled by the Shiites in the future. Reconciliation among the Kurds, Shiites and Sunnis cannot be imposed; rather it must be cultivated gradually as members of those groups interact in the years to come. Second, the less the United States attempts to micromanage the political process the better. Above all, it is the Iraqis who will reap the benefits and endure the costs of the success or failure of the transition to democracy. Their leaders, in turn, are sure to be held accountable by the populace throughout the process. Third, the political institutions Iraq adopts over the long term are not likely to be carbon copies of those in the United States or Western Europe, nor should they be. Striking a balance between Western and Islamic cultural, political and religious norms should thus be viewed as a necessary compromise in completing the transformation of Iraq.

Ultimately, each of these observations lead to several related conclusions. First, the Bush administration has acknowledged the indispensability of nation building to the war on terrorism as evidenced by the commitment it has made to the establishment of an enduring democracy in Iraq since the elimination of Saddam's regime. In short, the administration has recognized that following the reconstruction of Iraq through to completion is its only prudent course of action, particularly given the potential for that state to develop into in base for terrorist organizations should nation building fail. Second, it is clear that providing the necessary security safeguards to allow for the emergence of a vibrant economy and stable representative political system over the medium term and the maintenance of both over the long term will be difficult. The eruption of insurgent violence in April 2004 was especially illustrative of that point. Third, Bush's resolute commitment to nation building in Iraq has already entailed—and will undoubtedly continue to generate—substantial economic and physical costs. The more those costs (especially the loss of American lives and funds to maintain the military presence) rise, the more the pressure to reduce the US commitment will grow.

Nonetheless, no matter who occupies the White House, abandoning Iraq is simply not a realistic option given that American credibility and security will be on the line. Fourth, so long as the United States maintains its commitment, the situation is likely to improve rather than deteriorate over the long term. The aforementioned projections for economic growth suggest as much. Fifth, should nation building in Iraq succeed, it certainly has the potential to serve as a foundation for the broader democratization of the Greater Middle East, albeit over a period of decades rather than years.

Policy Prescriptions for the Persian Gulf

Put simply, there are two sets of actors with which the United States must deal in the Persian Gulf—adversaries and allies. Most significant among the former are one non-state actor (Al Qaeda) and one state (Iran). Each poses threats that fall within the level-one category touched on in the chapter's previous section. With respect to Al Qaeda, the United States must do all it can to prevent that organization from establishing a base of operations in the Gulf similar to the one it built in Afghanistan in the years preceding the 9/11 attacks. Above all, that requires the maintenance of stability in Iraq, which—absent the present American economic, military and political commitments there—would become the region's most likely candidate for state failure. As discussed previously, Al Qaeda has had some success in destabilizing Iraq, but the nation-building process is still underway in that state. So long as that process moves forward and US and Iraqi forces keep eliminating Al Qaeda's supporters there, America will continue to make progress in the war on terrorism.

Beyond Iraq, the United States must exert pressure on allies (especially Saudi Arabia) and adversaries (most notably Iran and Syria) to change their behavior in a manner that will contribute to the achievement of such progress in the future. The potential exists for the use of a range of tools in meeting the challenges presented by Iran specifically. Politically, Bush's characterization of Iran as a member of the "axis of evil" was designed to put the Iranians and American allies in and beyond the Middle East alike on notice as to the seriousness of his concerns over Tehran's development of WMD and sponsorship of terrorist groups. Those concerns still exist and may eventually demand the use of force. However, the United States should also focus on the reduction of transatlantic differences over the best manner to deal with Iran. One useful way Washington could proceed on this front would be by linking a de-emphasis of the 1996 Iran-Libya Sanctions Act with concrete improvements in the mullahs' treatment of advocates for domestic political reform as judged directly by European diplomats in Tehran. Those diplomats, in turn, would act as middlemen to enable the Bush administration to better express its support—rhetorical as well as financial—for reform-minded Iranian parliamentarians struggling to increase their influence relative to that of the all-powerful clerical Iranian executive branch.

Economically, sanctions emanating from Washington must reflect Iranian behavior (both positively and negatively), particularly with respect to WMD threats and the prosecution of the war on terror. Instead of concentrating exclusively on punitive measures, the United States should also impress upon Tehran the fact that American investment is possible if the mullahs elect to refrain from the development of WMD and sponsorship of terrorist groups in the future. One way the mullahs could demonstrate that kind of a shift would be by allowing the reformers more influence in domestic and foreign affairs. This type of change—albeit unlikely to occur in the short term—could help to clear the path for cooperative ventures (the piping of Caspian Sea oil and gas reserves through Iran to the West, for instance) over the long term.

Militarily, the United States should remain circumspect regarding the large-scale use of force against Tehran, at least until the task of nation-building in Iraq is much closer to completion. The potential for democratic change from within is greater in Iran than was ever the case in Saddam's Iraq. In addition, Iran's considerably larger relative geographic size and population would be sure to present daunting logistical challenges for US forces in the case that they are eventually deployed there. Thus, for now, America should not consider military action any more robust than launching air strikes against WMD developmental threats, if clearly identified, and continuing to pursue terrorist groups supported by the mullahs.

Policy Prescriptions for the Greater Middle East

Since the events of 9/11, American scholars, policymakers and laymen alike have focused their attention on a variety of issues related to the terrorist attacks on the World Trade Center and the Pentagon, ranging from the conduct of military operations in Afghanistan and Iraq to the escalating Israeli-Palestinian conflict. While distinctive individually, the particulars of such issues are ultimately the products of the evolving relationships among adherents to the world's three oldest monotheistic religions—Christianity, Islam and Judaism—as played out in the many contexts (whether local, national or international) within which Christians, Muslims and Jews interact on a daily basis.

In order to lay out a useful set of closing observations on the dynamics and practical consequences of these relationships and interactions effectively, it is necessary to address four questions. First, to what extent is the contemporary Islamic world (to include all states with Muslim-majority populations) a homogeneous or heterogeneous entity relative to the West (to include North America and Western Europe)? Second, what is the nature of the relationship between Islam and the West at present and how much has it changed historically? Third, what are the potential interactive courses for Muslim- and Christian-majority states and citizens to follow with respect to one another in the future? Fourth, what steps can American leaders and their Western European counterparts take to increase the likelihood that Islamic-Western relations evolve in a positive rather than a negative manner over the balance of the 21st century?

Regarding the initial question, the world's 1.2 billion Muslims and the states they populate—primarily but not exclusively in North Africa, the Middle East and Central and South Asia—exhibit both homogeneous and heterogeneous characteristics, of which the latter exceed the former markedly. These characteristics are best described in religious, ethnic, political and socio-economic terms. As to religious adherence, Islam is split into two predominant strains of followers—Sunnis (85 percent) and Shias (15 percent)—who profess a shared belief in the five fundamental "pillars" of the faith, but disagree on the historical right to leadership of the Muslim world. Additionally, each strain is interpreted in a variety of ways, leaving room for the governance of believers under myriad auspices, whether traditional, modern, secular, theocratic or a hybrid of these and other socio-religious precepts.

Ethnically, the Greater Middle East includes states with majority populations ranging from Arabs and Turks to Pakistanis and Iranians. While Arabic is the language of the Koran, a substantial minority of Islam's adherents do not speak or read Arabic fluently and thus rely on a wide array of interpretations of Koranic text that detract from its ability to deliver a universally accepted message. Such interpretive variety clouds the political landscape across an Islamic world that includes governmental structures as diverse in orientation as absolute military and civilian dictatorships (Libya, Pakistan, Syria and all five former Soviet Central Asian Republics) to putative democracies under de facto military control (Turkey and Algeria) to autocratic conservative religious monarchies (Saudi Arabia and Kuwait) to reforming religious-secular monarchies (Bahrain, Oman, Jordan, Morocco, Oman, Qatar and the United Arab Emirates) to a clerical theocracy (Iran).

Yet, there is at least one issue—the plight of the Palestinians, who have spent more than five decades attempting to carve a contiguous state out of territory presently controlled by Israel—that has consistently drawn the collective support of states and citizens across the Greater Middle East. This solidarity is largely a result of clever governmental propaganda campaigns emanating from capitals such as Cairo and Riyadh to shift domestic attention from the travails of the most economically marginalized elements of Middle Eastern societies to Washington's favoritism of Israel at the expense of the Palestinian Authority.

Historically, interactions among Christians and Muslims have often been adversarial in nature, as evidenced by Islamic invaders' capture of and eventual expulsion from the Iberian Peninsula between the 8th and 15th centuries and subsequent conflicts pitting Western and Central Europeans against the forces of the Ottoman Empire. In fact, the conception of European identity was itself in part a response to the initial appearance of Islam on the continent through the Umayyads' invasion of Spain in 711. Yet, the relationship between Islam and the West has grown perpetually more complex over time, most notably so as a result of the interconnected colonization and de-colonization of wide swaths of the Greater Middle East by European powers and the subsequent migration of individuals from those areas to states across Western Europe over the latter half of the 20th century. There are, for instance, as many as 15 million Muslims residing in EU member states at present, a number that is expected to grow to at least 23 million by 2015.[46]

Although interactions among adherents to the Islamic and Christian faiths have, on balance, proven adversarial in these contexts, such conflicts usually grow out of intra- as opposed to inter-civilizational issues. Examples range from attacks by far-right groups on Muslims in Western Europe to terrorist strikes against American interests—commercial, military and political alike—in states situated in the Greater Middle East. And, despite the fact that Islamic-Western relations have taken a turn for the worse over the past seven months (beginning with the events of 9/11 and continuing with the conduct of Operation Enduring Freedom and Operation Iraqi Freedom), there remain three potential courses for interfaith interactions in the future, whether measured at the global, regional, national, local or individual level: cooperation, confrontation or ambivalence.

Ultimately, in order to influence the character of the Islamic-Western relationship in a positive manner, one that pushes it toward cooperation rather than confrontation—and at least ensures ambivalence manifested in peaceful coexistence—American and European leaders would be prudent to consider the following policy prescriptions in the future.

First, the United States must maintain its commitment to the democratization of Iraq through nation-building operations there until that objective has been achieved. Second, the United States must take a carrot-and-stick approach to its relationships with states across the Islamic world, maintaining a hard line in confronting Iran over its development of WMD and sponsorship of terrorist groups, but also remaining open to economic and political engagement with both moderate Muslim regimes and those troubled states willing to take substantive action to alter their behavior favorably and verifiably. Third, Western governments and institutions must develop and maintain an even-handed approach in attempting to negotiate an end to the Israeli-Palestinian conflict through collaborative transatlantic mediation rather than either American or European unilateralism. Ideally, the EU will serve as an interlocutor to represent the collective interests of its member states in this process.

Fourth, Western European governments—especially those of France, Germany and the United Kingdom—must make concerted efforts to more fully integrate the presently marginalized Muslims residing within their borders, a perpetually increasing proportion of which hold EU citizenship. Coordination among municipal, national and EU officials and representatives from Islamic communities is the necessary point of departure toward achieving that end. Fifth, the United States must do a better job in representing American tolerance of a variety of Islamic interpretive viewpoints—provided they are expressed peacefully rather than via acts of terrorism within and beyond the Greater Middle East—to Muslims residing within states throughout both the Islamic and Western worlds. Islamic leaders in the West in particular could assist America in implementing this approach, which would add a constructive element of dual interest in, and responsibility for, a positive outcome. Sixth, American and European leaders must consistently press their counterparts in the Greater Middle East to take some of the difficult but necessary steps to further democratize their own societies. Deflecting criticism over backward domestic economic and social policies by shifting popular focus to the plight of the

Palestinians is a short-term fix that will only further radicalize Muslims to the long-term detriment of both the Islamic and the Western worlds.

Notes

1.　John Lewis Gaddis, *The Landscape of History: How Historians Map the Past* (New York: Oxford University Press, 2002), 3.
2.　John J. Mearsheimer, *The Tragedy of Great Power Politics* (New York: W.W. Norton & Company, 2001), 8-9.
3.　Hans Morgenthau, *Politics Among Nations: The Struggle for Power and Peace* (New York: Alfred P. Knopf, 1948).
4.　Kenneth Waltz, *Theory of International Politics* (Reading, MA: Addison-Wesley, 1979).
5.　P. Terrence Hopmann, *The Negotiation Process and the Resolution of International Conflicts* (Columbia: University of South Carolina Press, 1996), 28.
6.　David Dessler, "What's at Stake in the Agent-Structure Debate?" *International Organization* 43-1 (1989), 452.
7.　Huntington, *Clash of Civilizations*.
8.　Ibid., 20-21.
9.　Ibid., 36.
10.　Ibid.
11.　Fukuyama, *End of History*.
12.　Waltz, "The Emerging Structure of International Politics," 44-79; Mearsheimer, "Back to the Future: Instability in Europe After the Cold War," 5-56.
13.　Brzezinski, *Out of Control*; Kaplan, "The Coming Anarchy."
14.　Huntington, *Clash of Civilizations*, 36.
15.　Quoted in Daniel Pipes, *In the Path of God: Islam and Political Power* (New York: Basic Books, 1983), 107.
16.　Huntington, *Clash of Civilizations*, 78.
17.　Ibid.
18.　Ibid., 83-84.
19.　Shireen T. Hunter, *The Future of Islam and the West: Clash of Civilizations or Peaceful Coexistence?* (Westport, Conn.: Praeger, 1998), 166.
20.　Bernard Lewis, *Multiple Identities of the Middle East*, 99.
21.　Bassam Tibi, *The Challenge of Fundamentalism: Political Islam and the New World Disorder* (Berkeley: University of California Press, 1993), 6.
22.　Huntington, *Clash of Civilizations*, 84.
23.　Esposito, *Oxford History of Islam*, 683.
24.　Steven Metz, "Insurgency and Counterinsurgency in Iraq," *Washington Quarterly* (Winter 2003-04): 25-30.
25.　Lanier, "Low Intensity Conflict and Nation Building in Iraq"; "Iraqi Coalition Casualty Count."
26.　"Results in Iraq: 100 Days Toward Security and Freedom," *White House Office of the Press Secretary* (8 August 2003): 5.
27.　Robert Kagan and William Kristol, "Too Few Troops," *Weekly Standard* (26 April 2004): 7.
28.　Amir Taheri, "What to Do: The Problem in Iraq is neither political nor military; it is a security problem," *National Review* (24 November 2003): 18.
29.　Matthew Continetti, "Brother, Can You Spare $87 Billion," *Weekly Standard* (27 October

2003): 10-12; "Iraq and a Hard Place," *Economist* (20 September 2003).

30. Jonathan Weisman, "Iraq War May Require More Money Soon," *Washington Post* (21 April 2004).

31. Cordesman, "One Year On," 16; Michael E. O'Hanlon and Adriana Lins de Albuquerque, "Iraq Index: Tracking Variables of Reconstruction and Security in Post-Saddam Iraq," *Brookings Institution* (21 April 2004): 15.

32. O'Hanlon and Lins, "Iraq Index," 17.

33. Cordesman, "One Year On," 15.

34. Fred Barnes, "The Bumpy Road to Democracy in Iraq," *Weekly Standard* (5 April 2004): 21-23.

35. Cordesman, "One Year On," 10-11.

36. Reuel Marc Gerecht, "Democratic Anxiety," *Weekly Standard* (2 February 2004): 24.

37. Lanier, "Low Intensity Conflict and Nation-Building in Iraq."

38. "President Announces Intention to Nominate Ambassador to Iraq," *White House Office of the Press Secretary* (19 April 2004).

39. Cordesman, "One Year On," 10-11.

40. Victor Davis Hanson, *Ripples of Battle: How Wars of the Past Still Determine How we Fight, How we Live and How we Think* (New York: Doubleday, 2003), 44-45.

41. For a detailed account of the crisis from one of those directly involved at the time, see Robert F. Kennedy, *Thirteen Days: A Memoir of the Cuban Missile Crisis* (New York: W.W. Norton & Company, 1969).

42. For a detailed examination of the Reagan Doctrine, see Lagon, *Reagan Doctrine.*

43. Max Boot, "The Bush Doctrine Lives," *The Weekly Standard* (16 February 2004), 25.

44. For detailed examinations of NATO intervention in Kosovo in 1999, see Wesley K. Clark, *Waging Modern War: Bosnia, Kosovo and the Future of Combat* (New York: Public Affairs, 2001) and Ivo H. Daalder and Michael E. O'Hanlon, *Winning Ugly: NATO's War to Save Kosovo* (Washington, DC: Brookings Institution Press, 2000).

45. Clark, *Waging Modern War*, xx.

46. For an in-depth study on the issue of Islam in Europe, see Robert J. Pauly, Jr., *Islam in Europe: Integration or Marginalization?* (Aldershot, UK: Ashgate Publishing Limited, 2004).

Chapter 7

Conclusions

US Foreign Policy in the 21st Century: Focusing on the Persian Gulf

Over the course of American history, the United States has placed emphases on a variety of different regions of the world in developing and implementing its foreign policies. In the 19th century, for example, American presidents focused primarily on the Western Hemisphere, safeguarding US interests there by enforcing the Monroe Doctrine in order to counter European attempts to upset the status quo. In the 20th century, America's focus shifted to the European continent, where it fought in two global conflicts against Germany and faced the Soviet Union in a near half-century-long Cold War. It was also during the Cold War, however, that the United States began to pay greater attention to a pair of other places on the map—the Greater Middle East generally and the Persian Gulf specifically. That trend has continued in the post-Cold War era, especially so since the events of 11 September 2001 illustrated the centrality of the Arab and Islamic worlds to American security in the 21st century.

As stressed repeatedly in the previous chapters of this book, the past three US presidential administrations each had to deal with ever-more-serious threats emanating from the Persian Gulf and its periphery. First, the George H.W. Bush administration was forced to counter the aggression of Iraqi dictator Saddam Hussein, a tyrant America had supported in the 1980s. It did so through the successful conduct of Operation Desert Storm, expelling Iraqi forces from Kuwait, but leaving Saddam's regime in place in Baghdad. Second, the William J. Clinton administration found itself facing related threats posed by Saddam on one hand and Al Qaeda leader Osama bin Laden on the other. It confronted both; however, it failed to act decisively enough to eliminate Saddam or bin Laden, or even force either one to alter their behavior favorably. Third, the George W. Bush administration had to respond to Al Qaeda's attacks on the World Trade Center and the Pentagon and develop a new strategy to mitigate future threats posed to US interests at home and abroad by terrorists and their state sponsors. It did so by unveiling a doctrine of preemption it used to justify the liquidation of Saddam's regime and the subsequent conduct of nation-building operations in Iraq as the point of departure for a liberal democratic transformation of the Greater Middle East.

Given the extent of the present, and expected future, American economic, military and political commitments to Iraq, that state's progress, or lack thereof, will have a profound impact on Washington's pursuit of US interests in the Persian Gulf and broader Arab and Muslim worlds in the years to come. Those commitments are, in large part, the product of the Bush I, Clinton and Bush II administrations' respective policies toward the Gulf. Consequently, current and future American policy practitioners would be wise to reflect on the strengths and weaknesses of the manners in which each of the above administrations dealt with both state and non-state actors in the Gulf and surrounding Greater Middle East. This chapter provides some guidance on those issues by engaging in a concluding analysis of US policymaking toward the Gulf. It does so by presenting three sections that unfold in the following manner:

- The first section restates, and responds incisively to, the research questions posed in the book's introductory chapter.
- The second section restates and elaborates on the book's theses in light of the evidence put forward in its main chapters.
- The third section discusses the prospects for the future of the relationship between the United States and the Greater Middle Eastern and Islamic worlds.

Reconsideration of Research Questions

This section reconsiders the research questions stated in the introduction on the basis of the evidence presented in the book's main chapters. Each question is restated and then answered briefly.

- First, what were the fundamental economic, military and political causes of the 1990-1991 Persian Gulf War? Were such causes primarily regional or global in character?

The Persian Gulf War had a variety of related economic, military and political causes that, in combination, produced a confrontation between Iraq on one side and a broad coalition of Arab, European and Asian states led by America on the other. Economically, the conduct of the 1980-88 Iran-Iraq War drained Baghdad's financial resources to an extent that left Saddam in desperate need of funds. As a result, Saddam attempted to refill his state's coffers by using military force to annex neighboring Kuwait and seize the oil fields situated therein. However, he miscalculated politically, figuring incorrectly that the United States would not use force to expel the Iraqi army from Kuwait. While Iraq's invasion of Kuwait in August 1990 was a product of both economic desperation and political miscalculation within the Gulf, it also had potential global repercussions that led the George H.W. Bush administration to react militarily. Most significantly, neither America, or its European and Asian allies, were willing to take the chance that Saddam would limit his aggression to Kuwait and not consider attacking Saudi Arabia and appropriating that state's petroleum reserves (the most substantial such resources in the world) as well.

- Second, who were the principal actors—individual, national and international—in the contexts of the 1990-1991 and 2001-2003 Persian Gulf crises and conflicts? To what extent did each of these actors drive events in the Gulf from 1990-2004?

In general terms, the actors driving events in the Persian Gulf from 1990-2004—and in the contexts of the 1990-91 and 2001-03 crises therein in particular—were similar, albeit certainly not identical. Individually, Presidents George H.W. Bush, Clinton and George W. Bush and their foreign policy teams (a smaller inner circle of advisors for the two Bushs as opposed to Clinton) were responsible for managing US policy toward the Gulf between 1990 and 2004. All three had to deal with Saddam and the latter two also faced a related threat in bin Laden. In each case, the United States played the lead role in pressing Saddam to cease his development of WMD and sponsorship of terrorist groups and deliver unambiguous proof that he had done so. The support America received from its allies in confronting Iraq varied from administration to administration, ranging from the myriad states that joined Washington in opposing Saddam in the Persian Gulf War in 1991 to the joint US-British conduct of Operation Desert Fox in 1998 to the second Bush administration's use of a coalition of the willing to prosecute Operation Iraqi Freedom and move forward with nation-building efforts in Iraq in 2003-04. The UN also played a role in each of those endeavors, one that proved less and less useful to the interests of the United States and, for that matter, the vast majority of Iraqis, over time.

- Third, what roles did American leaders—and the policies they developed and implemented—play in both the 1990-1991 and 2001-2003 Persian Gulf crises and conflicts?

Presidents George H.W. Bush and George W. Bush—and comparably small groups of foreign policy advisors in each case—played the lead roles in managing the 1990-91 and 2001-03 Persian Gulf crises, respectively. In the former case, the elder Bush, Secretary of State James Baker, National Security Advisor Brent Scowcroft, Secretary of Defense Richard Cheney and Chairman of the Joint Chiefs of Staff Colin Powell managed the diplomatic prologue to, and prosecution of, Operation Desert Storm in a relatively seamless fashion. On balance, they were consummate realists and thus content to focus on the maintenance of the regional status quo once Saddam's aggression against Kuwait had been dealt with. In the latter case, Bush the younger had to choose between the slightly more dissimilar options vis-à-vis Iraq offered by the more—and less—hawkish Vice President Cheney and Secretary of Defense Donald Rumsfeld on one hand, and Secretary of State Powell on the other. He did so with plenty of assistance from National Security Advisor Condoleezzaa Rice, who helped bridge the gap between the two extremes. Collectively, they proved more determined to foster revolutionary change in the Gulf with the democratization of Iraq as the first step.

- Fourth, how effectively did the George H.W. Bush administration manage the 1991 Persian Gulf War and its aftermath?

Put simply, the Bush administration did an excellent job managing the run-up to, and prosecution of, the Persian Gulf War. Its policies toward Iraq in the aftermath of

Operation Desert Storm, on the other hand, were considerably less effective. The American-led diplomatic and military response to Iraq's invasion of Kuwait demonstrated to Saddam that the United States would not permit him to threaten his neighbors in the Persian Gulf. It also served as a warning to dictators in other regions of the world in which America had vital economic, military and political interests. Those effects were certainly beneficial. However, because the Bush administration chose not to engage in any practically feasible pursuit of regime change in Baghdad, the United States had to continue to maintain a substantial military presence in the Gulf in order to contain Iraq in the future. In addition to the economic and physical costs of that presence, it contributed to the genesis of a terrorist group known as Al Qaeda under the leadership of Osama bin Laden, who opposed the stationing of American troops in Islam's most revered state—Saudi Arabia.

- Fifth, how effectively did the Clinton administration define, articulate and pursue US interests in the Persian Gulf from 1993-2001? What were the short- and long-term costs and benefits of its diplomatic, economic and military policies toward the region?

Although Clinton failed to respond to Saddam's infractions of UN Security Council Resolutions as effectively as George H.W. Bush managed the Persian Gulf crisis, the outcomes in each case were not related exclusively to styles of policymaking and diplomacy. The interests of the actors differed in each case. Many of the states that joined the coalition against Saddam in 1990-91 felt Iraq posed less of a threat to their interests during the Clinton years than was true in the early 1990s. The reasons included desires to reap profits by helping to develop Iraqi oil resources and to quell potential unrest among growing domestic Muslim communities (France) and retain influence as a regional and global player (Russia). Nonetheless, in the end, the Clinton administration did little to mitigate the emerging threats to America presented by transnational terrorist networks (most notably Al Qaeda) and those states suspecting of sponsoring such groups (Iraq in particular). The half-measures Clinton did take only emboldened Saddam and allowed Al Qaeda to continue planning the 9/11 attacks that George W. Bush would have to deal with.

- Sixth, how effectively did the George W. Bush administration define, articulate and pursue US interests in the Persian Gulf from 2001-2004? What were the short- and long-term costs and benefits of its diplomatic, economic and military policies toward the region?

The greatest danger to American interests in the post-9/11 era is the acquisition of WMD by terrorist groups and the subsequent use of such munitions against the United States. Saddam's past behavior led to an understandable belief on behalf of Bush and his advisors that Iraq had the potential to present precisely that type of threat in 2002-03. In particular, Saddam's repeated violations of UN resolutions designed to curtail his WMD developmental programs, his proven willingness to use such munitions against his domestic and international adversaries, and his support for terrorist organizations rendered Iraq a legitimate target for regime change. Consequently, Bush chose correctly to demand that Iraq disarm and attempted to do so under the multilateral auspices of the UN rather than on an unambiguously unilateral basis. Ultimately, despite the UN's noble intentions to eliminate Iraq's WMD programs by way of weapons inspections, the United States had no choice but to remove Saddam from power in order to ensure that he fully dismantle his WMD programs and cease supporting terrorist organizations. However, the benefits of that action will exceed its costs only so long as Washington maintains a long-term commitment to democratic and economic progress in Iraq and the Greater Middle East.

- Seventh, what steps must American leaders take to safeguard US interests in the Persian Gulf in the future?

The extent to which the Persian Gulf is stable or unstable in the future will be conditioned primarily by the progress—or lack thereof—made in the transformation of Iraq. The maintenance of that stability, in turn, is in the interest of the United States for two reasons: to prevent terrorist groups from using the Gulf as a base for operations against American targets across the globe; and to ensure that the flow of oil from the region does not slow to a trickle or cease at any point in time. Consequently, it is essential that US leaders remain firmly committed to nation-building operations in Iraq. While bearing the economic, military and political burdens associated with those operations has been difficult, the costs of failure in Iraq would be considerably steeper.

Evaluation of Theses

This section revisits the theses presented in the introduction in light of the evidence presented in the book's main chapters. Each thesis is restated and then elaborated on incisively.

- First, the George H.W. Bush administration's management of the 1990-1991 Persian Gulf crisis was both prudent and effective when assessed in the short term. However, while the administration did a laudable job constructing a broad-based coalition and using that entity to expel Iraqi forces from Kuwait and thus reduce Baghdad's capacity to threaten regional stability in the short term, its failure to eliminate Saddam's regime has proven shortsighted and extraordinarily costly over the long term.

The evidence presented in Chapter 3 illustrates clearly that the Bush and his national security team did a commendable job in organizing the coalition of Arab, Asian and Western states that opposed Saddam's invasion of Kuwait in 1990 and restored the regional status quo through the prosecution of Operation Desert Storm in 1991. In particular, the Bush administration impressed upon the world the centrality of the Persian Gulf to American interests in the nascent post-Cold War era. Assessing the prudence of Bush's decision to cease military operations once Iraqi forces had been expelled from Kuwait rather than attempt to remove Saddam himself from power is somewhat more difficult. While appropriate at the time given the lack of support for regime change in Iraq among the members of the coalition—and reluctance of the American public to condone the casualties a drive to Baghdad would have entailed— it was indeed shortsighted over the long term. Saddam's reign of tyranny continued for an additional dozen years, costing hundreds of thousands of Iraqis their lives and postponing needlessly the commencement of a US-led effort to democratize the Greater Middle East.

- Second, the Clinton administration's reliance on the UN Security Council to enforce a series of resolutions proscribing Saddam's development of WMD programs and sponsorship of terrorist organizations, and its limited use of force in response to Iraq's repeated violations of those strictures, were relatively ineffective means to safeguard US interests in the Persian Gulf from 1993-2001.

The Clinton administration's record on Iraq, as examined in detail in Chapter 4, is reasonably straightforward. Put bluntly, the administration was content first to rely on UN weapons inspectors to convince Saddam to offer unambiguous proof that he had eliminated all of his state's WMD developmental programs and second to punish the Iraqi dictator for failing to do so with an occasional fusillade of limited air strikes. Although the evidence uncovered to date suggests that the extent of Iraq's WMD stockpiles was considerably less significant than UN and US intelligence assessments previously suggested, Saddam continued to support a variety of terrorist causes and repress his own people relentlessly throughout Clinton's time in office. Nothing Clinton did during that period convinced Saddam to moderate his behavior on either of the latter issues or even leave the impression that he had done so vis-à-vis Iraq's WMD programs. Furthermore, concurrent with its inability to produce any movement whatsoever toward its stated objective of regime change in Iraq, the Clinton administration failed to take the requisite action to either reduce the threats posed by an equaling threatening actor with roots in the Persian Gulf—namely bin Laden.

- Third, the George W. Bush administration's use of a preemptive strategy to confront Iraq over its development of WMD and sponsorship of terrorist groups and forcibly remove Saddam from power was both necessary and effective given the fundamental shift in the nature of the threats posed to the security of Americans at home and abroad in the aftermath of Al Qaeda's attacks on the World Trade Center and the Pentagon on 11 September 2001.

Preemption is, by design, intended to eliminate threats to the United States before such threats become imminent, and thus unavoidable. The events of 9/11 demonstrated tragically the consequences of allowing dangers to gather rather than taking adequate preventative action. By eliminating Saddam's regime through the prosecution of the Second Iraq War, President George W. Bush proved he was willing to put the doctrine of preemption into practice on behalf of American security interests. As discussed in detail in Chapter 5, the logic behind his action was sound. In light of Saddam's past behavior, it would have been imprudent to assume that he was at all likely to refrain permanently from either the development of WMD or the sponsorship of terrorist organizations such as Al Qaeda. As a result of the successful prosecution of Operation Iraq Freedom in 2003, at least one thing is now certain: Saddam will never again have an opportunity to threaten the United States in either of those ways.

- Fourth, ultimately, it is essential that US policymakers consider the liquidation of Saddam's regime and subsequent nation-building process in Iraq as useful first steps rather than endpoints in the democratization of the Persian Gulf and broader Greater Middle East over the long term. The pursuit of such a vision for change will ensure that history deems the Second Iraq War successful in both military and political terms.

Eliminating Saddam's regime was unquestionably an indispensable first step in providing an opportunity for the liberal democratization of Iraq—and, perhaps, the Greater Middle East—over the long term. But it is essential that, above all else, the transformation of Iraq, let alone the Persian Gulf and wider Arab and Muslim world, be viewed as a long-term objective. The Bush administration itself initially underestimated the daunting nature of many of the economic, military and political challenges it would face in postwar Iraq. Those challenges have become increasingly evident in the time that has passed since the conclusion of Operation Iraqi Freedom. In particular, the costs in American dollars and lives have led critics within, and outside of, the United States to question whether efforts to install free-market economic and representative political institutions in Iraq and, eventually, across the Greater Middle East are either prudent or desirable. For those opposed to the brand of repressive governance favored by Saddam, bin Laden and their ilk, the answers to both questions, however, should be definitively affirmative.

Islam and the West: Prospects for the Future

There are three potential interactive courses for the relationship between the United States and the Islamic world to follow in the future: cooperative, confrontational or ambivalent. Al Qaeda's attacks on the United States on 9/11 have reduced markedly the potential for the third of those options relative to the first or second. America now has no choice but to confront any states and non-state actors that are supportive of Al Qaeda or, for that matter, any other terrorist organizations in the future. Regrettably, at present, the vast majority of such actors are situated in the Greater Middle East. The choice for the other states therein is thus reasonably straightforward. Cooperate to at least some extent with the United States or risk creating the perception of sympathy for, if not outright collaboration with, the terrorists.

Although it is critical to impress upon the tyrants and extremists of the Islamic world—men such as Saddam and bin Laden—the consequences of confronting the United States, it is equally important to demonstrate the benefits of cooperation. America has taken the initial step in that direction through its economic, military and political commitments to nation-building operations in Iraq. Those commitments have been made in part to afford Iraqis opportunities to express themselves freely, improve their standards of living and participate in the selection and administration of representative political institutions. These outcomes, in turn, will help to enhance the security of the United States in two ways. First, they will produce a more politically stable and economically prosperous Iraq, one aligned with, rather than opposed to, America. Second, they will serve as an example to individuals across the Greater Middle East that beneficial change is possible, if not probable, in that region of the world. Such a realization has the potential to reduce the inclination of many to join Al Qaeda's war against the United States. While neither outcome is likely to occur in the immediate future, each is certainly a reasonable long-term objective. And, ultimately, positive change in any relationship rarely occurs without substantial effort over a lengthy period of time. The Cold War, for instance, lasted nearly a half-century. There is no reason to believe that victory in the war on terror will come any sooner or be any easier to achieve.

Bibliography

Documents and Official Sources

Bush, George W. Addresses and Speeches (various).

_____. "National Security Strategy of the United States of America." *White House Office of the Press Secretary* (September 2002).

CIA World Factbook (various country reports).

Clinton, William J. "A National Security Strategy for a New Century." *White House Office of the Press Secretary* (December 1999).

NATO Press Service. Communique S-I (90) 36 (6 July 1990).

NSC. "A Decade of Deception and Defiance: Saddam Hussein's Defiance of the United Nations." Background Paper for President Bush's UN Address. *White House Office of the Press Secretary* (12 September 2002).

Public Papers of the Presidents of the United States: George Bush, 1991, Book I, 1 January-30 June 1991. Washington: US Government Printing Office, 1992.

Rice, Condoleezza. Addresses and Speeches (various).

The Middle East, 7th ed. Washington: Congressional Quarterly, Inc., 1991.

UN. *Security Council Resolution 660*. S/RES/660 (2 August 1990).

UN. *Security Council Resolution 678*. S/RES/678 (29 November 1990).

UN. *Security Council Resolution 687*. S/RES/687 (3 April 1991).

UN. *Security Council Resolution 1441*. S/RES/1441 (8 November 2002).

US Congress, "Joint Resolution Granting Authorization for the Use of Military Force Against Iraq." *United States Congress* (10 October 2002).

US Department of State. *Basic Documents*. Washington, DC: US Government Printing Office, 1980.

US Senate Select Committee on Intelligence. "Report on the U.S. Intelligence Community's Prewar Intelligence Assessment on Iraq." *US Senate Select Committee on Intelligence* (July 2004).

Newspapers and Serials

Daily Telegraph.
Economist.
Guardian Weekly.
National Review.
Times.
Washington Post.
Weekly Standard.

Monographs

Albright, Madeleine, with Bill Woodward. *Madame Secretary: A Memoir*. New York: Miramax Books, 2003.

Baker, James A., with Thomas M. DeFrank. *The Politics of Diplomacy: Revolution, War and Peace, 1989-1992*. New York: G.P. Putnam's Sons, 1995.

Baram, Amatzia, and Barry Rubin, eds. *Iraq's Road to War*. New York: St. Martin's Press, 1993.

Benjamin, Daniel, and Steven Simon. *The Age of Sacred Terror*. New York: Random House, 2002.

Bergen, Peter L. *Holy War, Inc.: Inside the Secret World of Osama bin Laden*. New York: The Free Press, 2001.

Beschloss, Michael R., and Strobe Talbott. *At The Highest Levels: The Inside Story of the End of the Cold War*. Boston: Little, Brown and Company, 1993.

Brzezinski, Zbigniew. *Out of Control: Global Turmoil on the Eve of the Twenty-first Century*. New York: Touchstone Books, 1993.

Bush, George, and Brent Scowcroft. *A World Transformed: The Collapse of the Soviet Empire; the Unification of Germany; Tiananmen Square; the Gulf War*. New York: Alfred A. Knopf, 1998.

Christopher, Warren. *Chances of a Lifetime*. New York: Scribner, 2001.

Clark, Wesley K. *Waging Modern War: Bosnia, Kosovo and the Future of Combat*. New York: Public Affairs, 2001.

Clinton, Bill. *My Life*. New York: Alfred A. Knopf, 2004.

Cockburn, Andrew and Patrick. *Out of the Ashes: The Resurrection of Saddam Hussein*. New York: HarperCollins, 1999.

Coogan, Michael D., ed. *The Oxford History of the Biblical World*. New York: Oxford University Press, 1998.

Coughlin, Con. *Saddam: King of Terror*. New York: HarperCollins, 2002.

Daalder, Ivo H., and Michael E. O'Hanlon. *Winning Ugly: NATO's War to Save Kosovo*. Washington, DC: Brookings Institution Press, 2000.

Deger, Saadet, and Somnath Sen. *Military Expenditures: The Political Economy of International Security*. Oxford: Oxford University Press, 1990.

Esposito, John L., ed. *Oxford History of Islam*. New York: Oxford University Press, 1999.

Esposito, John L. *Islam: The Straight Path*. New York: Oxford University Press, 1998.

Fanning, Leonard M. *American Oil Operations Abroad*. New York: McGraw Hill, 1947.

Fukuyama, Francis. *The End of History and the Last Man*. New York: Avon, 1993.

Gaddis, John Lewis. *Surprise, Security and the American Experience*. Cambridge: Harvard University Press, 2004.

_____. *The Landscape of History: How Historians Map the Past*. New York: Oxford University Press, 2002.

Gold, Dore. *Hatred's Kingdom: How Saudi Arabia Supports the New Global Terrorism*. New York: Regnery Publishing, Inc., 2003.

Graham-Brown, Sarah. *Sanctioning Saddam*. London: I.B. Tauris, 1999.

Hanson, Victor Davis. *Ripples of Battle: How Wars of the Past Still Determine How we Fight, How we Live and How we Think.* New York: Doubleday, 2003.

Hart, Parker T. *Saudi Arabia and the United States: Birth of a Security Partnership.* Bloomington: Indiana University Press, 1998.

Hayes, Stephen F. *The Connection: How Al Qaeda's Collaboration with Saddam Hussein has Endangered America.* New York: HarperCollins, 2004.

History and Faith: Cradle and Crucible in the Middle East. Washington, DC: National Geographic, 2002.

Hourani, Albert. *A History of the Arab Peoples.* Cambridge: Harvard University Press, 1991.

Hopmann, P. Terrence. *The Negotiation Process and the Resolution of International Conflicts.* Columbia: University of South Carolina Press, 1996.

Hunter, Shireen T. *The Future of Islam and the West: Clash of Civilizations or Peaceful Coexistence?* Westport, Conn.: Praeger, 1998.

Huntington, Samuel P. *The Clash of Civilizations and the Remaking of World Order.* New York: Simon & Schuster, 1996.

Hutchings, Robert L. *American Diplomacy and the End of the Cold War: An Insider's Account of U.S. Policy in Europe, 1989-1992.* Washington: Woodrow Wilson Center Press, 1997.

Inalcik, Halil. *The Ottoman Empire: The Classical Age, 1300-1600.* London: Weidenfeld and Nicolson, 1973.

Kaplan, Lawrence F., and William Kristol. *The War Over Iraq: Saddam's Tyranny and America's Mission.* San Francisco: Encounter Books, 2003.

Kepel, Gilles. *Jihad: The Trail of Political Islam*, tr. Anthony F. Roberts. Cambridge: Harvard University Press, 2002.

Kennedy, Robert F. *Thirteen Days: A Memoir of the Cuban Missile Crisis.* New York: W.W. Norton & Company, 1969.

Lagon, Mark P. *The Reagan Doctrine: The Sources of American Conduct in the Cold War's Last Chapter.* Westport, CT: Praeger, 1994.

Lansford, Tom. *All for One: Terrorism, NATO and the United States.* Aldershot, UK: Ashgate Publishing Limited, 2002.

Lansford, Tom, and Robert J. Pauly, Jr. *Strategic Preemption: US Foreign Policy and the Second Iraq War.* Aldershot, UK: Ashgate Publishing Limited, 2004.

Lees, John R., and Michael Turner, eds., *Reagan's First Four Years: A New Beginning?* New York: St. Martin's Press, 1988.

Lewis, Bernard. *The Multiple Identities of the Middle East.* New York: Schocken Books, 1998.

_____. *The Middle East: A Brief History of the Last 2,000 Years.* New York: Touchstone, 1995.

Lowry, Rich. *Legacy: Paying the Price for the Clinton Years.* Washington, DC: Regnery Publishing, Inc., 2003.

Mann, James. *Rise of the Vulcans: The History of Bush's War Cabinet.* New York: Viking, 2004.

Mearsheimer, John J. *The Tragedy of Great Power Politics.* New York: W.W. Norton & Company, 2001.

Miniter, Richard. *Losing Bin Laden: How Bill Clinton's Failures Unleashed Global Terror.* Washington, DC: Regnery Publishing, Inc., 2003.

Morgenthau, Hans. *Politics Among Nations: The Struggle for Power and Peace.* New York: Alfred P. Knopf, 1948.

Morris, Dick. *Off With Their Heads: Traitors, Crooks & Obstructionists in American Politics, Media & Business.* New York: ReganBooks, 2003.

Mylroie, Laurie. *Study of Revenge: The First World Trade Center Attack and Saddam Hussein's War against America.* Washington, DC: The AEI Press, 2001.

Nisan, Mordechai. *Minorities in the Middle East*, second edition. Jefferson, NC: McFarland & Company, Inc., Publishers, 2002.

Palmer, Michael A. *Guardians of the Gulf: A History of America's Expanding Role in the Persian Gulf, 1893-1992.* New York: Macmillan, 1992.

Parrish, Thomas. *The Cold War Encyclopedia.* New York: Henry Holt and Company, 1996.

Pauly, Jr., Robert J. *Islam in Europe: Integration or Marginalization?* Aldershot, UK: Ashgate Publishing Limited, 2004.

Pipes, Daniel. *In the Path of God: Islam and Political Power.* New York: Basic Books, 1983.

Pollack, Kenneth M. *The Threatening Storm: The Case for Invading Iraq.* New York: Random House, 2002.

Pond, Elizabeth. *Beyond the Wall: Germany's Road to Unification.* Washington: Brookings Institution, 1993.

Powell, Colin, with Joseph E. Persico. *My American Journey.* New York: Random House, 1995.

Ross, Dennis. *The Missing Peace: The Inside Story of the Fight for Middle East Peace.* New York: Farrar, Strauss and Giroux, 2004.

Rubenstein, Alvin Z., Albina Shayevich and Boris Zlotnikov, eds. *The Clinton Foreign Policy Reader: Presidential Speeches with Commentary.* Armonk, NY: M.E. Sharpe, 2000.

Shannon, Vaughn P. *Balancing Act: US Foreign Policy and the Arab-Israeli Conflict.* Aldershot, UK: Ashgate Publishing Limited, 2003.

Shaw, Stanford Jay. *History of the Ottoman Empire and Modern Turkey.* New York: Cambridge University Press, 1976.

Shwadran, Benjamin. *The Middle East and the Great Powers.* New York: John Wiley and Sons, 1973.

Sick, Gary. *All Fall Down: America's Tragic Encounter with Iran.* New York: Random House, 1985.

Sifry, Micah L., and Christopher Cerf. *The Iraq War Reader: History, Documents, Opinions.* New York: Simon and Schuster, 2003.

Tibi, Bassam. *The Challenge of Fundamentalism: Political Islam and the New World Disorder.* Berkeley: University of California Press, 1993.

Tripp, Charles. *A History of Iraq* (Cambridge: Cambridge University Press, 2000).

Waltz, Kenneth. *Theory of International Politics.* Reading, MA: Addison-Wesley, 1979.

We Will Prevail: President George W. Bush on War, Terrorism and Freedom. New York: Continuum, 2003.

Woodward, Bob. *Bush at War.* New York: Random House, 2003.

Yetiv, Steven A. *Crude Awakenings: Global Oil Security and American Foreign Policy.* Ithaca, NY: Cornell University Press, 2004.

_____. *Explaining Foreign Policy: US Decision-making and the Persian Gulf War.* Baltimore: Johns Hopkins University Press, 2004.

_____. *The Persian Gulf Crisis.* Westport, CT: Greenwood Press, 1997.

Zakaria, Fareed. *The Future of Freedom: Illiberal Democracy at Home and Abroad.* New York: W.W. Norton & Company, 2003.

Zelikow, Philip, and Condoleezza Rice. *Germany Unified and Europe Transformed: A Study in Statecraft.* Cambridge: Harvard University Press, 1995.

Articles, Essays and Reports

Barram, Amatzia. "The Effect of Iraqi Sanctions: Statistical Pitfalls and Responsibility." *Middle East Journal* (Spring 2000).

Bengio, Ofra. "Baghdad Between Shi'a and Kurds." *Policy Focus* (February 1992).

Cordesman, Anthony H. "One Year On: Nation Building in Iraq." *Center for Strategic and International Studies* (April 2004).

Dessler, David. "What's at Stake in the Agent-Structure Debate?" *International Organization* (1989).

Fallows, James. "Blind Into Baghdad." *Atlantic Monthly* (January/February 2004).

Gaddis, John Lewis. "A Grand Strategy of Transformation." *Foreign Policy* (November/December 2002).

Haass, Richard N. "The Squandered Presidency: Demanding More from the Commander-in-Chief," *Foreign Affairs* (May/June 2000).

"Iraqi Coalition Casualty Count." <http://icasualties.org/oif> (15 August 2004).

Kagan, Robert. "America's Crisis of Legitimacy." *Foreign Affairs* (March/April 2004).

Kaplan, Robert D. "The Coming Anarchy." *Atlantic Monthly* (Summer 1994).

Kean, Thomas H., Lee H. Hamilton, Richard Ben-Veniste, Fred F. Fielding, Jamie S. Gorelick, Slade Gorton, Bob Kerrey, John F. Lehman, Timothy and James R. Thompson. *The 9/11 Commission Report: Final Report of the National Commission on Terrorist Attacks Upon the United States.* New York: W.W. Norton & Company, 2004.

Lanier, Stephen. "Low Intensity Conflict and Nation-Building in Iraq: A Chronology." *Center for Strategic and International Studies* (April 2004).

Mearsheimer, John J. "Back to the Future: Instability in Europe After the Cold War." *International Security* (Summer 1990).

Metz, Steven. "Insurgency and Counterinsurgency in Iraq." *Washington Quarterly* (Winter 2003-04).

O'Hanlon, Michael E., and Adriana Lins de Albuquerque. "Iraq Index: Tracking Variables of Reconstruction and Security in Post-Saddam Iraq." *Brookings Institution* (April 2004).

Powell, Colin L. "A Strategy of Partnerships." *Foreign Affairs* (January/February 2004).

Waltz, Kenneth N. "The Emerging Structure of International Politics." *International Security* (Fall 1993).

Index